MW01103474

PORTABLE POWER TOOLS

Delmar Publishers' Online Services

To access Delmar on the World Wide Web, point your browser to:

http://www.delmar.com/delmar.html

To access through Gopher: gopher://gopher.delmar.com

(Delmar Online is part of "thomson.com", an Internet site with information on
more than 30 publishers of the International Thomson Publishing organization.)

For information on our products and services:

email: info@delmar.com

or call 800-347-7707

THE USE OF
PORTABLE
POWER TOOLS

Copyright © 1980
BY DELMAR PUBLISHERS INC.

All rights reserved. Certain portions of this work copyright © 1962. No part of this work covered by the copyright hereon may be reproduced or used in any form or by any means — graphic, electronic, or mechanical, including photocopying, recording, taping, or information storage and retrieval systems — without written permission of the publisher.

20 19 18 17 16 15

LIBRARY OF CONGRESS CATALOG CARD NUMBER: 77-85761
ISBN: 0-8273-1100-1

Printed in the United States of America
Published simultaneously in Canada
by Nelson Canada,
A Division of International Thomson Limited

Leo P. McDonnell

Alson I. Kaumeheiwa

For more information address Delmar Publishers Inc.
3 Columbia Circle, Box 15-015
Albany, New York 12212-5015

PREFACE

New developments in building materials and their uses have brought about improvements in the tools of the building construction trades. New tools and changes made to older tools make it necessary to update courses of study dealing with this area of instruction. The purpose of this book is to fill the need for up-to-date coverage of portable power tools and their uses.

Careful research shows that the main occupational areas of carpentry include: (1) hand tools and portable machinery; (2) concrete form construction; (3) framing, sheathing, and insulation; and (4) interior and exterior trim. Because of the great increase in the use of power equipment in these modern carpentry practices, THE USE OF PORTABLE POWER TOOLS focuses on the various power tools basic to these areas.

The instructional units in the text include only basic operations common to a specific branch of carpentry work. Since each operation involves the teaching of basic trade theory and processes, both are included in the instructional units.

There are fifteen units of instruction in this publication. Unit 1 introduces basic components common to all electric power tools and explains the need for grounding or double insulation. The units that follow cover: circular hand saws; radial arm saws; refitting blades for circular and radial arm saws; sabre saws; reciprocating saws; electric drills; power planes; power block planes; router-shaper planers; floor and disc sanders; and belt and finishing sanders. The last three units cover automatic drivers, including: staplers; manual and pneumatic nailers; and powder-actuated drivers.

Related information, such as rules about carpentry practices, computations, and descriptions of tools, is presented before the basic process of the proper use of the tool is discussed. Thus, the student is acquainted with the rules for use of the tool prior to the instruction in their application. Also, safety precautions are highlighted at the point in the procedure where they must be observed.

Each unit is concluded with a review section presented in a variety of styles. This unit-end material allows the students to evaluate their mastery of the related technical information presented in each unit. The variety of types of testing techniques provides a more interesting review for the students.

NOTICE TO THE READER

Publisher does not warrant or guarantee any of the products described herein or perform any independent analysis in connection with any of the product information contained herein. Publisher does not assume, and expressly disclaims, any obligation to obtain and include information other than that provided to it by the manufacturer.

The reader is expressly warned to consider and adopt all safety precautions that might be indicated by the activities described herein and to avoid all potential hazards. By following the instructions contained herein, the reader willingly assumes all risks in connection with such instructions.

The publisher makes no representations or warranties of any kind, including but not limited to, the warranties of fitness for particular purpose or merchantability, nor are any such representations implied with respect to the material set forth herein, and the publisher takes no responsibility with respect to such material. The publisher shall not be liable for any special, consequential or exemplary damages resulting, in whole or in part, from the readers' use of, or reliance upon, this material.

CONTENTS

Unit 1 INTRODUCTION TO THE USE OF PORTABLE POWER TOOLS

This unit serves three purposes: (1) to present general information about all portable electric power tools, (2) to emphasize the need for a complete understanding of grounding methods, and (3) to acquaint the student with some valuable safety precautions.

BASIC COMPONENTS AND POWER FLOW

Fig. 1-1 is a cutaway of a portable electric drill which shall be used to trace the flow of power through electric power tools. The electric current enters the tool's switch and flows through the carbon brushes to the commutator and armature assembly. Electricity, acting upon the commutator, causes the armature assembly to turn, producing the tool's force.

The Motor

The armature-coil arrangement in portable electric power tools uses either alternating current or direct current. A motor that can operate on either alternating current (ac) or direct current (dc) is known as a "universal" type motor. It is designed to be used at a specified voltage. If too little or too much voltage is transmitted to the motor, the armature-coil arrangement will overheat and may burn out. A variation of more than 10 percent over or under the nameplate voltage will cause such overheating and possible burnout. Make sure, therefore, that the unit's line voltage is the same as that shown on the unit's nameplate: a 115-volt motor on a 115-volt line, or a 230-volt motor on a 230-volt line.

The motor is designed for a specified revolutions per minute (rpm) before the work load is placed on it. Manufacturers operation manuals will refer to this as *no-load speed.*

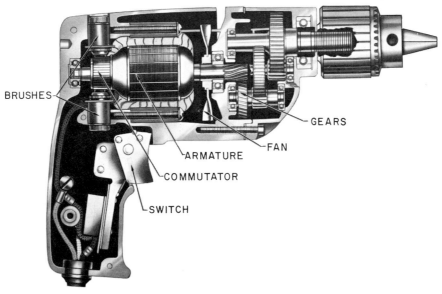

BRUSHES

GEARS

FAN

ARMATURE

COMMUTATOR

SWITCH

Fig. 1-1

Depending upon the requirements of the specific tool, motors are designed for no-load speeds ranging from about 500 rpm for large-capacity, heavy-duty drills to over 40 000 rpm for fast, smooth-cutting routers.

The Brushes

The electric current entering the portable power tool is fed through stationary brushes first to the commutator and then to the armature which drives the tool. If the brushes fail to make good contact with the commutator, the current will not reach the armature and the tool will not operate.

The brushes are held firmly against the commutator by a self-adjusting device such as the spring assembly shown in figure 1-2. These brushes will wear down by the constant rubbing against the revolving commutator.

The brushes should be inspected frequently. To do so, take away the brush caps and remove the brushes and springs. When the carbon on each brush is worn to about 1/4 inch in length, replace both brushes with new ones as specified in the manufacturer's instructions. If the brushes are satisfactory, return them to the same holders in the same position as before. Be sure that the brushes slide freely in the brush holders.

Brushes may be cleaned with a cloth dampened with turpentine and, when necessary, may be sanded to their proper shape. Such maintenance should be done each time the brushes are inspected. The commutator may be cleaned in a similar manner, inserting the dampened cloth through the brush-holder holes and revolving the commutator against it to remove surface dirt and carbon.

It is not unusual for universal motors to spark at the brushes. However, too much sparking may indicate a short or open circuit or a grounded motor. If the unit sparks a great deal, have it inspected at one of the manufacturer's authorized service stations.

The Fan

Universal motors used with electric power tools are generally cooled by a fan mounted on the armature shaft. When a tool is in operation, the fan draws air into the motor housing and passes it through the housing to cool the motor parts. Sometimes this stream of air is also used to keep saws' and routers' line of cut free from chips and sawdust.

It is important that the air passages be kept clean. Clean and unclogged air passages ensure a cooler running motor and contribute to a longer motor life. The air passages should be periodically cleaned out with compressed air. Common sense will indicate when too much dust and dirt have built up. The manufacturer's recommendations for cleaning and maintenance should be followed.

LUBRICATION

The revolving armature shaft transmits its force through a series of gears and bearings. The movement and action of the tool depend on the arrangement of gears. The circular force is used in

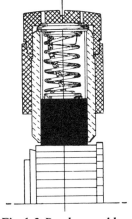

Fig. 1-2 Brush assembly

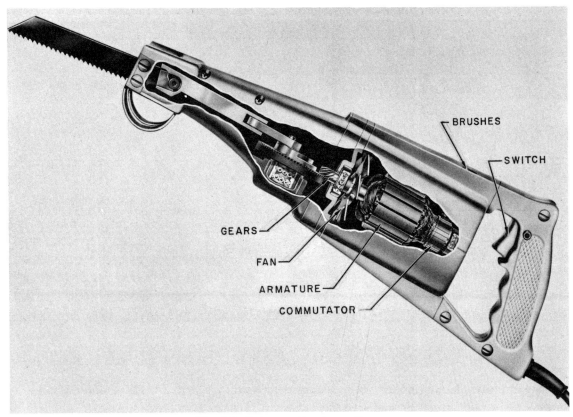

Fig. 1-3 Cutaway of reciprocating saw

power saws, drills, screwdrivers, and tools with revolving action. In other cases, the circular motion of the armature shaft is changed to a longitudinal motion. This reciprocating (back-and-forth) action is used in such tools as the reciprocating saw, figure 1-3, the sabre saw, and the power driver.

Regardless of their type of arrangement, gears and bearings need lubrication. If precision ball bearings are used in the machine, they are generally grease-sealed at the factory for the life of the bearing. No periodic lubrication is necessary in such cases. Where provision is made for lubrication, follow the manufacturer's recommedations. For oil wick holes which lubricate the motor bearings, two or three drops of light machine oil about once a month should be sufficient. Too much oil, in many cases, is just as harmful as too little oil.

GROUNDING

Portable or stationary electric power tools present a serious danger of electrical shock to the operator. An electrical shock is very likely to occur when the operator has wet hands or is standing on damp concrete. Wet hands and damp concrete decrease the resistance to the flow of electricity.

Electrical circuits that operate at up to 150 volts are usually of the *grounded system* type. The grounded system conforms with the National Electrical Code. In this system one of the circuit (supply) wires is grounded at the transformer furnishing power to a building.

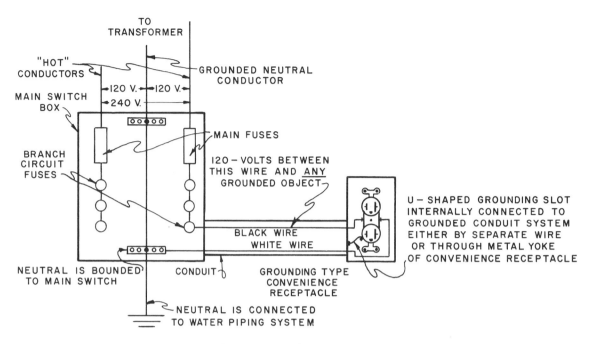

Fig. 1-4 Diagram of grounded system

This same circuit is then grounded at the main service-entrance switch inside the building by a wire connected to the main service-entrance switch and the water piping system which is usually connected ahead of the water meter. In this grounded system, one wire is commonly called the *grounded neutral conductor.*

Figure 1-4 shows that there are 120 volts between any of the *hot conductors* (current-carrying) and the grounded neutral conductor. The narrow slot of any convenience outlet is connected to the hot circuit wire (usually black) and the wide slot is connected to the grounded neutral conductor (usually white). This is basically how a voltage of 120 volts between the slots of a convenience outlet is obtained. However, since the voltage between the hot wire and the grounded wire is 120 volts, the voltage between the hot wire and *any grounded object or surface will also be 120 volts.*

Electrical tools are manufactured so that all current-carrying parts are insulated from the housing and handles. Underwriters' Laboratories, Inc. tests these portable electrical tools to see that they are well-insulated and safe to operate. However, if the motor is overloaded to the point of possible burnout; the tool is dropped; the switch is damaged; the supply cord is pulled roughly; or improper use brings the live, hot conductor in contact with the tool's housing, the operator will receive an electrical shock if he touches a ground surface.

The danger of electrical shocks can be reduced by using a low-resistance grounding circuit between the tool's housing and the ground. Then, if one of the above faults should occur, the current will flow through the grounding wire, not through the body of the operator. The fuse or circuit-breaker will also blow under this condition if their proper sizes are used in the branch circuit. Circuit-breakers or fuses rated at 15 or 20 amperes are used in circuits to which portable electric power tools are connected.

Fig. 1-5 Three-wire cord with three-wire grounding type attachment plug cap

Fig. 1-6 Grounding type convenience outlet

> While in use or connected to a power source, the metal frames and/or housings of all portable electric tools must be grounded to protect the operator against electric shock if a fault should occur.

METHODS OF GROUNDING PORTABLE POWER TOOLS

Preferred Method

The National Electrical Code specifies that portable electric power tools must be grounded. Underwriters' Laboratories requires that these tools be manufactured with three-wire cords, one wire serving as grounding conductor. This conductor is covered by a green insulating jacket. One end is connected to the tool housing when the tool is made. The other end is connected to the longer prong of a three-prong plug.

When the three-wire, grounding-type cord and outlet are correctly installed, the operator is protected from electrical shock.

It is important that the wires in the cord be connected to the plug and the tool according in the the electrical color code. If the green and black wires were to be crossed (that is, connecting the green wire where the black wire should be connected or vice versa), the entire housing and/or frame of the tool would become *live* (an electrical charge of 120 volts between the housing and ground).

The whole purpose of a grounding system would be defeated if the wires were crossed. Remember, green is the code for a grounding conductor. It is *not* a current-carrying conductor. The color-coding of three-wire cords (one black, one white, one green) and the color coding of attachment plug caps and convenience outlets must be followed for the protection and safety of the operator.

If an extension cord is used, it should be a three-wire type so that the ground is continued from the tool to the outlet. The conductor must be large enough to prevent an excessive voltage loss. Voltage loss in a conductor results in a low-voltage condition at the motor. Low voltage is a common reason why motors burn out.

Alternate Method #1

Cord — Three-wire

Outlet — Two-wire

In order to use machines having thee-wire cords with three-prong grounding-type plug caps on two-wire outlets, a special adaptor is available. To use the adaptor, the extending green wire is connected to the outlet plate retaining screw (in the case of switch boxes), or the cover mounting screw (in the case of outlet boxes).

**RECOMMENDED EXTENSION CORD SIZES
FOR USE WITH PORTABLE ELECTRIC TOOLS**

(For Rubber Types S, SO, SR, SJ, SJO, SV, SP & Thermoplastic Types ST, SRT, SJT, SVP, SPT)

Name-plate Amperes	CORD LENGTH IN FEET																			
	25	50	75	100	125	150	175	200	225	250	275	300	325	350	375	400	425	450	475	500
1	16	16	16	16	16	16	16	16	16	16	16	16	16	16	16	16	16	16	16	14
2	16	16	16	16	16	16	16	16	16	16	14	14	14	14	14	12	12	12	12	12
3	16	16	16	16	16	16	14	14	14	14	12	12	12	12	12	12	10	10	10	10
4	16	16	16	16	16	14	14	12	12	12	12	12	12	10	10	10	10	10	10	10
5	16	16	16	16	14	14	12	12	12	12	10	10	10	10	10	8	8	8	8	8
6	16	16	16	14	14	12	12	12	10	10	10	10	10	8	8	8	8	8	8	8
7	16	16	14	14	12	12	12	10	10	10	10	8	8	8	8	8	8	8	8	8
8	14	14	14	14	12	12	10	10	10	10	8	8	8	8	8	8	8	8	8	
9	14	14	14	12	12	10	10	10	8	8	8	8	8	8	8	8	8			
10	14	14	14	12	12	10	10	10	8	8	8	8	8	8	8					
11	12	12	12	12	10	10	10	8	8	8	8	8	8	8						
12	12	12	12	12	10	10	8	8	8	8	8	8	8							
13	12	12	12	12	10	10	8	8	8	8	8	8								
14	10	10	10	10	10	10	8	8	8	8	8									
15	10	10	10	10	10	8	8	8	8	8										
16	10	10	10	10	10	8	8	8	8	8										
17	10	10	10	10	10	8	8	8	8											
18	8	8	8	8	8	8	8	8	8											
19	8	8	8	8	8	8	8	8												
20	8	8	8	8	8	8	8	8												

NOTES: Wire sizes are for 3-cdr Cords, one cdr of which is used to provide a continuous grounding circuit from tool housing to receptacle.
Wire sizes shown are A.W.G. (American Wire Gauge).
Based on 115V power supply; Ambient Temp. of 30°C, 86°F.

NOTE: The metal switch box or outlet box must be grounded. In some cases it may be necessary to run a ground wire to a known permanent ground, such as a water pipe. In some water systems an insulated meter is used, thus isolating the pipes behind the meter from ground. In such cases, the ground connection is made to the water pipe ahead of the meter.

A rod or pipe driven into the ground can serve as a ground connection if no other ground connection is available. However, this method is not nearly so effective as a grounded water system.

The use of adaptors is not advised since they are effective only if the ground lead is properly connected to an adequate ground. For this reason, their use in Canada is prohibited by the Canadian Electrical Code.

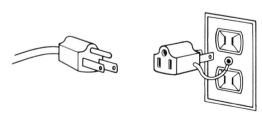

Fig. 1-7

Alternate Method #2

Cord — Three-wire cord having a two-prong attachment plug cap

Outlet — Two-wire

Some of the older electrical tools came furnished with a three-wire cord which was attached to a two-prong attachment plug cap. The green grounding wire was brought out of the side of the plug cap. This green grounding wire must be connected to the outlet plate retaining screw or to the outlet cover mounting screw.

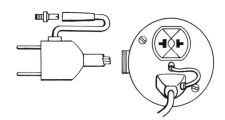

Fig. 1-8 Grounding a portable power tool

Alternate Method #3

Cord — Two-wire cord

Outlet — Two-wire

On tools having only a two-wire cord, it is strongly recommended that the cord be replaced with a three-wire cord. In this case, proper grounding can be accomplished as in method #1, #2, or #3.

It is possible to ground such tools by running a separate ground wire from the housing of the tool and connecting this ground wire to a ground. But, since such a procedure exposes the loose separate ground wire to mechanical damage or the possibility of being pulled, kicked, or torn apart, such a method is not recognized by the National Electrical Code.

Importance of Grounding

Reviewing the case of proper grounding of portable electric tools, it can be seen that the user may not want to take the time to connect the extra ground wire mentioned in the alternate methods. Many operators ignore safety precautions even though their life is in danger every time they use a portable electric power tool without first establishing a good ground. The use of a properly connected three-prong grounding type attachment plug cap connected to a properly installed three-wire grounding type convenience outlet is by far the surest and safest method of all.

It is also recommended that the power tool be checked often to be sure it is still grounded. Every time the tool is used it is assumed to be grounded, yet the tool may have an open (broken) ground wire or a loose connection at a terminal. An open or loose ground wire could cause the operator to receive a serious electric shock.

Double-Insulation

Grounding portable electric power tools does not remove the possibility of electric shock. Other precautions are being taken by manufacturers. Some portable electric power tools are *double-insulated.* These tools have two separate insulations. For example, the switch may have a standard insulation. In addition, the switch would be mounted on a second insulating assembly. Thus, the term double-insulated is used. Both insulations would have to fail before the operator would receive a shock.

Many portable power tools are now being manufactured with high-impact plastic housings. These cases are natural insulators. With both double-insulation and nonconducting plastic housings, insulation, rather than grounding, is the safety feature. These insulated tools are manufactured with two-wire cords instead of three-wire cords. To avoid confusion, these tools are marked indicating their insulation qualities.

GENERAL SAFETY PRECAUTIONS

When working with power tools, a certain amount of hazard is involved for the operator. Using the tools with proper respect and caution lessens the possibility of personal injury. However, if normal safety precautions are overlooked or ignored, injuries can occur.

While safety precautions for individual machines are discussed in their respective instructional units, the following general precautions should always be observed when using electric power tools.

1. KEEP THE WORK AREA CLEAN. Cluttered areas and benches invite accidents.
2. AVOID DANGEROUS ENVIRONMENTS. Don't use power tools in the rain or in any damp or wet location. Don't use power tools in the presence of combustible liquids or gases.
3. WEAR PROPER APPAREL. Don't wear loose clothing or jewelry; either could get caught in moving parts. Rubber gloves and rubber-soled shoes are recommended when working outdoors.
4. CHECK ELECTRICAL CONNECTIONS. Make sure the power tool is properly connected and the circuit is properly grounded.
5. DON'T ABUSE THE CORD. Check to see that the cord does not get tangled with the machine. Don't carry the tool by the cord or yank the cord from the receptacle. Keep the cord from heat, oil, and sharp edges.
6. SECURE THE WORK. Use clamps or a vise to hold the work in place. This is safer than using your hand and frees both hands to operate the tool.
7. USE THE TOOL CORRECTLY. Operate a power tool only at the designated voltage. Do not modify the tool; use it in the way it was intended.
8. MAINTAIN TOOLS WITH CARE. Keep tools sharp and clean for best performance. Protect tools from dampness and dirt. Check for loose parts that should be tightened. Follow instructions for lubricating and changing accessories.
9. USE SAFETY GUARDS. Use/safety guards provided with the machine. Check to be sure that they are in good working condition.
10. DISCONNECT TOOLS. Disconnect all power tools when not in use; before servicing; and when changing accessories such as blades, bits, or cutters.
11. KEEP VISITORS AWAY. All onlookers, especially children, should be kept a safe distance away from where work is being done with power tools.
12. STORE IDLE TOOLS. When not in use, tools should be stored in dry, high or locked cabinets – out of children's reach.

13. DON'T FORCE THE TOOL. A power tool will do a better and safer job when it used at the rate it was intended to be used.

14. WEAR SAFETY GLASSES. Wear safety glasses while operating power tools. Wear a face mask if the operation creates dust.

15. DON'T OVERREACH. Keep proper footing and balance at all times.

16. REMOVE ADJUSTING KEYS AND WRENCHES. Always check to see that keys and wrenches are removed from tools before they are turned on.

17. AVOID ACCIDENTAL STARTING. Don't carry tools that are plugged in. Develop the habit of keeping fingers off the switch until it is time to use the tool.

18. USE THE CORRECT EXTENSION CORDS. Use properly rated cords. Check the cord for worn or torn insulation. If the tool is to be used outdoors, use a cord that is marked "suitable for use with outdoor appliances".

19. THINK. Most accidents are caused by simple thoughtlessness. Common sense can prevent injuries.

REVIEW QUESTIONS

A. Short Answer or Discussion

1. Descibe how the electric current goes through an electric power tool to produce the tool's force.

2. What parts of the power tool should be inspected from time to time?

3. What precautions should the operator of an electrical power tool take to prevent electrical shock?

4. Using an extension cord that cannot handle the current (amp) required by the tool could cause a low voltage condition. Why is a low voltage condition a problem?

5. What are manufacturers of portable electric power tools doing to eliminate or reduce the danger of electrical shock?

6. What kinds of protective devices should the operator use when working with power tools?

7. What precautions should be taken with clothing and jewelry when operating power tools?

8. What might cause the motor of the power tool to spark excessively?

9. What precaution should be taken if the metal switch boxes and outlet boxes are grounded to water pipes?

B. Completion

1. RPM before the work load is placed upon the tool is known as _____ speed.

2. Insulated tools are manufactured with _____ wire cords.

3. In a three-wire cord, the color of the grounding wire is _____ .

4. The color of the "hot" wire is usually _____ .

5. To prevent a fire or possible explosion, do not use electrical power tools in an environment where _____ are present.

6. To obtain and keep proper footing and balance when using power tools, do not _____ .

7. Besides protecting your tools from theft, locking tools away in a cabinet keeps them out of the reach of _____ .

8. Cluttered areas and benches invite _____ .

9. Portable electrical power tools are tested for safety in operation by the _____ .

10. Most accidents are caused by _____ .

Unit 2 CIRCULAR SAWS

The most economical, practical, and accurate method of cutting structural and finish lumber is by the use of electric power machinery. In carpentry work there are many hand cutting operations that can be done with power-driven equipment. Portable power tools for carpentry should be selected with care. Several factors should be considered in selection: cost, upkeep, safety, and labor-saving efficiency.

TYPES AND SIZES

The size of a circular saw is determined by the diameter of the blade it uses. Saw sizes range from 4 1/2 inches to 12 inches. The depth of cuts range up to 4 3/8 inches with a 12-inch blade. Horsepower (hp) ratings range from 1/2 hp to 2 1/2 hp. Most manufacturers report the amperage (amp) rating rather than horsepower. To calculate horsepower, multiply volts by amperes and divide by 746. Seven hundred and forty-six is the number of watts required to do 1 hp of work. The specifications for the following example are: 115 volts ac and 10 amps. Using the formula, horsepower is calculated as:

$$\frac{\text{volts x amps}}{746} = \text{hp} \qquad \frac{115 \times 10}{746} = 1.54 \text{ hp}$$

The result is a rated horsepower of 1 1/2 hp.

As new motors and power tools are produced motor ratings will be measured in watts and kilowatts rather than amps or horsepower.

$$1 \text{ hp} = 746 \text{ watts}$$

Therefore, to convert the above example to the metric equivalent, multiply as follows:

$$1.54 \text{ hp x } 746 = 1\,148.84 \text{ watts per hp}$$

If 1 000 watts equal 1 kilowatt (kW), then

$$1\,148.84 \text{ watts} = 1.15 \text{ kW}$$

The result in metrics is a motor rating of 1.15 kW.

The saw shown in figure 2-1 is a heavy-duty 7 1/4-inch circular saw. Its universal motor is rated at 12.5 amps and operates on 120 volts ac. The blade is 7 1/4 inches in diameter with a 5/8-inch arbor hole. At 90 degrees, the depth of cut is 2 7/16 inches. At a 45-degree angle, it is 1 29/32 inches. No-load or idle speed is 5 800 rpm. The machine has precision ball bearings. The saw is 10 inches long, weighs 12 pounds, and is double-insulated.

Unlike handsaws, portable power saws cut from the near to the far edge of the work and from the underside of the board up. The handle is generally located on the top, on the back, or on an angle between the top and back, depending upon the manufacturer.

Control of the saw is usually by means of a trigger switch located in the handle and operated by the forefinger of the right hand.

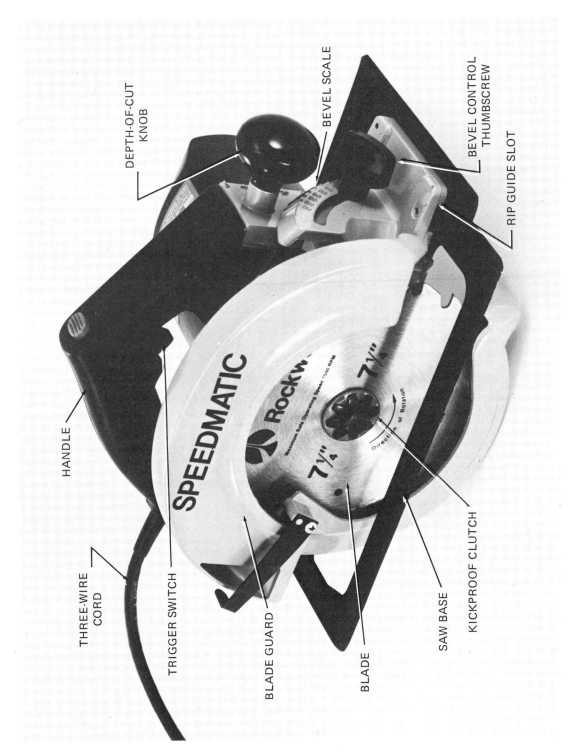

DEPTH-OF-CUT KNOB

BEVEL SCALE

BEVEL CONTROL THUMBSCREW

RIP GUIDE SLOT

HANDLE

SPEEDMATIC

Rockw

7 1/4"

7 1/4"

Direction of Rotation

Maximum Safe Operating Speed 7500 RPM

THREE-WIRE CORD

TRIGGER SWITCH

BLADE GUARD

BLADE

SAW BASE

KICKPROOF CLUTCH

Fig. 2-1 7 1/4-inch Circular saw

Two adjustment devices are built into the saw. A large handlock knob provides for depth of cut adjustment. A thumbscrew allows for angular adjustment of the blade from zero (90 degrees) to slightly more than 45 degrees. The graduated angle scale above the thumbscrew clearly shows these settings, figure 2-2 (A).

A third adjustment is provided through use of a rip guide. Two small knurled screws on the front of the saw base allow quick installation and adjustment of the rip guide and hold it firmly in position. The guide is graduated in 1/8-inch increments up to 5 inches. Aligning the desired width of rip as graduated on the rip guide, with the rip guide mark on the saw base, ensures a uniform, measured cut. Figure 2-2 (B) shows the guide set for a 1 1/4 inch width of rip.

Safety guards differ among manufacturers but usually blade guards are provided in the front and bottom of the blade. In the saw illustrated, these are telescoping guards which return to the positions shown through spring action.

One additional feature of the saw illustrated is the kickproof clutch. This relieves motor strain and possible burnout. It also protects the operator from possible kickback of the saw.

DESCRIPTION OF PORTABLE SAW BLADES

The selection of the proper circular saw blade ensures the success of the cutting job. Using the right blade contributes to the safety of the operator and maximum efficiency of the machine. It saves time, expense, and energy.

There are three basic types of blades for the portable electric saw: crosscut, rip, and combination. It is important that the right blade be used for a given job. A

Fig. 2-2 (A) Knob A controls the depth of cut. Thumbscrew B controls the bevel adjustment.

Fig. 2-2 (B) Rip guide set for 1 1/4" width of rip. Broken arrow shows direction of blade motion.

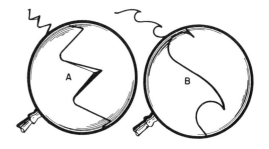

Fig. 2-3 Circular crosscut and ripsaw blades

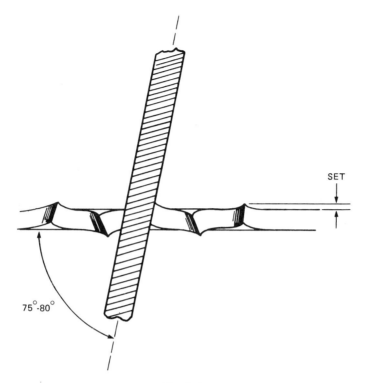

Fig. 2-4

crosscut blade is illustrated in figure 2-3 (A), page 13. A ripsaw blade is shown in figure 2-3 (B), page 13.

The teeth of a circular saw blade are *set* (tips of the teeth are bent slightly outward) alternately left and right. By setting the teeth of the saw, the *kerf* (sawcut) is slightly wider than the thickness of the blade. Crosscut teeth are filed to an angle of 75 to 80 degrees producing a knife-edge on the side to which they are set, figure 2-4. The result is that the cutting action resembles that of a knife, slicing fibers of the wood. The ripsaw blade has flat-faced teeth more like a chisel. It scoops out larger chips than the crosscut.

The combination blade, figure 2-5, combines features of both the crosscut and ripsaw blades. It has two outstanding advantages for rough work: it operates on less power and can be sharpened very easily.

For special work, special types of blades are available. Figure 2-6 shows a planer or miter blade, which is a type of combination blade. It consists of a series of four cutting

Fig. 2-5 Combination blade for rough work   **Fig. 2-6 Planer blade for smooth work**

teeth and one raker tooth. The cutting teeth resemble crosscut teeth and are set to obtain clearance of the blade. The raker teeth are similar to ripsaw teeth, but are not set. This type of blade makes an especially smooth cut and is very suitable for cutting inside trim. It should be used on dry wood only.

Another special type of blade is called the flooring blade or nail blade. This is ruggedly constructed and designed for use where random nails may be encountered. They are commonly used for cutting old flooring, reclaimed lumber, and packing cases.

Carbide-tipped blades hold a sharp edge longer than regular steel blades. Tungsten-carbide tips brazed onto a hard alloy steel blade give these blades their durability. They are generally used to cut very hard materials which might rapidly dull the standard steel blade.

A final group of special blades are the abrasive cutoff wheels. They are designed for sawing, slotting, and grooving hard dense material. There are three types of abrasive cutoff wheels: one for nonferrous metals; one for masonry, brick, stone, tile, concrete, and cinder block; and one for ferrous metals.

Take special care not to twist the saw when cutting with abrasive cutoff wheels, figure 2-7. Although very strong, they are also brittle and can break with dangerous results if the saw is twisted while cutting. It is also important that the air passages be cleared of dust immediately after using these blades. Metal, concrete, or mortar dusts are very abrasive and can severely damage the motor assembly.

Fig. 2-7 **Sawing with an abrasive cutoff wheel**

THE CARE OF CIRCULAR SAW BLADES

To keep blades in good condition, the operator should observe the following precautions.

1. Use crosscut saw blades for crosscut work only. Use ripsaw blades for ripsaw work only.

2. If the cutting process require the constant changing of saws, use a combination saw blade.

3. Do not use a saw unless there is sufficient set in the teeth to make a saw kerf through which the body of the blade will move freely.

4. Do not use a blade after you sense that it is dull, needs setting, or has come in contact with metal.

5. Do not twist the saw from a straight line while it is making a cut.

6. If a saw becomes cracked, some mechanics drill a small hole through the blade at the end of the crack. This will prevent the crack from extending. However, when the

injury it might cause to the operator if it is sprung again is considered, it is better to have the saw ground below the crack or to dispose of the blade.

7. If the blade becomes coated with resin from cutting resinous woods, remove it with a little turpentine and fine sandpaper.

How to Change Blades

1. Be sure the saw is disconnected from the power source.

2. Block the blade by inserting a piece of wood against the teeth at the front of the saw. Then loosen the retaining screw by turning it counterclockwise with the wrench provided for the saw, figure 2-8.
   NOTE: Some saws have (a) a milled flat on the shaft so that it may be held stationary with a second wrench, or (b) a hole in the saw blade and one in the gear housing, through which a nail is inserted, or (c) a built-in blade lock which holds the shaft while the retaining screw is loosened.

3. Push the circular guard back until it stops in the open position.

4. Remove the retaining screw and clutch spring washer. Lift the old blade from the shaft and slide down through the bottom opening, figure 2-9.

5. Clean the bearing surface of the collars. Add a film of grease, smoothing it over the bearing surface with the finger, figure 2-10.

6. Place the new blade on the arbor, making sure the teeth point up at the front of the saw. Add a film of grease around the hole in the blade.

7. Place the clutch spring washer in position against the blade. Place the retaining screw in position and tighten by turning clockwise, leaving the clutch spring bowed out slightly. Allow the circular blade guard to swing back in place, figure 2-11.

Fig. 2-8

Fig. 2-9

Fig 2-10

CROSSCUTTING

Cutting across the wood grain may be done with the combination blade if smoothness of the cut is not a factor. The combination tooth is really a compromise between the ripsaw tooth and the crosscut tooth. For rough or wet lumber, use the combination blade. Where a smoother cut is required, use the crosscut blade.

How to Crosscut

1. Be sure the work to be cut is solidly supported.

2. Adjust the depth of cut so that the blade will extend through the material to be cut to the extent that the gullets of the teeth clear the thickness of the material, figure 2-12.

3. Be sure the angle-adjustment thumbscrew is set and locked at zero.

4. See that the saw guard is in proper position.

5. Plug the saw into the power outlet and make certain the electric cord is properly grounded and is positioned so that it will not become tangled during the sawing operation.

6. Grasp the handle firmly with the forefinger ready to operate the starting trigger. Keep the other hand well out of danger.

7. Place the front of the saw base on the work so that the guide mark on the front plate and the line of cut are in line.

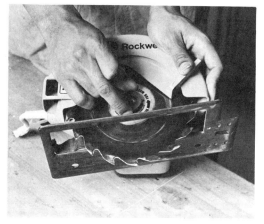

Fig. 2-11

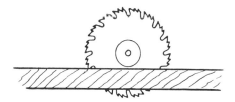

Fig. 2-12

Fig. 2-13 **Using a protractor guide to make a square crosscut**

8. With the blade well clear of the work, start the saw and allow the blade to attain full cutting speed.

9. Advance the saw into the wood, following the line of cut with the guide mark. Save the full cutting line. As skill improves, only half the width of the line should be saved. NOTE: Beginners may use a squaring template to guide the saw. After practice, simply use a square to mark the material.

10. Guide the saw steadily through the cut. If the saw stalls, do not release the starting trigger, but back out the saw until it resumes cutting speed, then continue cutting. A wedge placed in the saw kerf will help prevent the saw's binding when cutting a wide board.

NOTE: If the saw stalls excessively, disconnect the power source and check the blade for dullness or lack of set.

11. When the end of the cut is reached, release the trigger switch and allow the blade to follow through as you lift the saw out and away from the work. Twisting the saw as it is removed may score the work.

RIPPING

Cutting with the grain, or ripping, can be done with the combination blade or with the ripping blade. The ripping blade will give a smoother cut. The rip cut is generally more difficult to make than the crosscut because of the length of the cut.

Important items to bear in mind when ripping with the portable saw are:

- The board you are ripping must be well supported to prevent sagging.

- The board must be securely held in position.

- The saw blade must not cut into the wrong material.

How to Rip

1. Insert the rip guide in the frame, figure 2-14. The guide may be inserted into either side of the frame for wide or narrow widths.

2. Adjust the rip guide to the desired width by aligning the proper graduation on the guide with the mark on the saw base. Tighten the two thumbscrews to lock the guide in position.
   NOTE: If the rip guide contains no graduations, adjust it so that the guide mark on the front plate of the saw aligns with the proposed line of cut. The side of the board against which the guide rides must be straight. For cuts wider than the scope of the guide, a straight board clamped to the workpiece will serve as a guide.

3. Proceed as in crosscutting, steps 2 through 11. If the saw kerf seems to close and bind the blade, insert a wedge to open it and give clearance to the blade.

If the ripping is so long that it will be necessary to walk beside the board while cutting, make the following additional preparations before making the cut:

a. Support a 2-inch x 10-inch plank at least as long as the proposed cut, on two horses or other solid foundation at a comfortable height for cutting.

b. Place the board to be cut on the 2-inch x 10-inch plank. Allow its edge to

Fig. 2-14 Cutting with the guide

project beyond the edge of the plank about 1 inch more than the width of the proposed cut. Tack the board to the plank in this position using nails that will hold securely at each end.

c. Be sure to have a clear, unobstructed place to walk while pushing the saw along the required length, and see that the saw cord will not become fouled while making the cut.

BEVEL CUTS

A bevel cut with the portable electric saw is made in much the same manner as a crosscut. These cuts, however, require the additional adjustment of the angle segment thumbscrew to set the blade at the angle desired. A *simple miter cut,* figure 2-15, is actu-

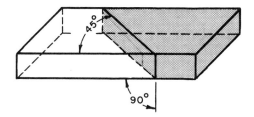

Fig. 2-15 Miter cut

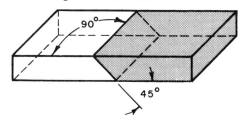

Fig. 2-16 Bevel cut

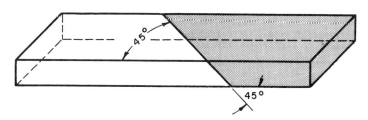

Fig. 2-17 Compound miter or compound bevel cut

ally nothing more than a straight-blade cut made at a 45-degree angle across the board. A *bevel cut,* figure 2-16, is one on which the saw blade is set at the required angle and the cut is made straight across the board. A *compound miter* or *compound bevel cut,* figure 2-17, is one in which the saw blade is set at the required bevel angle, and the line of cut across the board is also laid out at an angle. Such cuts are used for ridge cuts of hips, valley jacks, and cripple rafters.

How to Make a Simple Miter Cut

1. Lay out the line of cut on the material to be cut, using a sliding T bevel, framing square, or protractor to obtain the 45-degree angle.

2. An angle gauge may also be used and is the best method. This gauge contains a protractor and, when set to the proper angle, provides a guide against which the saw base is pushed as the cut is made.

3. Cut as in crosscutting.

How to Make a Bevel Cut

1. Loosen the angle segment thumbscrew and rotate the saw frame until the pointer on the angle indicator rests at the desired angle of bevel. Tighten the thumbscrew securely.

2. Adjust the depth of cut so that the saw blade will penetrate the bevel thickness of the material to be cut.

Fig. 2-18 Notching a rafter

Fig. 2-19

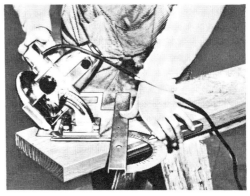

Fig. 2-20 Compound bevel cut

NOTE: The bevel thickness will be greater than the straight thickness and it may be necessary, if the blade will not clear the bevel thickness, to make a cut on each side of the wood to cut through it. If so, reduce the depth of cut to a little more than half of what is ordinarily required.

3. Proceed to cut as in crosscutting. If a cut must be made on each side of the wood, turn the piece over and maintain the same saw adjustments as with the first cut. Guide the second cut so that the two kerfs will be in line.

How to Make a Compound Bevel Cut

1. Lay out the line of cut on the material to be cut, using a sliding T bevel, framing square, protractor, or best, an angle gauge.

2. Loosen the angle segment thumbscrew, rotate the saw blade to the desired bevel angle as indicated by the pointer, and tighten the thumbscrew securely.

3. Adjust the depth of cut so that the blade will penetrate the bevel thickness of the material to be cut. Tighten the depth adjustment knob securely.

4. Make a trial cut on scrap lumber and check the accuracy of the bevel angle and the line of cut angle using a protractor or an angle gauge.

5. If all adjustments are accurate, proceed to cut as in crosscutting, except the saw should be guided along the outside of the line of cut with reference to the guide mark on the saw base for miter cuts.

CUTTING DADOES, GROOVES, AND RABBETS

Rabbet and dado cuts with the portable electric saw are made in much the same manner as cross cuts and rip cuts except that the depth adjustment is set so the blade cuts only to the depth of the rabbet or groove desired. A gauge or straightedge is helpful for both types of cuts.

How to Make a Dado Cut

1. Mark the outlines of the required dado on the board to be cut, figure 2-21.

2. Adjust the saw blade (crosscut) to the required depth of the dado. Tighten the adjustment knob securely, figure 2-22.

3. Use a square or angle template to guide the saw across the cut, figure 2-23.

4. First, cut along the two outside marks of the dado, leaving both marks on the board.

5. With a series of cuts about 1/16 inch apart, proceed across the dado from one side to the other, figure 2-24.

6. Clean out the dado with the saw. When all the slender strips have been removed, move the saw sideways while it is running so that the entire dado is cleaned out to a uniform depth. Take care not to let the saw blade touch the sides of the dado.
   NOTE: Groove cuts are made in the same manner as described above except that a ripping blade is used since cutting is done with the grain.

How to Make a Rabbet Cut

NOTE: For edge rabbet cuts (with the grain), use a ripping blade; for end rabbets, use a crosscut blade.

1. Mark the required rabbet outlines along the edge and face of the board to be cut.

2. Secure the board to be cut on its edge.

Fig. 2-21

Fig. 2-22

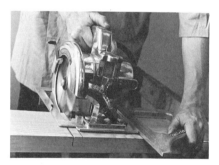

Fig. 2-23

Fig. 2-24

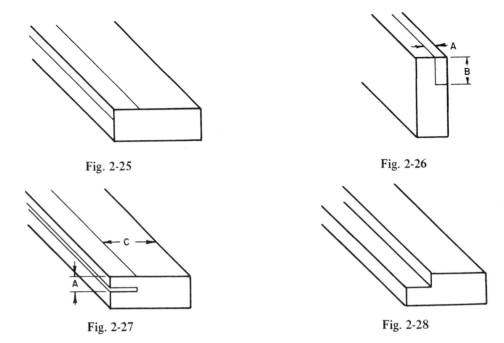

Fig. 2-25   Fig. 2-26

Fig. 2-27   Fig. 2-28

3. Attach the rip guide to the base of the saw and adjust the guide to the depth of the desired rabbet (A in figure 2-26).

4. Adjust the depth of cut so it will cut the full width (B in figure 2-26) of the desired rabbet.

5. Make the cut.

6. Now place the board flat with the rabbet outline mark face up. Secure it firmly.

7. Set the ripping guide so the blade will follow along the outline mark of the rabbet (C in figure 2-27).

8. Set the depth of the cut so the blade will cut the full depth of the rabbet (A in figure 2-27) and will meet the previous cut.

9. Make this second cut. The surplus wood should easily be removed.

CUTTING A POCKET

The pocket or interior cut is one which starts and ends within the width or length of a board, floor or wall. When starting this cut, it is necessary to hold the circular blade guard out of the way. Once the cut is started, the guard stays out of the way without being held.

How to Make a Pocket Cut

NOTE: Since cutting will be done both with and across the grain, a combination blade is best used.

1. Mark the area to be cut. Use clear sharp lines and mark exactly to the corners.

2. Set up temporary guides along these lines to aid in guiding the saw accurately. Narrow wood strips tacked in position can be used.

3. Adjust the depth of cut so the blade will cut though the material only.
   NOTE: Make sure there are no nails or other obstacles in the cutting paths.

4. Push the telescoping guard lever forward so the lower edge of the blade is exposed.

5. Starting near a corner limit, tilt the saw forward until the front edge of the blade rests on the surface on the waste side of the line of cut, figure 2-29.

Fig. 2-29 Starting the pocket cut

6. With the blade clear of the material, start the motor and when it has reached full speed, lower the blade into the surface until the base rests on it firmly.

7. Advance the saw to the corner. Remove it from the cut, turn it around, and cut in the opposite direction to the corner.

8. Proceed in this manner around the other sides of the opening.
   NOTE: The circular blade will extend slightly beyond the corner on the top of the work if a full cutout is made. This can be avoided by stopping the cuts when the blade just reaches each corner on the top surface, then finishing the corners with a keyhole or handsaw.

SPECIAL CUTS

Many types of cuts can be made with the portable electric saw and its standard equipment. With additional accessories, which can be readily attached to the saw frame, and with skill on the part of the operator, this type of saw has the capacity to make any type of cut required by the woodworker. Special blades such as were described earlier in the unit make possible the cutting of every type of material in modern construction.

REVIEW QUESTIONS

A. Short Answer or Discussion

1. How are circular saws identified?

2. How is the saw adjusted for depth of cut?

3. How is the saw adjusted for bevel cuts?

4. Suppose a 60-degree bevel is desired. How would you set the saw for such a cut? Explain with a sketch.

5. How is the saw adjusted for width of rip?

6. How does the depth of cut differ in vertical and angle positions of the saw blade?

7. Where are blade guards desirable for utmost safety?

8. What is the purpose of a kickproof clutch? What safety features does it provide?

9. What are the three basic types of blades used in the circular saw? What is the purpose of each?

10. When might a planer combination blade be used?

11. What type blades will give the longest service?

12. What special type of blade is used for cutting material such as cement block, slate, sheet metal, etc.?

13. Describe two important precautions for using the type of blade described in question 12.

14. What is a possible cause for excessive stalling of the saw?

15. In making a compound bevel cut, what unusual procedure is followed in guiding the cut of the saw?

B. Completion

1. If cutting requires constant changes from crosscut to rip, use a _____ type blade.

2. A _____ saw blade should never be used.

3. Depth of cut should be adjusted so the _____ of the teeth clear the thickness of the material.

4. The bevel thickness of a cut will be _____ than the vertical thickness.

5. The blade is aligned with the line of cut when the _____ on the front plate and the _____ are in line.

6. Twisting the saw while the blade is revolving may _____ the work.

7. In making a long rip cut, it is sometimes necessary to insert a _____ in the _____ to keep the blade from binding.

8. In cutting along the two outside guide lines of a dado, both marks should be _____ the board.

9. Subsequent cuts for a dado should be about _____ apart.

10. When starting a pocket cut, the _____ must be held out of the way.

C. Identification and Interpretation

  1. Identify the numbered parts of the circular saw illustrated.

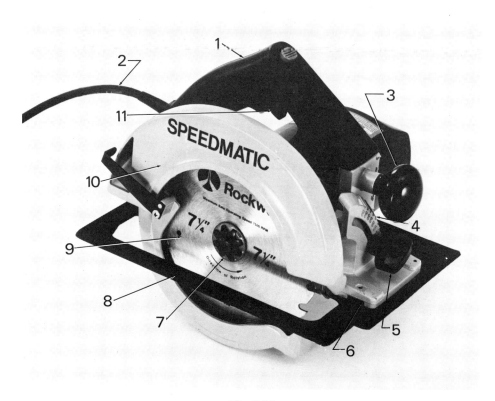

Fig. 2-30

Unit 3 THE RADIAL ARM SAW

Radial arm saws are made in a range of sizes from 3/4 horsepower (0.56kW) to 10 horsepower (7.46kW). The smallest is the most popular for residential construction and home shop use. The larger types are used in all types of industrial construction, maintenance work, and the fabrication of an almost unlimited range of materials.

Figure 3-1 shows a 10-inch radial arm saw with the following cutting capacities: crosscut, 14 1/2 inches; rip, 24 11/16 inches; depth of cut, 3 inches. This saw is typical of radial arm saws and shall be used for purposes of explanation and illustration throughout this unit.

DESCRIPTION OF THE RADIAL ARM SAW

The yoke cradles the motor and is supported by the cantilever (radial) arm. It travels on a track located on the cantilever arm and may be rotated horizontally 360 degrees. The arm is supported by a column which is bolted to the metal base of the saw table. The yoke

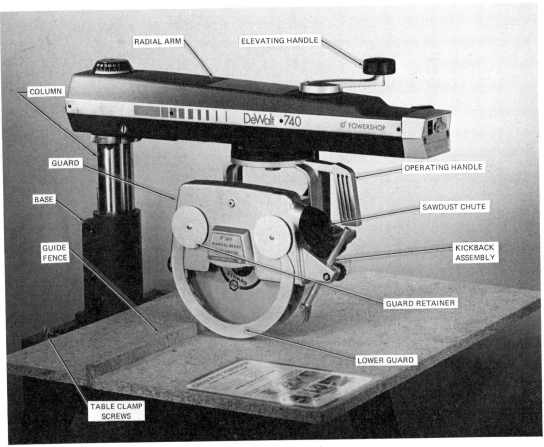

Fig. 3-1 (A) A 10-inch radial arm saw

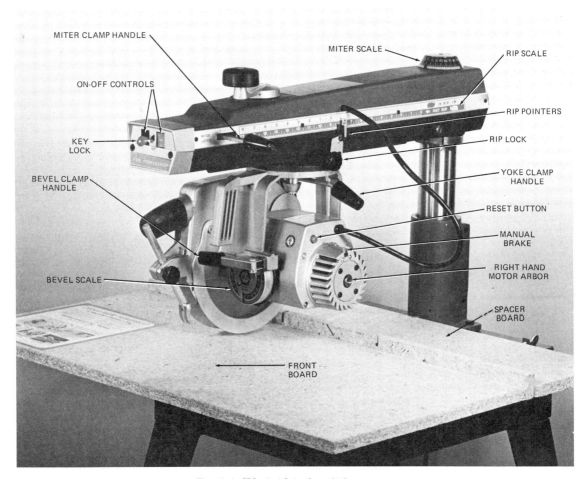

MITER CLAMP HANDLE

ON-OFF CONTROLS

KEY
LOCK

BEVEL CLAMP
HANDLE

BEVEL SCALE

MITER SCALE

RIP SCALE

RIP POINTERS

RIP LOCK

YOKE CLAMP
HANDLE

RESET BUTTON

MANUAL
BRAKE

RIGHT HAND
MOTOR ARBOR

SPACER
BOARD

FRONT
BOARD

Fig. 3-1 (B) A 10-inch radial arm saw

and arm may be raised or lowered on the column as well as rotated. Depth of cut is controlled by the elevating handle. Each turn of the handle raises or lowers the saw 1/8 inch.

The miter clamp handle holds the arm to the column at any angle. The miter latch engages slots in the column to lock the arm in position at 45 and 90 degrees. The rip block releases so the yoke may turn the saw to position for ripping or crosscutting. The miter scale locates the arm at the desired angle to the right or left. The bevel clamp positions the saw blade to make bevel cuts indicated on the bevel scale.

Safety guards include the safety key lock; floating ring guards which enclose the blade and are self-adjusting to depth of cut; and the kickback guard.

The motor for the model shown in figure 3-1 operates at 3 450 rpm and is available in 120 208/240 volts, single-phase, 60 hertz ac. The totally enclosed motor has sealed-for-life bearings which never require oiling. It also has an electromechanical brake which stops the blade quickly after power is shut off. The motor is protected against overload by a manual-reset, overload device which reacts when the motor becomes overheated. To reset the motor, press the STOP switch and let the motor cool. Press the reset button and listen for an audible click. If there is no click, let the motor cool longer before attempting to reset the motor.

The radial arm saw gets its name from the arm's ability to be pivoted a full 360 degrees to the right or left. Figure 3-2 shows the controls used to rotate the arm. To adjust positions, pull the miter clamp and swing the radial arm right or left to the desired angle. The calibrated miter scale is at eye-level and shows the exact angle of the arm. With the handle released, the miter latch will automatically locate at 0 and 45 degrees. After positioning the arm to the angle desired, push the clamp to lock the arm.

The yoke which cradles the motor can also be rotated 360 degrees. Pull the yoke clamp handle against the pin lifter and the entire yoke can be swiveled to any position for ripping. (See figure 3-4.) The yoke automatically stops at four 90-degree positions.

Besides the ability of the radial arm to pivot and the yoke to swivel, the saw may be tilted for bevel cuts and raised or lowered for depth cuts. Figure 3-3 shows the elevating handle being turned. Figure 3-5 shows the saw being tilted. To tilt the saw, elevate the arm 2 1/2 inches (18 turns). Pull the bevel clamp handle and tilt the saw to the desired angle. With the handle released, the bevel-locating pin automatically locates 0-, 45-, and 90-degree bevel positions. When the desired bevel angle is obtained, push the clamp handle locking the bevel angle. NOTE: Always leave the kickback guard in place. Adjust it to barely clear the work piece in crosscutting operations and about 1/8 inch below the top of the stock during all ripping operations. Do not feed the stock from the kickback guard side of the saw when ripping.

Fig. 3-2 Pivoting the radial arm

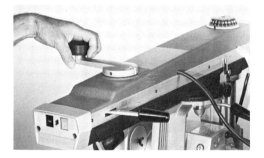

Fig. 3-3 Elevating handle to raise and lower saw

Applications

The types of carpentry work to which the radial arm saw may be applied are almost unlimited. Crosscutting, bevel crosscutting, ripping, and compound mitering may be done with common saw blades by making the proper adjustments of the saw carriage. Dado cuts, shaping, routing, tenoning, and special cuts can be done with special cutters that can be fitted to the arbor.

SAFETY FEATURES

Maximum safety is provided in radial-arm machines. The saw blade rotates down and away from the operator. This holds

Fig. 3-4 Saw swivels 360 degrees for rip cuts

the board down on the saw table and against the rear fence when crosscutting. The operator's hands are protected by the guards, which encircle the saw blade on both sides, and by the kickback rod, which incorporates a safety splitter to eliminate binding of the saw when ripping. The directional spout controls the flow of sawdust away from the operator. An electromechanical brake stops the saw blade from rotating within seconds after the switch is turned off. The handles used for relocation and

Fig. 3-5 Tilt saw for bevel cut

adjustment of the saw are not within the danger zones of the operator's hands. The table top is designed to eliminate saw overhang at any angle, and gives maximum work area. An automatic safety return device prevents the motor and carriage from accidentally moving forward along the tracks of the arm when the motor is running, and automatically returns the motor and carriage behind the guide fence after the cut is completed. The cam-type switch which delivers power to the saw when turned either right or left can be removed only when the power is shut off. The controls, Start and Stop, are located at the end of the radial arm, convenient to the operator and safely out of the way of the revolving blade.

SAFETY PRECAUTIONS

- Be sure that the saw is located in a position so that the electric lead line running from the saw to the electric supply box or socket will not be in the way during movements of the operator or the saw arm.

- Check the electric voltage and cycle of the motor on the saw; also check the source of power for the correct voltage. Be sure that the machine is grounded.

- Do not stand directly in front of the saw blade. Be sure the floor is clean of debris. Grasp the saw handle and pull the saw out to its full travel on the radial arm. Do this several times and find the most convenient footing that will enable you to bend your arm naturally without strain on your body, maintain your foot position of the floor, and also allow you to watch the operation of the saw.

- Always return the saw and motor to the column at the rear of the radial arm.

- Check all clamping and locking handles involved in cutting operations; tighten them and secure the guards properly.

- Never leave the key in the machine unless it is operating and always turn the power off before making adjustments.

- Be sure the saw table is clean so that the material to be cut may be placed in a solid flat position against the guide fence. When this is done, it can safely be held in such a position during the cutting operation. Never move the cut material away from the saw until the saw blade is pushed back to the rear and entirely out of the material.

- Do not wear gloves or loose clothing. They may become caught in the moving parts of the machine and cause injury.

- Remember that in crosscutting operations, the saw blade should rotate down and away from the operator and the saw blade should be pulled slowly into the stationary material.

- Remember that in ripsawing operations, the ripsaw rotates up and toward the operator and that the material to be cut is pushed into the saw, as the motor is stationary on the radial arm.

- Do not let the saw blade lose speed during a cutting operation. Use less pressure on the saw or the material to be cut. Get used to the sound of the free running blade and when it sounds different, stop the saw and find the cause.

- Do not use dull or damaged blades or cutters of any type on the machine. A dull tool is a dangerous tool, especially when driven at high speed.

- Keep the machine free of sawdust. Use a good grade of motor oil to lubricate the elevating screw threads, swivel, miter, and bevel latches, about every 48 hours of motor operation. Wipe off all surplus oil. Do not try to oil the motor. Keep the arm tracks and roller bearing surfaces clean and dry. Periodic cleaning with a dry cleaner is recommended.

GENERAL INSTRUCTIONS FOR OPERATION AND ADJUSTMENT

The following general conditions are most important before operating the radial arm saw:

- Study the manufacturer's description of the machine and its adjustments for the type of cutting expected to be done.

- Make the adjustments on the machine while the power is disconnected and go through all the operations required to make the complete cut to be sure that the adjustments have been made properly.

- Check all the adjustments that are not involved in the cutting to be sure that they are secure and that the safety guards will work for your protection throughout the operation.

- Revolve the saw blade, or cutter, by hand to be sure it runs clear and cannot become fouled.

- Check the saw table to see that it is at the proper angle with the face of the saw blade.

- Check the table fences and stops that will be used in making the cut to see that they are secured to the table. Clear all loose material from the table.

- Be sure the electric switch is in the off position, then connect the cord to the source of current. Start the saw and be sure that the saw blade rotates in a direction down and away from the handle of the machine and the operator. If it rotates in the opposite direction, stop the machine and check the wiring in the motor connecting box.

Today, many larger pieces of equipment are purchased unassembled. All such equipment is assembled and job-tested at the factory, then partially disassembled for shipment. Usually, the only tools needed for assembly are a screwdriver, pliers, and hammer. Wrenches and special tools generally come with the machine. If assembly is required, follow each direction carefully and proceed according to the instruction manual.

If the machine comes assembled, then it has been carefully adjusted at the factory and should require no additional adjustment, unless it is so indicated by the manufacturer. After a period of operation, however, it may be necessary to make adjustments for the continued proper operation of the equipment. The detailed adjustment procedures in this unit are provided primarily for this maintenance and should not be attempted by inexperienced operators.

> Do not use adjustable claw-type wrenches or ordinary tools to make adjustments. Use tools that are similar to those indicated in the specific adjustments discussed in this unit.

How to Mount the Saw Blade

1. Remove the saw guard, the arbor nut (which has a left-hand thread), and arbor collars. Now place the 3/8-inch thick collar on the arbor so that the recessed side of the collar faces out. To remove the arbor nut, fit a large open-end wrench on the flat section of the arbor shaft, and a second similar wrench on the nut. Holding the first wrench steady with the right-hand, use downward pressure of the left hand on the second wrench to loosen the nut.

2. Place the saw blade on the arbor so that the teeth of the saw nearest the saw table top point toward the elevating column of the machine. Generally, blades are marked "this side out" to avoid mounting the blade backwards. Remember that the motor shaft rotates clockwise.

3. Place the 1/4-inch thick arbor collar on the arbor with the recessed face against the saw blade, figure 3-6.

4. Tighten the arbor nut using two wrenches as shown in figure 3-7.

Fig. 3-6

Fig. 3-7

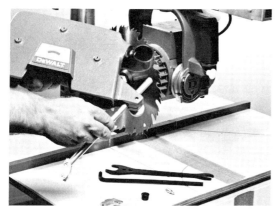

Fig. 3-8

Fig. 3-9

5. Assemble the guard kickback and elbow, figure 3-8.

6. Enclose the blade with the guard and lock in place with the wingnut, figure 3-9. Rotate the saw blade by hand to see that it runs clear and free.

How to Adjust the Saw Table

The top of the saw table should be in perfect alignment with the travel track in the radial arm so that when the saw cuts through a board on the table top, the depth of the saw kerf at the entering edge of the board will be exactly the same depth throughout the full length of the cut in all cutting positions.

NOTE: This adjustment is handled differently with different models. Wherever a question exists, it is wise to consult the manufacturer.

1. Remove the guard, the blade, and the washers from the motor.

2. Raise the arm about 20 turns.

3. Release the bevel-lock lever and pull the bevel locating pin.

4. Turn the motor until the arbor (shaft that holds the saw blade) is perpendicular (90 degrees) to the table.

5. Release the miter lock and locator so the arm can move freely to the left and right.

6. Lower the arm until the end of the arbor is just over the table.

7. Bend over so the table top is eye level. Move the arm to the right and left and push the roller head back-and-forth. Check for any change in the distance between the end of the arbor and the table top.

8. If the clearance is the same over the entire surface of the table, the arm is parallel to the table.

9. If there is a difference in the clearance, remove the four spring pins (if provided) and adjust as follows:

   Position the end of the arbor directly over the highest point of the table. Look under the table and you will notice four locking nuts that hold the cleats to the frame. Position the end of the arbor directly over the locking nut nearest this high point. Lower the arbor until it touches the table. Now move the arbor directly over another locking nut. Loosen the locking nut and push the table up until it touches the end of the arbor. Tighten the locking nut. Adjust the other locking nuts in the same way. Repeat step #7 to check the clearance between the end of the arbor and the table.

Fig. 3-10 Adjusting the saw table

How to Square the Face of the Saw Blade with the Table Top

1. Set the radial arm in position for 90-degree crosscutting. Be sure when mounting the saw blade on the motor shaft that the collars and saw blade are clean and properly placed on the shaft. Tighten the nut to bring the saw and collars to their proper positions on the shaft. Make sure that the bevel latch is properly seated at 90 degrees.

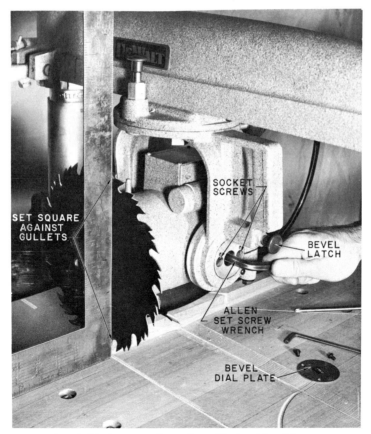

Fig. 3-11 Squaring face of saw blade with table top

2. Place the steel square against the face of the saw and table top as shown in figure 3-11, page 33. Be sure the square is placed against the gullets of the blade, not directly against the teeth.

3. Remove the bevel dial plate using a phillips screwdriver.

4. With an allen wrench, loosen the two socket screws about two turns.

5. Twist or tilt the motor head so that the saw blade aligns with the edge of the square as shown.

6. Tighten the allen key socket screws and replace the bevel dial plate and saw guard.

How to Adjust the Fences on the Saw Table

The guide fence is adjustable to three positions on the table by means of spacing strips and clamps located at the rear of the table.

1. For ordinary width boards that are to be crosscut or ripped, loosen the clamps that hold the spacer boards and place the guide fence in front of the spacer strips and against the edge and flush with the ends of the solid table. Be sure the spacer strips and fence are solid on the steel frame. Then tighten the metal clamps to hold the guide fence in place.

2. To place the fence for wider board cutting, loosen the metal clamps, place the 2-inch wide spacer strip in front of the guide fence, and tighten the clamps.

3. To place the guide fence for maximum width cutting or ripping, loosen the metal clamps. Then place all the spacer strips in front of the guide fence and against the solid saw table. Be sure the spacer strips lie flat on the frame and flush at the ends. The metal clamps should be tight to hold the spacer strips and fence in proper position.

If the guide fence should become cut with many different saw kerfs, as it will with continual use, it is a good idea to replace it with a new and similar one. Special fences may be made for this use with special cutters.

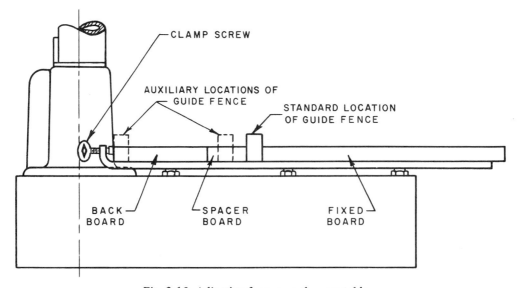

Fig. 3-12 Adjusting fences on the saw table

It is a good idea to cover the saw table with a hard-faced plywood or composition board 1/4 or 3/8 inch thick. If this covering becomes scarred, it can be replaced more readily than the original saw table.

How to Square the Crosscut Travel of the Radial Arm

The crosscut travel of the radial arm must be perfectly square with the rear fence guide to ensure making square cuts.

To check if this adjustment is needed, lay a steel square flat upon the saw table, straight against the guide fence and against the side of the sawblade which should be lowered to the top of the table. (See A in figure 3-13.)

Move the saw forward and backward along the radial arm. If the blade moves along the edge of the square equidistant in all positions, no adjustment is required. If the distances differ, adjustment should be made as follows:

1. Loosen the arm clamp handle (B) and the latch key (C).

2. Loosen both socket set screws (D) with a 1/4-inch allen key wrench.

3. If the saw blade moves <u>toward</u> the edge of the steel square as the saw is moved forward along the radial arm,
   a. loosen the rear adusting screw where the screwdriver is shown (E).
   b. tighten the opposite front screw (F) to take up the slack.
   c. check the adjustment for accuracy by moving the saw back and forth. If correct, tighten both allen key setscrews (D), the latch (C), and the arm clamp handle (B).

4. If the saw blade moves <u>away</u> from the steel square as it travels along the radial arm, make opposite adjustments as follows:
   a. proceed as in Steps 1 and 2.
   b. loosen the <u>front</u> adjusting screw <u>opposite</u> the screwdriver (F).
   c. tighten the rear adjusting screw (E).
   d. check adjustment for accuracy and, if correct, tighten the allen key set screws (D), the latch (C), and the arm clamp handle (B).

How to Adjust the Column Gripping Tension and Alignment

To check if this adjustment should be made, tighten the arm clamp handle (A, figure 3-14), and with ordinary hand pressure, check to see if there is any side-to-side motion at the end of radial arm (B).

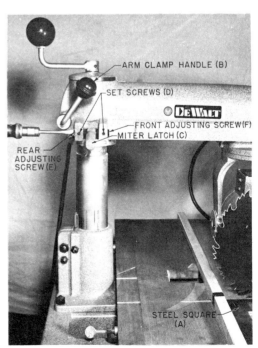

Fig. 3-13 Adjusting crosscut travel with guide fence

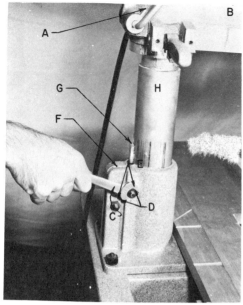

Fig. 3-14 Adjusting base to column

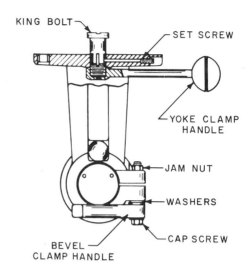

Fig. 3-15 Adjusting bevel clamp handle

If there is no motion, adjustment is unnecessary. If there is motion, proceed as follows:

1. Loosen the pinch bolt (C), the hex jam nuts (D), and the allen key setscrews (E).

2. Rotate the elevating crank handle to raise and lower the column. Tighten the pinch bolt (C), so that the column is snug and can be raised and lowered freely without play.

3. Push the adjusting gib (F), against the column key (G), so that the gib and key are held tightly against the column (H).

4. Tighten all the allen key setscrews until there is no play or side motion in the column.

5. Tighten all the hex jam nuts with a wrench.

How to Adjust the Bevel Clamp Handle

The purpose of the bevel clamp handle is to hold the motor swivel plate rigid in its yoke at any angle, even though the bevel latch may be disengaged from the locating holes in the dial plate. The bevel latch locates 90-degree crosscuts, 45-degree crosscuts, and 0-degree vertical position.

1. Loosen the handle and the hex jam nut.

2. Turn the cap screw clockwise until the bevel clamp handle rigidly clamps the motor in its yoke.

3. Tighten the hex jam nut.

How to Take Heel Cutting Out of the Saw Kerf

A good way to check for heel cutting is to watch the back of the saw blade as the teeth come up through the board. If the teeth are kicking up the top wood fibers on one side

Fig. 3-16 Adjusting crosscut travel parallel to arm tracks

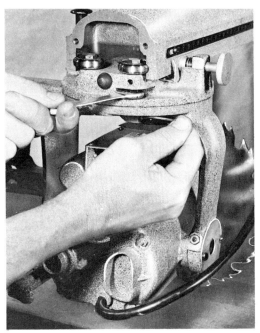

Fig. 3-17 Adjusting yoke clamp handle

of the saw kerf more than on the opposite side, the blade is not rotating parallel to the radial arm track (heeling).

If the saw is heeling on the <u>right side</u> of the saw kerf, proceed as follows:

1. Loosen setscrew (A), about 1/6 of a full turn, and tighten setscrew, (B) to take up the slack. Use a 5/16-inch allen wrench. (See figure 3-16.)

2. After adjusting, place the saw guard in position and make a few trial cuts on a board 10 inches wide.

3. Test for saw heeling on the square cut, and right- and left-hand bevel cuts.

If the saw is heeling on the <u>left side</u> of the saw kerf, proceed as follows:

1. Loosen setscrew (B), and tighten setscrew (A), with the 5/16-inch allen wrench, figure 3-16.

2. With saw guard in position, make trial cuts on a board 10 inches wide, and test for square cuts and right- and left-hand cuts, as above.

If the saw is heeling on the <u>bottom side</u> of the saw kerf, proceed as follows:

1. Loosen both setscrews (A and B), and tighten setscrew (C), figure 3-16.

2. Make trial cuts and test for heeling as above.

If the saw is heeling on the <u>top side</u> of the saw kerf, proceed as follows:

1. Loosen setscrew (C), and tighten both setscrews (A and B), figure 3-16.

2. Proceed to test adjustment as described above.

How to Adjust the Yoke Clamp Handle

There should be no play between the swivel plate and the yoke plate. The yoke clamp handle, together with the king bolt, should securely lock the saw carriage to the yoke. If, at any time, the yoke clamp handle can be moved so that it strikes the rear portion of the yoke, it is not in proper adjustment. Its proper position for machine operation is approximately 90 degrees or less to the hand grip of the yoke. To correct the adjustment:

1. Remove the arm end cap.

2. Remove the yoke, saw carriage, and motor assembly from the arm.

3. Loosen the dog screw located in the milled slot in the side of the king bolt.
   NOTE: The dog screw keeps the king bolt from turning when the yoke clamp handle is loosened or tightened.

4. Turn the king bolt clockwise about 1/6 turn so the dog screw can be located in the next slot of the king bolt.

5. Tighten the dog screw, then back it off slightly so that the king bolt can slide freely up and down as the yoke clamp handle is loosened or tightened.

6. Replace the saw carriage into the arm.

7. Check the rollerhead bearing adjustment.
   NOTE: There should be no play in the roller bearings when the saw carriage travels along the track of the arm.

8. To take up slack between the bearings and the track, adjust the hex nuts above and below the swivel plates.

9. Secure the end plate on the radial arm.

BASIC TECHNIQUES

There are only six basic cuts in sawing: crosscut, miter, rip, bevel crosscut, bevel miter or compound bevel, and bevel rip. All other cuts, no matter how intricate, are simply combinations or adaptions of these fundamental techniques.

CUTTING ACROSS THE GRAIN

The operations described for crosscutting are basic for all general cutting across or diagonal to the direction of the wood grain, and for cutting that involves the traveling of the motor along the radial arm. There are many special cuts that also include these basic operations; the only difference is that special cutters are used.

How to Make a Crosscut

1. Check to be sure a crosscut blade is mounted on the saw and that the teeth are pointing toward the back of the machine and away from the operator.

2. Check the miter scale to see if it reads 0 degrees. If not, pull the miter clamp handle and set the radial arm to 0 degrees.

3. Check the blade depth. The blade should penetrate the surface of the table not more than 1/32 to 1/16 inch.

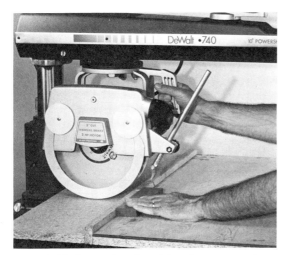

Fig. 3-18 Proper hand position for crosscutting   Fig. 3-19 The miter cut

4. Place the stock against the fence and move it to the position or mark where the cut will be made.

5. Hold the stock with the left hand, four fingers on the stock and the thumb tucked under the palm, figure 3-18. Keep fingers of the left hand at least 3 inches from the blade.

6. Turn on the saw and with the right hand on the saw handle draw the saw towards you just far enough to cut through the stock. Push the saw back behind the fence.
    NOTE: If the saw is drawn too far past the stock, the stock to the right of the saw may move into the path of the saw. When you try to return the saw back behind the fence the teeth will hit this piece and lift it over the fence with quite a bang.

How to Make a Crosscut on Wider Lumber

With the fence in the forward position, the average capacity of a crosscut is 13 inches. If the piece is 15 or 16 inches wide, draw the saw as far back as possible. With the saw held in this position, lift the back edge of the stock up toward the motor bottom. If the board is too wide, the fence must be moved to the rear of the table. When performing this operation be very careful to keep your lifting hand clear of the blade. Be sure you lift the entire back of the board, not just a corner of the board.

How to Make a Miter Cut

The miter cut is a crosscut made on the diagonal. The stock is cut at an angle other than 90 degrees with the fence, and 90 degrees with the surface of the table.
NOTE: The working surface (surface in front of the fence) is covered with a sheet of 1/4-inch plywood which may be removed after many uses. The portion behind the fence will be lower than the working surface. When the yoke is behind the fence the radial arm may be moved without elevating the blade.

1. To set the saw for a miter cut, release the miter lock lever and move the radial arm to the desired angle.

2. Lock the arm in position by pushing the miter lock lever.

3. Place the stock on the table against the fence and slide it to the position or mark where the cut is to be made.

4. Hold the stock in your left hand, if the cut is to be made diagonally from left to right. Hold it in your right hand, if the cut is to be made diagonally from right to left.

5. Turn on the saw and draw the saw only far enough to cut through the piece and push the saw back behind the fence.

How to Make a Bevel Cut

The bevel cut is a crosscut made at some angle other than 90 degrees to the table and an angle that is 90 degrees to the fence.

1. Set the saw for the bevel cut by drawing the saw forward. Elevate the saw 18 or 19 turns.

2. Release the bevel lock and with your left hand on the kickback rod rotate the saw to the desired bevel angle, counterclockwise. Any bevel angle may be selected, but the saw has an automatic 45-degree bevel locator.

3. Lower the radial arm until the blade is in its groove, 1/16 inch below the surface of the table. If the table does not have a groove, establish one with the saw running.

4. With the saw behind the fence, position the stock up against the fence.

5. Hold the stock with the right hand and pull the saw with the left hand until the blade is about 1/2 inch past the stock, figure 3-21.

Fig. 3-20 Incorrect

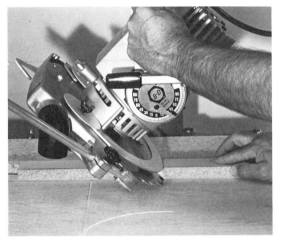

Fig. 3-21 Correct

Fig. 3-22 Compound miter

The bevel cut is made with the right hand holding the stock because the tilt of the saw tends to move the stock away from the blade before it is completely cut, figure 3-20 inset. Figure 3-20 also shows that if the left hand is used, it will be hidden from the operator's vision as the saw is drawn through the stock.

How to Make a Horizontal Crosscut

This operation is used for cutting across the end of stock and requires that the saw be positioned at 90 degrees from the vertical position. The operation is identical to a bevel crosscut but the saw is swung to the full 90-degree bevel position. The cut is made as in crosscutting.

How to Make a Compound Bevel Cut

This cut is simply a combination of the bevel and miter cuts. The saw blade is tilted to the bevel angle and the radial arm is revolved to the miter angle. The cut is then made as in crosscutting.

Miscellaneous Crosscut Techniques

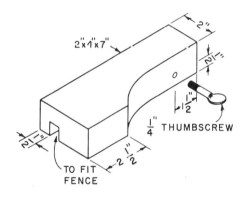

1. To cut lumber thicker than the normal depth-of-cut capacity of the saw blade, make the first cut with the blade set to cut slightly more than half the wood thickness. Turn the piece over and complete the cutting with a second pass. The stock should be marked on three sides for easier alignment when it is turned over for the second cut.

Fig. 3-23

2. To cut multiple pieces to length, fasten a stop block to the fence. The distance between the stop and the blade will be the length of the work. A wood clamp will suffice as a stop, or the type shown in figure 3-23 may be constructed. It is dadoed to ride on the fence and is clamped in position by the thumbscrew.

RIP CUTTING

In general, when making cuts that run parallel to the grain with the radial arm saw, the saw carriage is held stationary on the radial arm. The saw blade is turned so that its face is parallel to the direction of the wood grain. The wood is fed into and agianst the revolving saw, rather than the revolving saw being fed into the wood as in crosscutting.

How to Make a Straight Rip Cut

1. With kerfs properly cut into the table top, pull the saw out toward you. If a kerf for ripping has not been established, the saw must be elevated to set the rip width and lowered to penetrate the surface of the table.

Fig. 3-24 (A) Unlocking the yoke clamp

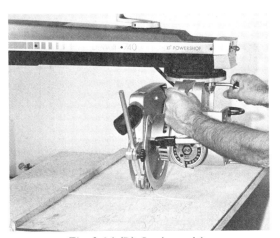

Fig. 3-24 (B) In-rip position

2. Release the yoke lock and yoke locator pin and swing the roller head to the "out-rip" or "in-rip" position. Figures 3-24 (B) and 3-24 (C) show these positions.

   NOTE: With the saw in the "in-rip" position, material must be fed from the right side against the teeth of the blade. With the saw in the "out-rip" position, material must be fed from the left side.

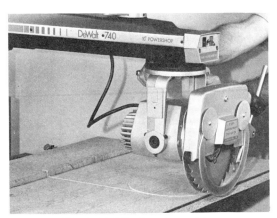

Fig. 3-24 (C) Out-rip position

3. The locator pin will fall into place when the blade is parallel with the fence. Lock the yoke lock and position the saw to the desired rip width. When the saw is in position, lock track by tightening the rip-lock clamp.

4. The upper blade guard must be positioned. Place the stock to be cut next to the blade. Lower the front of the guard until it is about 1/8 inch above the stock. Lower the anti kickback until it is 1/8 inch below the surface of the stock. Figures 3-25 and 3-26 show the correct way to position the blade guard.

5. Before operating the machine, be sure that all the adjustments are correct and tight. The guard should be adjusted and the kickback rod should be in position. Remember to feed the stock from the side opposite the kickback rod, figures 3-25 and 3-26.

6. When feeding the material into the saw, hold it firmly and guide it along the back fence of the saw table and into the revolving saw with a slow, steady motion.

7. Do not force the material into the saw to the extent that it decreases the speed of the saw. If the speed decreases with normal pressure, it is evident that the saw blade needs refitting or the saw carriage is not adjusted properly. Release the material from the saw before trying to shut off the power.

Fig. 3-25

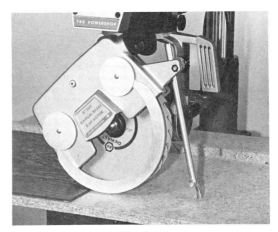

Fig. 3-26

8. If narrow strips are to be cut and there is little room between the saw blade and the rear fence guide, use a pusher stick instead of the hands. Place the pusher stick against the board section that goes between the saw blade and the guide fence.

9. When ripping long lumber, if the edge of the material is not straight, place the hollow edge against the fence rather than the crowned edge. If the ripping is to be very accurate and straight, always plane one edge of the stock straight and place this edge against the fence.

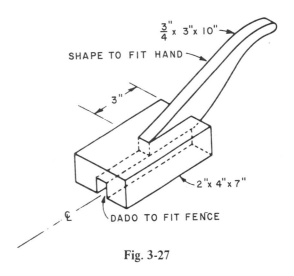

Fig. 3-27

10. To rip short pieces of stock, set up the saw in the crosscutting position and rip the board as in crosscutting.

11. To adjust the saw for bevel ripping, tilt the motor head by adjusting it as when cutting bevels for crosscutting.

How to Cut Dadoes, Grooves, or Rabbets

1. Select the dado head required. Place an outside cutter (A), figure 3-28, page 44, of the dado head on the arbor as for a crosscut or ripsaw.

2. Place the inside chippers (B, C, and D) of the dado head on the arbor. The number of chippers needed depends on the width of the cut to be made. Example: Assume that a 1-inch dado or groove is to be made. The combined width of the two outside cutters would make up 1/4 inch and the three 1/4-inch inside chippers would make up 3/4 inch. Thus, the assembled dado head would be 1 inch wide.

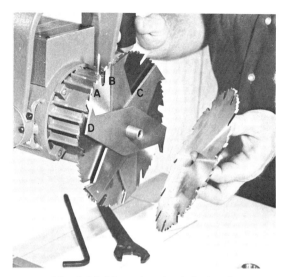

Fig. 3-28 Mounting the dado head

Fig. 3-29 Cross dado

3. When assembling the inside chippers of the dado head, be sure the cutting edges are opposite the gullets of the two outside cutters and that they are equally spaced around the circumference of the blade. In other words, place one outside cutter on the arbor first (A), figure 3-28. Place an inside chipper next as indicated at (B), and other chippers as shown at (C and D). Then put on the other outside cutter with the teeth opposite cutter (A). If additional inside chippers are necessary, for wider cuts, place more of them on the arbor before placing the second outside cutter.

4. Place the outside washer and nut and the thumbnut on the arbor and tighten the assembled dado head.

5. To make dadoes, use the machine the same way as for crosscutting. Move the dado into the lumber carefully. When making wider dadoes than can be cut with the dado head, make two or more cuts as required. If three cuts are required, make the outside cuts first and then clean out the center, figure 3-29.

6. To groove cuts with the grain, adjust the saw carriage and use the dado head as when ripping lumber with the ripsaw.

7. To make multiple parallel dadoes, as for shelving, use a trigger or surface stop mounted on the fence. This should click in the groove as shown by the stop in figure 3-30.

8. Ploughing can be done by putting the machine in a ripping position. Special care must be taken to cut against the rotation of the saw, or the dado head will pull the piece out of the operator's hands.

9. To cut dadoes at an angle, as for window frames, set up for the mitering position.

10. The end of a door or window frame can be trimmed and the dado cut in one operation as shown in figure 3-31. Place a crosscut blade on the arbor, then the dado head. A similar combination for cutting a half-lap joint is shown in figure 3-32.

Many other types of cuts may be made with the dado head. Some of these are shown in figures 3-33 through 3-42. The previous instructions given in the basic adjustments and operation of the saw should act as a guide in doing the operations.

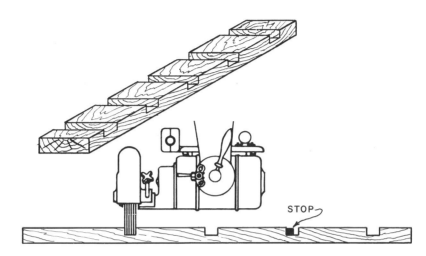

Fig. 3-30 Multiple grooving or dadoing

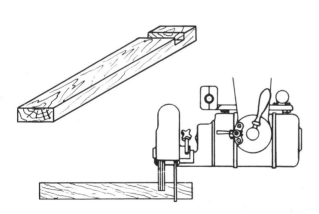

Fig. 3-31 Combination dado and crosscut

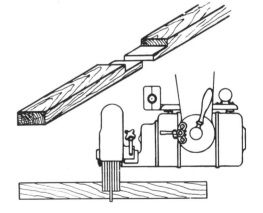

Fig. 3-32 Cutting half-lap joint

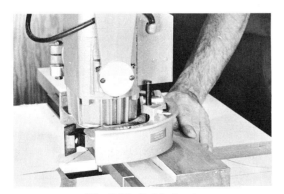

Fig. 3-33 Rabbet cut

Fig. 3-34 Tennoning

Fig. 3-35 Grooving

Fig. 3-36 Tongue-and-groove cut

Fig. 3-37 Bevel rabbet cut

Fig. 3-38 Scalloping

Fig. 3-39 Panel sinking

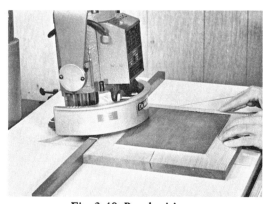

Fig. 3-40 Panel raising

Fig. 3-41 Cutting a radius

Fig. 3-42 Fluting

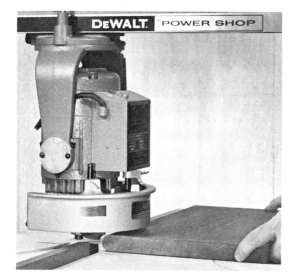

Fig. 3-43 Using a nosing cutter for stair tread

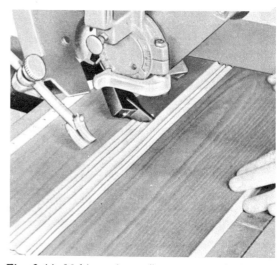

Fig. 3-44 Making a butterfly pattern with shaper cutter

Fig. 3-45 A full bead and rabbet cut in one operation

Fig. 3-46 Notice the special safety guard in this shaping operation

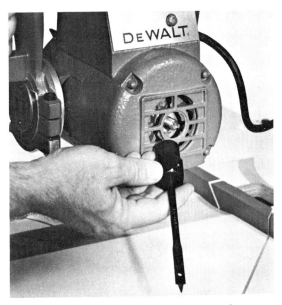

Fig. 3-47 Mounting the boring tool

Fig. 3-48 Edge drilling

USING THE RADIAL ARM SAW AS A SHAPER

Figures 3-43 through 3-46 show shaping-type cuts. These cuts are made with a "shaper head" which is a solid head into which special cutters may be inserted. These form special contours on the edges and faces of the boards. The head is mounted on the motor shaft similar to the dado head and is used in much the same way.

USING THE RADIAL ARM SAW AS A DRILL

The operation of precision drilling in woodworking is made easy because of the flexibility of the machine, the almost un-limited number of adjustments which may be made, and the various types of drills which may be used. Figure 3-47 shows how to mount the adapter.

Fig. 3-49 Parallel drilling

USING THE RADIAL ARM SAW AS A SANDER

Figures 3-55 through 3-60 show sanding operations. The two general types of sanding adapters shown are the disc type and the spindle type. Both may be obtained in other sizes but these will suffice for most kinds of work. The disc type is a circular plate which can be mounted on the motor shaft. The spindle sander is an expandable cylinder which is

Fig. 3-50 Radial drilling

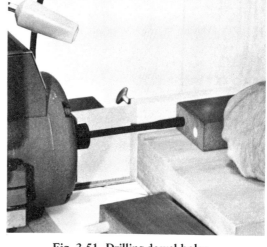

Fig. 3-51 Drilling dowel holes

Fig. 3-52 Miter drilling dowel holes

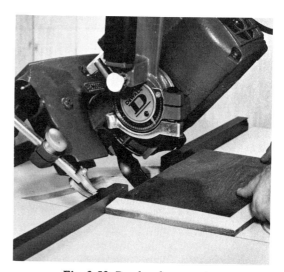

Fig. 3-53 Bead and cove cut

Fig. 3-54 Router cutting

Fig. 3-55 Mounting the sand disc

Fig. 3-56 Straight edge sanding

Fig. 3-57 Butt sanding

Fig. 3-58 Sanding outside curves

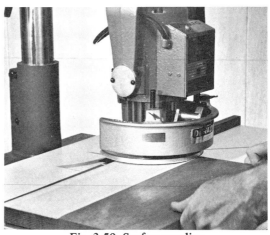

Fig. 3-59 Surface sanding

Fig. 3-60 Spindle sanding

Fig. 3-61 Planing a surface

Fig. 3-62 Using a grinding head

Fig. 3-63 Cutting light metal with special blades

also mounted in the same way. Sandpaper of any grit can be easily attached to both of these. These two types will sand most straight or curved surfaces.

OTHER ADAPTATIONS OF THE RADIAL ARM SAW

There are many other operations which can be performed on this machine. Special adaptors may be utilized to make possible operations performed by other types of machines such as grinders or buffers.

Curved sawing of all types may be done with a special sabre-type saw that can be attached easily to the radial arm

Fig. 3-64 Polishing with the buffing wheel

saw. The sabre saw is capable of cutting wood two inches thick. Because of the many different angles to which the radial arm and motor head can be adjusted, both vertical and bevel curves may be cut. Because of the many types of saws that are available for use in the sabre saw, most types of material may be cut, filed, or finished. Figure 3-65 shows the sabre saw doing piercing work, an operation that cannot be performed with a typical bandsaw. Figure 3-66 shows curves being cut similar to bandsawing. In figure 3-67 the sabre saw is being used to cut a circular disc with a bevel or undercut edge.

Figure 3-68 shows another phase of woodworking to which the radial arm saw may be adapted. This lathe attachment is readily fastened to the machine and to the table. Power is transferred by a V-belt pulley attached to the motor shaft and to a cone-type pulley on the lathe. This provides various speeds for faceplate and spindle-type wood turning. The

Fig. 3-65 Using the scroll saw blade

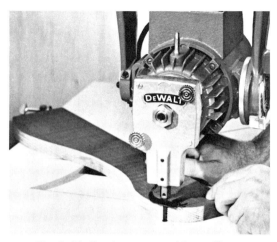

Fig. 3-66 Cutting curves with scroll saw

Fig. 3-67 Cutting bevel curves

Fig. 3-68 Using the lathe attachment

lathe bed, center bearing supports, and all other typical lathe attachments are precision-made so that accurate work may be done.

REVIEW QUESTIONS

A. Short Answer or Discussion

1. What are the three primary features that give the radial arm saw its versatility?

2. In the crosscut position, what is the direction of rotation of the blade?

3. When ripping, what important precaution must be observed and why?

4. Describe the safety features desirable in a radial arm saw.

5. a. What is the difference between the "in-rip" and the "out-rip" positions?

    b. How is width of cut determined for each position?

6. Describe the differences in the way the saw is set up for a straight crosscut, miter cut, bevel crosscut, and compound bevel cut.

7. Where should the kickback device be located for crosscutting? For ripping?

8. When cutting stock beyond the capacity of the saw's depth of cut, thus requiring more than one pass, how should the stock be marked for cutting?

9. Describe two methods of crosscutting 12 pieces, 1 inch x 6 inches x 8 inches long.

10. At what angles should the miter latch automatically lock into position?

11. At what angles does the bevel latch automatically lock?

12. Describe a technique for making multiple parallel dadoes.

13. What device is advisable when ripping with less than 5 inches between the blade and the rear fence guide?

14. How would you assemble a dado head for a 7/8-inch dado?

15. When cutting dadoes or grooves, how should the speed of the cut be adjusted?

16. Describe two different methods of cutting a rabbet with the radial arm saw.

17. How can "climbing" be avoided when cutting an extra-wide dado?

18. In addition to sawing, what are the other uses of the radial arm saw?

19. At what points and how often should the saw be lubricated?

20. What type of clothing should not be worn when using this saw?

B. Completion

1. Depth of cut is adjusted by the _____, each complete turn representing _____.

2. Release of the _____ allows the arm to be swung left or right. The angle to which it is swung is shown on the _____.

3. To position the saw for ripping, the _____ must be disengaged.

4. To locate the saw for a bevel cut, the _____ must be disengaged and the bevel angle is shown on the _____.

5. The safety device which brings the revolving blade to a quick stop when the power is turned off is the _____.

6. If the saw becomes overheated by overloading, the _____ stops the machine to prevent motor damage.

7. The guide fence is adjustable to _____ positions on the saw table.

8. _____ is an action that occurs when the back teeth of the blade are not cutting on the same line as the front teeth.

9. A dado is cut _____ the grain; a groove, _____ the grain.

10. Whenever adjustments are made to the saw, it is good safety practice to remove the _____ from the saw so that the power cannot accidently be turned on.

C. Indicate what action should be taken to remedy each of the problems listed:

1. The crosscut is not square.

2. The kerf is wider than normal.

3. The depth of the dado is not uniform.

4. The crosscut results in a slight cross bevel.

5. The radial arm wobbles slightly from side-to-side.

6. On bevel cuts, the motor slips off the angle set for the bevel.

7. The saw carriage does not lock properly to the yoke.

D. Identification and Interpretation

1. On the following illustration of a 14-inch radial arm saw, identify the lettered parts.

2. From manufacturer's literature, identify the differences between this model and the 10-inch model in terms of location of parts, horsepower, and rpm and cutting capacities.

3. Compare other makes of radial arm saws with the one illustrated and note their similarities and differences.

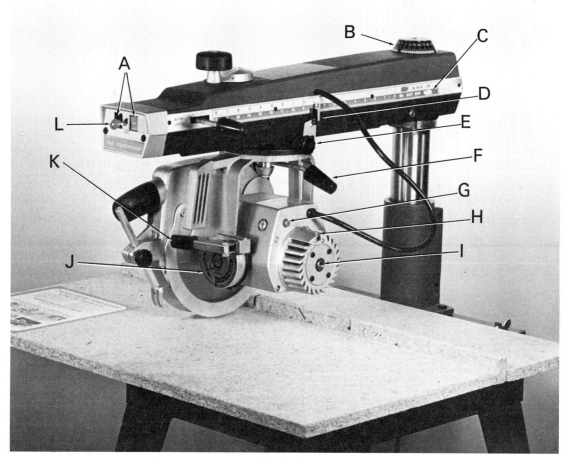

Fig. 3-69

Unit 4 REFITTING BLADES FOR CIRCULAR AND RADIAL ARM SAWS

To get the best performance and to avoid accidents, saws must be kept round and sharp. This means that saws must be refitted periodically. Complete refitting or reconditioning of flat ground saw blades consists of rounding, gumming, setting or swaging, and filing. These are performed in the order listed.

For a better understanding of the descriptions and procedures of refitting operations which follow, a review of the terms applied to saw teeth is presented in figure 4-1.

Rounding is simply jointing the teeth, that is making the points of all of the teeth the same distance from the center of the blade. Rounding is done when wear and repeated sharpenings have caused the points on the saw to become out of round — generally before each third or fourth filing.

Gumming is the process of grinding or filing the saw teeth to the same depth. It is done when wear and repeated sharpenings have caused the gullets to become too shallow for proper removal of chips. This operation also helps to correct the balance of the blade.

Setting is the process of bending the teeth alternately right and left to provide clearance for the blade. The need for setting is indicated by the tendency of the blade to bind. It is done after the saw has been jointed and gummed and before filing.

Swaging is another method of preparing the teeth to provide blade clearance. It involves spreading the point of every tooth with a swaging tool. Swaging is not done if the points have been set and, conversely, setting is not done if the points have been swaged.

Filing, the last refitting operation, puts the final edge on the teeth so they will cut fast and clean. However, a blade may be filed three or four times before it is necessary to perform any of the operations mentioned above. The filing operation is the one most often performed by the carpenter.

NOTE: Setting or swaging is not necessary for refitting hollow ground blades because the blade is made with a portion of it reduced in thickness to provide the needed clearance. All others are performed in the order listed.

The refitting operations performed by the carpenter are often limited to rounding and filing. When it is necessary to have the blade completely refitted, it is usually sent to a saw manufacturer or saw filing specialist.

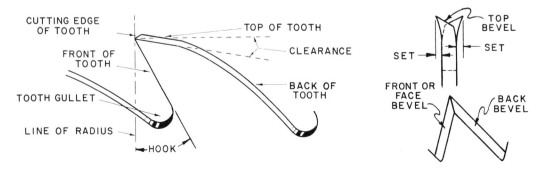

Fig. 4-1 Terms applied to saw teeth

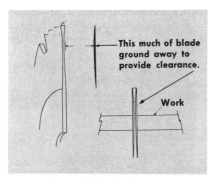

Fig. 4-2 Blade clearance

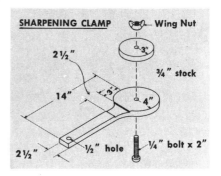

Fig. 4-3 Sharpening clamp

REFITTING BLADES FOR PORTABLE ELECTRIC SAWS

How to Touch up the Teeth on a Circular Saw

The types of blades used with portable electric saws are flat ground with the teeth set at a greater angle than for other types of saws. The refitting operations which follow apply to these blades.

Blades are touched up to restore original sharpness, to get the best performance, and to keep the blade from becoming dull too rapidly. It is not a technique that is used on a very dull blade. Such a blade must be rounded before filing.

1. A device for holding the blade for filing is illustrated in figure 4-3. When the long handle is clamped in a vise, the blade is held snug and chatter-free as it is worked on. Another method is to clamp the blade in a vise between two circular pieces of wood which clear the teeth.

2. Have on hand an 8-inch cant file, a mill file with two round edges and a 6- or 8-inch slim taper file. The cant file is used on blades with large teeth; the mill file on gullets, fronts, and backs of ripsaw and raker teeth; and the slim taper is used on small teeth.

3. Place the file so that it forms the angle of the bevel on the tooth; then file just enough to brighten the metal, usually 2 or 3 firm strokes. Use the same number of strokes on each tooth so the height of each tooth will remian equal.

4. File every other tooth on one side all around the saw. File with the set. Following this technique will lessen the filing as the direction of the file does not need to be reversed until half the teeth have been sharpened.

5. Then, reverse the saw in the vise and file the unsharpened alternate teeth.

How to Round a Blade for a Portable Electric Saw

Generally a saw is rounded by a carpenter when its teeth are still in a condition where the only other requirement for refitting the blade is filing.

The technique of rounding described as follows applies to all types of blades used on portable electric saws.

1. Cut a saw kerf through a smooth flat board so that the blade comes through the face of the board.

2. Take the saw off the arbor and put it on backward (that is, reverse the direction in which the teeth point). Tighten the blade into place.

3. Clamp the board to the saw frame, figure 4-4. Adjust the bottom plate of the saw so that the blade projects through the saw kerf not more than 1/64 inch beyond the face of the board.

4. Turn the saw upside down and clamp it firmly to a bench, figure 4-4.

5. Start the saw. When it is running at full speed, pass an abrasive stone back and forth across the top of the revolving teeth.

Fig. 4-4 Jointing a circular saw

NOTE: A portion of a discarded abrasive wheel is suitable for this operation. Take extreme care when passing the stone over the blade.

6. Stop the saw and inspect the teeth. If all the teeth have been touched by the stone, the saw is properly jointed. If not, adjust the saw so that the blade again protrudes 1/64 inch and repeat the stoning operation. Continue to do this until a small flat spot or *land* appears on the top of each tooth.
   NOTE: Round the blade only to the extent that is necessary. Excessive rounding will require the blade to be gummed and set before filing.

7. The blade is now ready to be removed from the arbor for filing.
   NOTE: Before taking the saw off the arbor, mark the blade (on some blades a mark is already etched on the blade) and mark the arbor so that the two marks are in line. When replacing the saw on the arbor after sharpening, again be sure these two marks line up. By putting the saw blade back on the arbor in the same relative position (but with the teeth pointing in the direction of cutting) a round, true running saw is ensured.

How to File a Circular Crosscut Saw

1. Secure the blade firmly in a vise between two circular pieces of wood or within the blade holder previously described. Place the blade so that the teeth point in a clockwise direction.

2. Select an appropriate file. For blades with 1/4-inch tooth spaces and finer, use an 8-inch cant saw file or 6-, 7-, and 8-inch slim taper files.

3. Place the file in a gullet at the top of the blade and file both the right side of the tooth set toward the operator and the left side of the tooth set away from the operator. The file should be held at angles shown in figure 4-6. Notice that the file points to the left at a 10- to 15-degree angle and upward at about a 10-degree angle with the horizontal.

4. File until half the flat (produced from rounding) on top of the tooth to the left and half of the flat on the tooth to the right disappear.

5. File each alternate gullet in this manner until the first side is completed. In general, use the same number of file strokes across each gullet. Reposition the blade in the vise as filing progresses so that filing is done at the upper part of the blade.
   NOTE: Every tooth should have the same amount of bevel. In soft fibrous woods, a somewhat longer bevel than 10- to 15-degrees is sometimes used, but in dry hardwoods, a shorter face bevel is preferred. The long bevel does not stay sharp long in hardwood. Do not file too wide a bevel on the face of cut-off teeth because this produces lateral strains and causes cracks.

6. Reverse the saw so that the teeth point in a counterclockwise direction. Position the file so that it points to the right 10 to 15 degrees, and the handle is tilted up 10 degrees to the horizontal.

7. File until the remaining flat sections at the top of the teeth to the right and left disappear at the same time each gullet is filed.
   NOTE: If one side requires more filing than the other in order to remove the flats at the same instant,

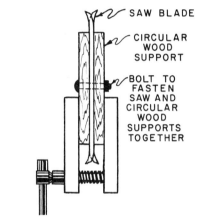

Fig. 4-5 Method of holding saw in vise for filing

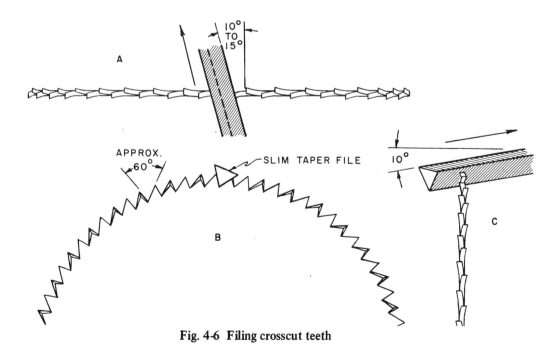

Fig. 4-6 Filing crosscut teeth

Fig. 4-7 Face bevel gauge

push the file more to one side than the other. However, keep the file tilted at the same angles. The angle of the face bevel can be checked with a prepared gauge as illustrated in figure 4-7.

8. To check the completed filing, slowly revolve the blade on a dowel rod and view the top of the teeth. The inside edges of the teeth should appear to form a "V" (B), figure 4-8. A further check for correctness of sharpening can be made by making a trial cut. The kerf produced should appear as shown in (A), figure 4-8.

    NOTE: Figure 4-9 shows several views of how the teeth should appear when filing is complete. Figure 4-10 shows teeth incorrectly filed with sharp corners in the gullets. Fractures often begin in gullets that are filed to a sharp "V". In all cases, the gullets should be rounded to avoid this. The size of the round will vary with the size of the teeth.

How to File Circular Ripsaw Blade with Set Teeth

The filing operation for this type blade is made easier by using a templet of the tooth shape as a guide, figure 4-11. The templet should be made from a thin piece of sheet metal when the blade is new.

1. Clamp the saw in a vise like the one described for sharpening crosscut teeth. Begin with the teeth pointing in a clockwise direction.

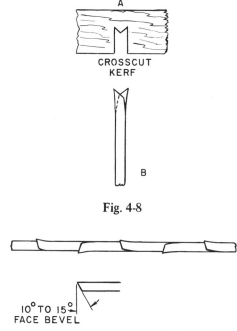

Fig. 4-8

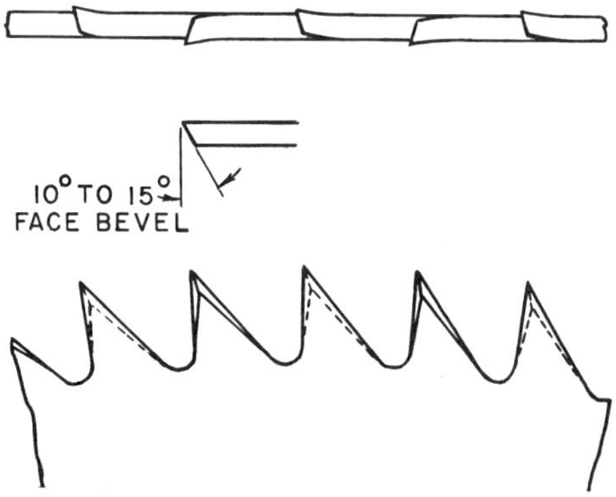

Fig. 4-9 Crosscut teeth correctly refitted

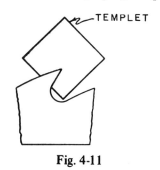

Fig. 4-10 Gullets improperly sharpened

Fig. 4-11

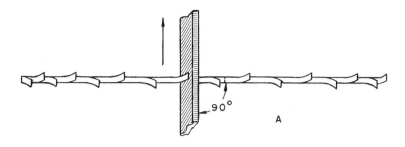

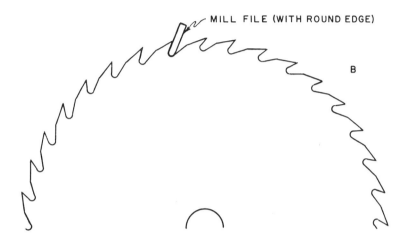

Fig. 4-12 Filing the front of a ripsaw tooth

2. Select an 8- or 10-inch mill, bastard-cut file with one or two round edges. Hold the handle with one hand and the tip of the file between the thumb and forefinger of the other hand.

3. Place the file flat against the front of a tooth that is set or bent away from the handle of the file. Hold the file horizontally and at a 90-degree angle to the face of the saw (A and B), figure 4-12.

4. Push the file straight forward, taking a full stroke with a light pressure. Maintain the file at the angle shown in (A), figure 4-12, to keep the original hook to the teeth.

5. Repeat the operation until a point is formed at the top of the tooth.

6. File every other tooth in the same manner.

7. Use a light stroke with a round file (or with the round edge of a mill file) to clean out the gullets.

8. Reverse the saw in the vise and file the front of the teeth that have not already been filed.

9. Then, begin filing the backs of the teeth. File every other tooth on one side all around the saw. File in the direction of the set as illustrated in figure 4-13, page 62.

10. Reverse the saw in the vise and file the backs of the other alternate teeth. Again, file in the same direction as the set.

Fig. 4-13 Filing back of tooth

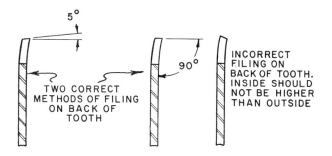

Fig. 4-14

NOTE: A ripsaw cuts with the grain as the teeth chisel through the wood. For general work, the teeth should be filed straight across. Some carpenters prefer a slight bevel on the top. Care should be taken not to bevel too much on the top of ripsaw teeth as a beveled tooth may split the fiber instead of cutting it squarely. Too much bevel also produces a lateral motion which causes the teeth to chatter and vibrate in the cut. This, in turn, results in a rough cut and will eventually cause cracks in the blade.

11. After the filing is complete, inspect the teeth by slowly rotating the blade on a dowel rod. If the points have been filed straight across (without a top bevel) the teeth should appear as in figure 4-15 (B). The kerf produced should appear as shown in figure 4-15 (A). Other views of how the teeth should appear are shown in figure 4-16. Teeth that are not sharpened correctly are shown in figure 4-17.

How to File a Combination Circular Saw

NOTE: Steps 1 through 4 apply to combination blades with teeth arranged as shown in figure 4-19.

1. File the raker teeth first. Use the same technique as described for sharpening the teeth of a ripsaw blade — file the front of the tooth first and then the back.

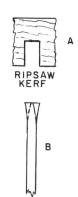

Fig. 4-15

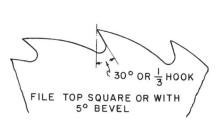

Fig. 4-16 Correctly filed crosscut teeth

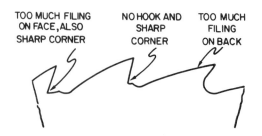

Fig. 4-17 Incorrectly filed crosscut teeth

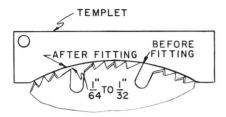

Fig. 4-18 Checking raker tooth size

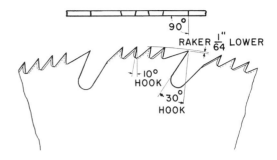

Fig. 4-19 Combination teeth crosscut and raker

2. When filing the back of the raker teeth, file the point 1/64 to 1/32 inch below the points of the cutting teeth.

   NOTE: Raker tooth height can be checked by preparing a templet from light-gauge metal as illustrated in figure 4-18. The radius of the arc is the same as the radius of the saw.

CORRECT. RAKERS SHORTER THAN CUTTING TEETH

A

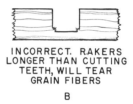

INCORRECT. RAKERS LONGER THAN CUTTING TEETH, WILL TEAR GRAIN FIBERS

B

Fig. 4-20

3. File the crosscut (cutting) teeth as was described for sharpening a crosscut blade.

4. The shape of the cut produced by a correctly sharpened blade is shown in figure 4-20 (A). A cut made with a blade that was not sharpened correctly is shown in figure 4-20 (B).

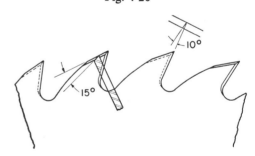

Fig. 4-21 Combination W – tooth

5. For sharpening the type of combination blade shown in figure 4-21, file the face of each tooth with a 10-degree bevel first. Alternate the bevel direction of each tooth and file in the direction of the set.

6. File a 15-degree top bevel on each tooth, again alternating the direction of the bevel.

7. Clean out the gullets with an 8- or 10-inch round, second-cut file.

Fig. 4-22 Plywood combination

8. To sharpen plywood combination saws with teeth as illustrated in figure 4-22, first file the face of the teeth lightly, maintaining the original face bevel and hook.

9. Then file the top of the teeth to a sharp point, maintaining a 15-degree top bevel.

REFITTING BLADES FOR RADIAL ARM SAWS

The type of blades refitted for radial arm saws include those which are flat ground with set and swaged teeth, varieties of hollow ground blades, and dado heads.

How to Round Circular Saw Blades (All Types) on the Radial Arm Saw

1. Install the blade backwards (that is, with the teeth pointing upward) and tighten the arbor nut.

2. Lay an oilstone on the saw table and against the rear fence.

3. Lower the saw carriage until the saw blade just touches the stone. Hold the stone firmly against the fence and revolve the blade carefully by hand.

4. After several revolutions, inspect the teeth to see whether all have been jointed.

5. Repeat the process of lowering the carriage very slightly and revolving the blade until a small flat appears on the points of all the teeth.

6. Prior to removing the blade for filing, mark the blade and arbor so that the blade may be replaced in the same position on the arbor as when rounded, but with teeth pointed in the direction for cutting.

How to File Flat and Hollow Ground Blades

1. For filing flat ground blades, use the same techniques as was described for sharpening similar blades for the portable electric saw.

2. For sharpening hollow ground blades, the same techniques also apply. Disregard, however, the directions which refer to filing with the set.

How to Round Dado Heads

Dado heads should be rounded after every fourth or fifth filing to maintain efficient performance.

1. To joint the dado head, put all the inside chippers between the outside cutters on the arbor backwards. Joint the entire head and all the chippers together in the manner previously described for all circular saws.
    NOTE: Every time the head is sharpened, both cutter saws and all chippers in the set should be rounded and sharpened together whether they have been used or not. This is necessary in order to keep them uniform in diameter.

How to File Dado Heads

1. Remove the dado head and file the two outside cutters. File the raker or cleaner teeth like those of a ripsaw and small teeth like those of a crosscut saw. Raker tooth heights should be 1/64 to 1/32 inch less than crosscut teeth.
    NOTE: A templet, as previously described for use with combination blades, may be used to check raker tooth heights.

2. File each tooth of the inside chippers exactly like an individual tooth of a circular ripsaw. File to the same height as the raker teeth on the outside cutters.

NOTE: A correctly filed dado head, outer blades and chippers included, will produce a cut as shown in figure 4-23.

REFITTING CARBIDE-TIPPED BLADES

Carbide-tipped blades are best refitted by returning them to the saw manufacturer. Sharpening is done solely by grinding with diamond impregnated abrasive wheels. To attempt to sharpen carbide-tipped blades by filing or with the conventional type abrasive wheels (aluminum oxide or silicon carbide) would result only in damaging the sharpening tools.

Refitting services by saw manufacturers of these blades also includes replacement of individual carbide-tipped teeth when necessary. Sharpening costs are generally rated on a cost-per-tooth basis.

REFITTING BLADES WITH SWAGED TEETH

Swaging, spreading the point of every tooth, is sometimes done instead of setting teeth. A swaged saw will cut more wood than a set saw. This is because every tooth is cutting the full width of the kerf. However, swaging is not a simple operation and not many carpenters do it.

A hand swaging tool, shown in figure 4-24, is one type of device used to swage teeth. It consists of two dies, one which is convex and another which is flat.

The convex die is placed on the tooth first and struck several light blows with a small hammer. This spreads the tooth as in (1) figure 4-25.

After completing the swaging, the saw is again slightly rounded. The face and

Fig. 4-23 Dado cut

Fig. 4-24 Swaging tool

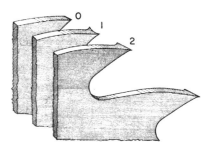

Fig. 4-25 Swaged teeth

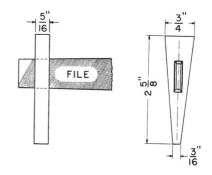

Fig. 4-26 Tools for side filing swaged teeth

Fig. 4-27 Side filing swaged teeth

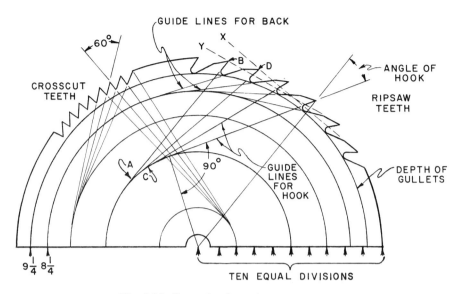

Fig. 4-28 Gumming layouts

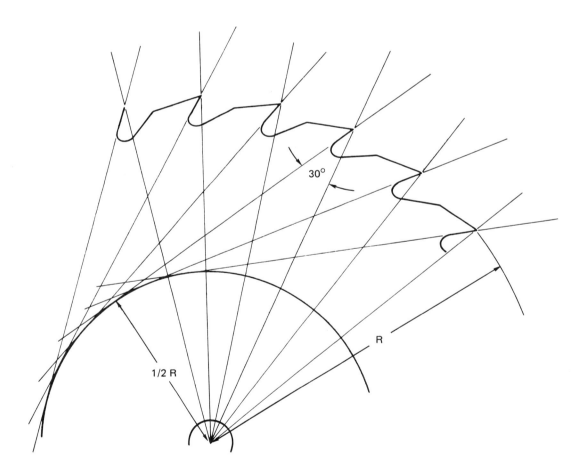

Fig. 4-29 Significance of hook given as an angular or linear dimension

back of the teeth are then filed in the same manner as raker teeth on a combination saw. Finally the teeth are side-filed so the saw will cut smoothly. The tools and technique for doing this are shown in figures 4-26 and 4-27, page 65.

DESCRIPTION OF GUMMING

Gumming requires that all of the teeth be laid out so that they may be filed or ground to a uniform shape and size. The layout for each type of blade (ripsaw, crosscut, etc.) varies.

An example of layouts for gumming of ripsaw and crosscut teeth is shown in figure 4-28.

The ripsaw layout consists of scribing a circle that will touch the deepest gullet to serve as guide lines for filing the gullets to the same depth, and filing the hook, top, and back of the tooth. Hook guide lines are laid out by first drawing a circle with a radius equal to one-half the radius of the saw and then scribing lines A-B, C-D etc., from the point of each tooth tangent to this circle.

The hook may also be obtained from tables prepared by saw manufacturers for this purpose. Note that in the table, hook may be given as a degree or an inch dimension. Figure 4-29 shows how the information on the table below is used.

HOOK IN DEGREES TO HOOK IN INCHES			
DIAM.	10° HOOK IS EQUAL TO	13° HOOK IS EQUAL TO	30° HOOK IS EQUAL TO
6"	1/2"	5/8"	1 1/2"
8"	3/4"	7/8"	2"
10"	7/8"	1 1/8"	2 1/2"
12"	1"	1 3/8"	3"
14"	1 1/4"	1 5/8"	3 1/2"
16"	1 3/8"	1 3/4"	4"
18"	1 1/2"	2"	4 1/2"
20"	1 3/4"	2 1/4"	5"
22"	1 7/8"	2 1/2"	5 1/2"
24"	2 1/8"	2 3/4"	6"

Guide lines for filing the top of the tooth are found by drawing lines (X, Y, etc.) across spacings of every four points, from point-to-point or by laying out the included angle of the tooth. Guide lines for the backs of the teeth are found by drawing tangents to the 8 1/4-inch circle as illustrated.

The layout for crosscut teeth can be determined from figure 4-28. Layouts for combination blades involve layout for both types of teeth.

Following the layout, the teeth are filed to the gumming lines with a round-edge mill file or, if the gullets are large, with a suitable size round second-cut file.

The gullets may also be shaped by using a power grinder with an abrasive wheel faced to fit the gullets. The wheel is mounted on the grinder and a flat surface is provided on which to rest the saw while it is being ground. See figure 4-30, page 68.

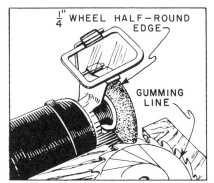

Fig. 4-30 Gumming with a power grinder

SETTING THE SAW TEETH

Setting (bending the teeth alternately right and left to provide clearance on a saw blade) is sometimes done by carpenters. To set the teeth of a saw blade, it is necessary to know the amount of set required on various gauges and size of blades and the tools that are used for setting.

The amount of set for circular blades is usually 2 gauges of set on each side of the saw for dry wood, and 2 1/2 gauges for green softwood. The set for blades on portable electric saws for general cutting is 2 1/2 gauges because the additional clearance is needed for better control of the direction of cutting and to keet the blade from binding.

An example of the gauge system of setting is shown by the following example.

Example: To set a saw for cutting dry softwood, allow two gauges per side. If the saw is 16 gauge (.065 inch), two gauges per side would make the saw kerf 12 gauge (.109 inch). See figure 4-31 and the table which follows. Note that as the gauge number decreases, the thickness of the blade increases; therefore, the total amount of gauge set (4) is subtracted from the gauge thickness (16) of the blade.

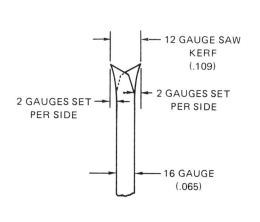

TABLE BELOW SHOWS AMOUNT OF SET FOR DIFFERENT GAUGE SAWS		
Thickness of Saw	With 2 Gauges Set per Side Saw Kerf Will Be	With 2½ Gauges Set per Side Saw Kerf Will Be
10 ga	6 ga (.203)	5 ga (.220)
11 ga	7 ga (.180)	6 ga (.203)
12 ga	8 ga (.165)	7 ga (.180)
13 ga	9 ga (.148)	8 ga (.165)
14 ga	10 ga (.134)	9 ga (.148)
15 ga	11 ga (.120)	10 ga (.134)
16 ga	12 ga (.109)	11 ga (.120)
17 ga	13 ga (.095)	12 ga (.109)
18 ga	14 ga (.083)	13 ga (.095)
19 ga	15 ga (.072)	
20 ga	16 ga (.065)	

Fig. 4-31 Saw gauge size and set applied

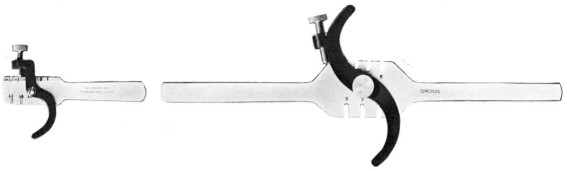

Fig. 4-32 Combination saw set

From a practical standpoint, carpenters on the job would have difficulty in setting a blade as precisely as indicated by these figures, however, this information should help them picture the amount of set that is needed.

Setting may be performed with any of the various types of saw sets shown in figure 4-32.

The pistol-grip type of saw set is used in the same manner as a smaller version used for setting handsaw teeth. It is used on small circular saws of 11 gauge and thinner, whereas the other types illustrated are used for setting larger and heavier gauge blades.

Setting with an anvil and stake involves placing the teeth over the anvil so that one-fourth to one-third of their depth projects over the bevel on the anvil and then striking the tooth with a hammer and punch or with a special setting hammer. The top surface of the anvil is beveled to various angles and may be revolved to provide different degrees of set for different saws.

The combination saw sets have a gauge attachment for regulating the set. They are provided with setting slots which are graduated to give the desired depth to the set in each gauge teeth they are intended to set.

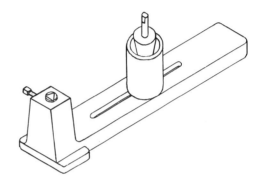

Fig. 4-33 Anvil and stake

Fig. 4-34 Pistol-grip saw set

Fig. 4-35 Setting with an anvil and stake

When the saw set is placed on the tooth, it is fitted so that the point of the tooth touches the bottom of the slot. The tooth is then bent over until the gauge touches the side of the saw.

SUMMARY OF REFITTING CIRCULAR SAWS

- Saws are usually sharpened for all-around cutting. If work is mostly in softwood, a wider bevel may be carried on the teeth.

- In filing, do not reduce the length of the teeth; simply bring them up to a sharp point. If the teeth are uneven, the saw cannot cut properly. Have all teeth of the same shape, with gullets of even depth.

- Do not file sharp corners or nicks in the bottom of the gullets. This usually results in cracks in the gullets.

- Bevel the teeth in crosscut saws on both the face and back edges. More bevel, however, is filed on the face than on the back of the teeth.

- File ripsaw teeth straight across to a chisel-like edge. Then file the top of the teeth straight or with a very slight bevel.

- When filing saws, take care that the bevel does not run down into the gullets. The bevel on both the face and back should be about one-third the length of the teeth.

- In filing a flat ground combination saw, which crosscuts, rips and miters, use the same method for beveling the scoring teeth as is used in sharpening a cut-off saw.

- Some combination saws have rakers or cleaner teeth, to remove the material left in the cut by the beveled cutting teeth, hence the points of these rakers or cleaner teeth should be filed 1/64 inch shorter for hardwood, 1/32 inch for softwood, than the points of the beveled cutting teeth. After filing these teeth shorter, square the face of each raker tooth and bring it to a chisel-like edge by filing on the back of the tooth only.

- In sharpening a hollow ground combination saw, follow the method used for a flat ground combination saw. Do not set the teeth, since the hollow grinding provides ample clearance.

REVIEW QUESTIONS

A. Short Answer or Discussion

1. What operations are involved in refitting saw blades? In what order should these operations be performed?

2. Which operation is most often performed by the carpenter?

3. How does the refitting of hollow ground blades differ from flat ground blades and what is the reason for the difference?

4. Under what conditions may a flat ground blade be touched up?

5. Describe two methods for holding the circular saw blade when performing the touching up operation.

6. What three files are required for touching up and how is each used?

7. When rounding a blade, at what distance should the blade protrude above the face of the clamping board for stoning the blade?

8. What technique is suggested for ensuring that the rounded blade will be placed back on the arbor in the same relative position as it was before rounding?

9. In filing a crosscut blade, how is the length of bevel affected by the kind of wood which will be cut?

10. When filing is completed, how should the blade be checked?

11. What is the danger in filing too much bevel on the top of ripsaw teeth?

12. In what way does filing of a combination blade differ from filing both crosscut and ripsaw blades?

13. Why is swaging sometimes preferred to setting?

14. What type of blades are best returned to the manufacturer for any refitting required? Why?

15. What is the purpose of gumming layouts for ripsaw and crosscut teeth?

16. Describe two methods of shaping saw teeth to the gumming line.

17. Why is the amount of set greater for portable electric saw blades than for circular saw blades?

18. Describe the tools that may be used for setting blades.

B. Completion

 1. Jointing saw teeth so that all points are equidistant from the center of the blade is called _____.

 2. _____ is the process of bending the teeth alternately left and right.

 3. Grinding and filing the teeth to the same depth is _____.

 4. The final edge is put on saw teeth by _____.

 5. The bevel of a saw tooth should be about _____ the length of the tooth.

 6. In sharpening hollow ground blades, it is not necessary to _____ the teeth.

 7. In filing a combination blade, the _____ teeth should be filed first.

 8. The two operations most frequently performed by the carpenter in refitting blades are _____ and _____.

 9. The amount of set a saw blade requires is dependent upon the _____ of the blade.

10. In general, the tops of ripsaw teeth should not be filed with a _____.

C. Identification and Interpretation

 1. Identify the terms used to describe each of the parts of the saw tooth indicated by arrows in the illustration below:

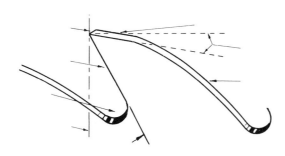
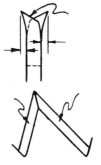

Unit 5 THE SABRE SAW

The sabre saw, or bayonet saw as it is sometimes called, is similar to a portable electric jigsaw. It can perform a variety of sawing operations, the most distinctive of which is plunge cutting. Blades are available for cutting practically every type of common construction material. This broad range of work capacity makes this saw an ideal tool for woodworking shops, millwork and cabinet shops, carpenters, contractors, plumbers, electricians, general repairers, and home craftspeople.

The action of some sabre saw models is an orbital or oval motion rather than the reciprocating or straight up-and-down motion of other models. Orbital motion allows the blade to cut only on the upstroke and to relieve itself of accumulated chips on the return stroke. This tends to eliminate *blade drag.* As a result, the teeth stay sharp longer, and the blade stays cooler, cuts faster, and breaks less often than in reciprocating action.

The saw illustrated in figure 5-2 is a typical sabre saw. It has a 3.5 amp universal-type motor that operates on 115 volts ac-dc.

The motor is cooled by a fan located on the armature shaft. Air is drawn in through ports at the rear of the motor housing and released through ports at the front. One exhaust port is positioned so that the exhaust keeps the cutting line clear of chips.

The blade drive is through a worm gear which operates the blade at 4 500 strokes per minute when idle and 4 250 strokes per minute under normal load. The motor starts and stops by control of the trigger switch located directly under the first-finger position of the handle, giving instant power control in all positions of operation. The length of the stroke of the blade is 7/16 inch, and the relief of the orbital motion is 3/64 inch. The long, shaped handle at the top of the motor housing permits the greatest possible control of the cutting action as the blade enters and cuts through the work. In addition, the handle remains cool, even during long cutting operations.

The base of the sabre saw can be adjusted for bevel cuts. A rip fence accessory is available on certain models.

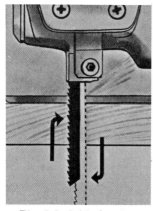

Fig. 5-1 Orbital action

Fig. 5-2 Sabre saw

Fig. 5-3 (A)   Fig. 5-3 (B)

Figure 5-3 (A) illustrates a saw in which the adjustable base is an accessory which replaces the standard base for bevel cutting. Figure 5-3 (B) shows a saw in which adjustment is made as an integral part of the base.

ELECTRICAL WIRING AND GROUNDING PRECAUTIONS

The precautions in unit 1 should be reviewed carefully and strictly adhered to when handling the sabre saw. The sabre saw, like all other portable electric equipment, must be adequately grounded. The voltage of the circuit on which it is to be used must be the same as that shown on the saw's nameplate, and the correct size of wire must be used in the circuit. All of these requirements are fully covered in unit 1.

MOTOR MAINTENANCE

Since the sabre saw is equipped with a universal type ac or dc motor, the characteristics and maintenance described in unit 1 apply.

LUBRICATION

Manufacturers provide detailed instructions for the lubrication of their specific saws. Most saws are factory-lubricated, which is adequate to cover a specified number of hours of operation (such as 50 hours). In all cases, however,

Fig. 5-4 Double insulated barrel handle sabre saw

Fig. 5-5 (A) Brushes are located at back of motor housing

Fig. 5-5 (B) Keep air ports clean at rear of motor housing

Blade Length (Inches)	Teeth Per Inch	Blade Width (Inches)	APPLICATIONS
3	10	5/16	Fast Cutting Set Tooth — Wood
3	6	5/16	Faster Cutting Shark Tooth
4 1/4	10	1/2	Fast Cutting Set Tooth
4 1/4	6	1/2	Faster Cutting Shark Tooth
4 1/4	10	1/4	Scroll and General Smooth Cutting Soft and Hard Grain Woods — Plywood — Masonite
4 1/4	6	1/4	Fast Scroll and Rough Cutting Soft and Hard Grain Woods
4 1/4	10	3/8	General Wood Cutting — Asphalt Tile Fiber — Paper — Plastic — Laminates — Lucite — Plexiglass
4 1/4	6	3/8	General Rough Cutting Roof Rafters and General Frame Cutting — Plunge Cutting
3 1/2	10	1/4	Smooth Scroll and Circular Cutting Masonite — Plywood — Soft and Hard Grain Trim Stock — Plastics
3 1/2	6	1/4	Fast Scroll and Circular Cutting Solid Grain Wood — Masonite — Plastics
3 1/2	10	3/8	General Straight and Large Curvature Cutting — Solid Grain Wood Plywood — Masonite — Plastics — Soft Aluminum Extrusions
3	10	1/4	Smooth Scroll and Circular Cutting — Plywood, Straight Grain Wood, Masonite — Plastics — Plunge Cutting
3	6	1/4	Fast Scroll and Circular Cutting — Plunge Cutting Straight Grain Woods — Hard Board
3	10	3/8	General Wood Cutting, Fiber, Paper and Plastic Laminates Plexiglass, Rubber Linoleum
3	6	3/8	Rough Cutting Wood
2	10	13/64	Smooth Finish Cutting of Straight, Curvature, Round Finish and Trim Materials and Plunge Cutting
2	—	5/16	Cutting — Cardboard —Cloth — Leather Rubber and Sponge Type Plastics
4 1/4	6	3/8	Cutting Fiberglass — Fiberglass Bonded to Plywood Sheet Rock — Asphalt Tile — Plastics — Plaster
2 5/8	6	3/8	Cutting Fiberglass — Fiberglass Bonded to Plywood Sheet Rock — Asphalt Tile — Plaster
3 1/2	6	3/8	Cutting Fiberglass, Asphalt Tile, Plastics, Sheet Rock, Plaster and General Wood Cutting
3 5/8	14	3/8	Cutting Brass — Bronze — Copper and Nonferrous Metals 5/32 to 1/4'' Thick Angle Iron — Mild Steel Sheets and Tubing 5/32 to 1/8'' Wall Thickness
3 1/2	24	1/2	Cutting Window Openings in Steel Core Fire Doors — Copper — Brass and Steel Tubing to 1 7/8'' Diameter
3	10	3/8	Cutting Brass — Bronze — Copper — Aluminum to 1/2'' Thickness Steel — Cast Iron to 3/16'' in Thickness
3	14	3/8	Cutting Nonferrous Metals to 1/4'' in Thickness — Cutting Angle Iron Mild Steel Sheets and Tubing to 1/8'' Wall Thickness
3	24	3/8	Cutting Steel Sheets to 1/8'' Cutting Tubing Thin Wall to 1 3/8'' Diameter
3	24	1/4	Cutting Steel Sheets and Tubing 3/32 to 1/8'' Wall Thickness
1 3/4	14	1/4	Cutting Steel Sheets and Tubing 3/32 to 1/8'' Wall Thickness
1 3/4	24	1/4	Cutting Steel Sheets and Tubing 3/32 to 1/8'' Wall Thickness

Fig. 5-6

Fig. 5-7 Inserting blade firmly

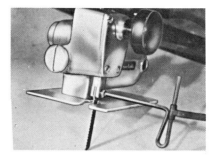

Fig. 5-8 Tighten with allen wrench

the instructions of the manufacturer must be followed, because different makes require different methods of lubrication.

SABRE SAW BLADES

As with any other saw, it is important that the correct blade be used for a specific job. Sabre saw blades are made in three general types: wood cutting, metal cutting, and knife blades.

Wood-cutting blades are made of fine tool steel, taper-ground and machine-filed to razor sharpness. They range from six to twelve teeth per inch. Some manufacturers provide two lengths; long, for greater stiffness on deep cuts, and short, for small radius curves and intricate cutting jobs.

Metal-cutting blades are made of high-quality hacksaw stock and range from six teeth per inch to thirty-two teeth per inch. In general, the blade with more teeth per inch is used for cutting thinner sections of metal.

Knife blades are adapted for cutting paper, leather, cloth, rubber, and corrugated board. Knife blade edges are precision ground to keen, durable cutting edges.

The table, on page 75, recommends the selection of blades for a variety of cutting jobs.

How to Install Sabre Saw Blades

NOTE: This procedure is for the specific saw illustrated.

1. Slide the slot in the back of the blade onto the blade holder screw, making sure it is fully inserted against the screw, figure 5-7.

2. Tighten the screw with the allen wrench provided for this purpose, figure 5-8. Be sure the blade is locked securely.

A base insert is used with the saw illustrated where a cut with an especially fine finish is desired. The insert is used only with the ten-tooth short blade and is especially recommended to obtain a fine, smooth cut in plywood, figure 5-9.

How to Install the Base Insert

1. Remove the blade by loosening the blade holder screw with the allen wrench.

2. Place the insert in the base with the dimpled side up and the blade clearance slot forward.

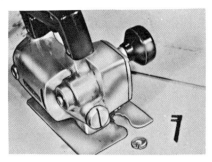

Fig. 5-9 Base insert and short blade

Fig. 5-10 Base insert in position

3. Slide the insert toward the back onto the supporting web of the base, figure 5-10.

4. Install the ten-tooth short blade in the usual manner.

How to Operate the Sabre Saw

1. Hold the material in a bench vise or with clamps to the work table. This is especially important when sawing small pieces of material. As the

Fig. 5-11 Left hand guides saw
through intricate cuts

work progresses in scroll or curved cutout pieces, the material can be readjusted to accommodate the movement of the saw. If the work is large enough, it may be held by hand across saw horses.

2. Mark the line of cut clearly.

3. Place the forward edge of the saw base firmly on the edge of the material to be cut. Start the motor by closing the first finger against the trigger switch, and move the blade into the work.

4. Move the machine forward just fast enough to keep the blade cutting. Do not use force. Use the left-hand knob for greater control of the saw, figure 5-11.

   NOTE: To lock the saw motor on for long or tedious cuts, press the lock button on the left side of the handle above the trigger switch. To release this lock mechanism, simply snap the trigger switch and release it immediately. This releases the lock and stops the motor immediately.

PLUNGE CUTTING

One of the most useful features of the sabre saw is that an inside or pocket cut can be made without drilling holes first. This feature is especially helpful for cutting doors and wall or floor openings for plumbing fixtures.

How to Plunge Cut

1. First measure the area to be cut out and mark it clearly with a pencil, chalk, or scriber. Choose a convenient starting point and hold the saw over that point and inside the line of the waste.

Fig. 5-12 **Starting the plunge cut**

Fig. 5-13 **Freehand pocket cut**

Fig. 5-14 **Cutting sharp corners**

Fig. 5-15 **Starting plunge cut through synthetic resin**

Fig. 5-16 **Notice the sawdust being blown off line of cut**

2. Tip the machine forward until the front edge of the base rests firmly on the surface of the material and the top of the blade is well clear of the work surface, figure 5-12.

3. Start the motor. As the blade reaches its full speed, lower the back of the machine and the blade will cut smoothly into the surface and down to its full depth. Do not move the machine forward until the base is fully seated on the surface of the work.

4. Now guide the saw along the inside of the marked area. If sharp corners are necessary, cut up to the corner of the marked edge. Stop and back up slightly, start the turn, and cut along the side. Do the same at each corner until you end up where you started.

5. Then go back and cut into each corner from the opposite direction. The base of the machine is wide enough so that there will be a solid guiding surface on either side of the cut.

CUTTING SYNTHETIC RESINS AND PLYWOOD

The sabre saw is particularly suited for cutting plywood and synthetic resin board such as Formica® or Texolite®. For counter top or sink installations, it can plunge into such materials without blade breakage. The ten-tooth wood cutting blade is recommended for cutting synthetic resins.

Fig. 5-17 Notching 2 x 4s on sawhorse

Fig. 5-18 Notching rafters overhead

Plywood is most easily handled using the base insert with a ten-tooth short wood cutting blade. This combination cuts with a smoother finish.

NOTCHING HEAVY LUMBER

The sabre saw can cut 2-inch material when notching rafters, floor joists, wall studs, corner bracing, or when angle-cutting fire stops and cut-in bracing.

Fig. 5-19 Cutting out flooring for installing pipe

The six-tooth blade is used for work of this nature. No particular devices or methods are necessary except that it is necessary to hold the material firmly across the saw horses or other working surface.

Notching or cutting of floor joists is often a problem for plumbers, electricians, and heating system mechanics. Since the distance from the edge of the saw base to the front edge of the blade is only 1 1/8 inch, this saw can work to within 1 1/8 inch of the underside of the floor or other barriers. This makes it especially suited for pipe and conduit installation. Plunge cutting allows cutouts for heating ducts and ventilator openings to be made after the carpenter has completed roughing, providing the necessary blocking and supports are correctly placed.

METAL SAWING

Metals of many types are used in house construction, cabinet work, window and door installation, and home shop work. This is due partly to the general use of aluminum and its alloys and to the improvement of metal cutting tools. The sabre saw can be used with a variety of metals for many types of construction and shop purposes. With the assortment of metal cutting blades available, this saw can handle most materials with ease.

Soft aluminum can be cut with the ten- and fourteen-tooth metal cutting blades, although a much finer cut is possible with the twenty-four-tooth metal cutting blade. For all types of angles, tubing, and screen-frame stock, the fine tooth blade is recommended.

Sawing tubing presents no problem when the diameter of the tube is larger than the length of the blade. Start the cut at one point, then insert the tip of the blade in the hole and proceed around the top side, cutting through the wall as the tube is turned.

Fig. 5-20 Cutting aluminum in vise

Fig. 5-21 Slitting pipe

Fig. 5-22 Cutting thin sheet metal

Fig. 5-23 Cutting flat or bar-steel

NOTE: When sawing metal over 1/8 inch thick, care must be taken to start turns slowly. The blade should not be twisted or bent sharply. Hold the work firmly and cut close to the holding point so vibration is kept to a minimum.

Thin sheet metal material is hard to cut because it bends very easily and is likely to tear. To cut thin sheet metal, use plywood or other such material on both sides of the work. Clamp it tightly in position on the table so that the metal sheet lies between the scrap supports. Be sure the outside or scrap edge is clamped so that layers do not vibrate as the saw moves into the work. The pattern or line of cut is drawn directly on the top part of the sandwich and the saw cuts through the entire pile. In this way, the metal sheet will be cut smoothly and accurately without tearing. Such cuts can be made to exact size without the need for filing or other finishing.

Clogging the teeth of the blade with small chips is a common problem when cutting soft metals. If this occurs, use a stiff brush to clear the teeth and change to a coarser, more open-tooth blade. Start the new blade from the outer edge of the work, or at a point other than where you stopped. The reason for this is that the new blade will be thicker and will not operate smoothly in the original kerf.

Sawing heavy metals such as solid bar stock, rod, or thick sheets requires more care. Stick wax applied to the blade before making the cut will result in smoother work and a longer, trouble-free performance of the saw.

Any time the saw shows a tendency to bounce when cutting metal, change to a blade with finer teeth. A bouncing action is an indication that the teeth are straddling the edge of the work. At least two teeth of the blade must contact the work at all times.

PLENTY OF CHIP
CLEARANCE

FINE TEETH, NO
CHIP CLEARANCE
TEETH CLOGGED

TWO OR MORE TEETH
ON SECTION

COARSE PITCH
STRADDLES WORK

Fig. 5-25   Installing the angle adjusting base

Fig. 5-24   Angle adjusting base

Fig. 5-26   Bevel cutting with sabre saw

Most of the difficulty encountered in metal sawing is the result of trying to rush the job.   Do not force the saw.   Move it forward with a steady and even pressure, but let the saw and blade do the work.

THE ANGLE ADJUSTING BASE

On some sabre saws, an angle adjusting base, figure 5-24, may be substituted for the regular base.   This permits accurate sawing of angles up to 45 degrees to the plane of the surface.   Installation is simply accomplished by removing the three screws which hold the standard base to the frame, placing the angle base in the same position over the screw holes, and replacing the screws securely, figure 5-25.

REVIEW QUESTIONS

A.   Short Answer or Discussion

1.   Describe the orbital action of some types of sabre saws.

2.   Where are the exhaust ports located?   What functions do they serve?

3.   How does the sabre saw provide for bevel cuts?

4.   Describe the three common types of blades available.

5. What is the purpose of the base insert?

6. For what purposes are blades made in long and short lengths?

7. What is the primary feature of this type of saw?

8. What blade is recommended for cutting synthetic resins?

9. When cutting thin wall tubing, what blade is generally used?

10. What action indicates that the saw teeth are straddling the work when cutting tubing? What remedy is called for?

B. Completion
   1. Orbital action tends to eliminate _____.
   2. The most commonly used wood cutting blade has _____ teeth.
   3. Smooth cuts in plywood are best made with a _____ blade.
   4. For notching 2 x 4s, a _____ blade is recommended.
   5. Application of _____ to the blade enables easier sawing of heavy metals.

C. Identification and Interpretation
   1. Identify the lettered parts of the sabre saw illustrated.

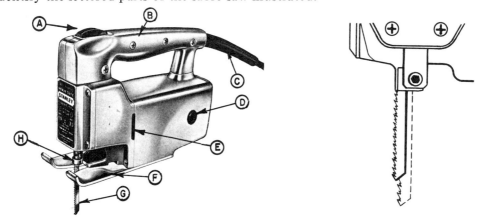

   2. On the right-hand sketch above, dimension the length of stroke and the relief of the orbital motion.

Unit 6 RECIPROCATING SAWS

Reciprocating saws are manufactured so the cuts may be made in any direction. They are more versatile than the sabre saw. They also have a blade action which is different from that of the sabre saw. In the sabre saw, the blade moves at right angles to the base. In the reciprocating saw, the blade is in line with the body of the saw. Their construction is somewhat different and the power factor is increased so that heavier and more varied work may be done.

The manufacturers state that these saws may be used by carpenters, millwrights, electricians, plumbers, equipment installers, and others. Saw blades are available for cutting wood, metals, plastics, compositions, and other kinds of materials.

RECIPROCATING SAWS WITH VARYING FEATURES

One saw, figure 6-1, has fingertip speed control from 0 to 2 300 strokes per minute (spm). This feature makes it easier to cut a wide range of materials from paper to metals.

It has a two-position shoe, adjustable for vertical or horizontal cutting. When the shoe is moved in or out, a dif-

Fig. 6-1 Stanley 90 459 All-purpose saw

ferent section of the blade is brought to bear on the work. This increases the life of the blade.

A handle near the front of the saw swings 180 degrees. This permits the operator to obtain a better hold on the handle when making flush or similar cuts. It also offers better control of the saw when in use.

The saw blades may be turned horizontally or vertically. Figure 6-2 shows the saw positioned for vertical flush cutting, up and down. Figure 6-3 shows the saw positioned for horizontal flush cutting, right and left.

Fig. 6-2 Vertical flush cutting

The specifications for this saw indicate that the length of the stroke is 3/4 inches; 0-2 300 spm; overall length 11 3/4 inches; and the net weight is 6 pounds. It has a 2.7 amp ac motor that operates on 115 volts.

Another type of reciprocating saw is a dual action, 2-speed, all-purpose saw, figure 6-4. It has an 8-amp, universal-type motor. It operates at 1 900 and 2 800 spm with a 1-inch stroke. The overall length is 17 1/2 inches and weighs 9 pounds. It has

Fig. 6-3 Horizontal flush cutting

Fig. 6-4 Rockwell tiger saw

Fig. 6-5 Millers Falls reciprocating saw

Fig. 6-6

an auxiliary handle that may be attached to either side of the saw. A lever located at the side of the saw converts the cutting motion from reciprocating to orbital. Orbital cutting reduces heat and blade breakdown due to friction and provides faster cutting and longer blade life. A pivoting guide shoe provides stable, accurate flush cutting.

Another example is of a heavy-duty type which may be used for a large number of utility and other jobs, not only by carpenters but by workers in other trades. It has a rocker-type shoe which helps to roll the blade into starting cuts, figure 6-5. A cutaway view of this same saw was shown in unit 1, figure 1-3.

Instead of a handle at the blade end of the saw, as on other saws, the nosepiece is tapered to provide a handhold.

An attachment for flush cutting is provided. It is reversible for right- or left-hand cuts, figure 6-6.

This saw has a 1/2-horsepower universal-type, 5-amp motor. It operates on 115-125 volts, ac-dc and produces 2 500 strokes per minute. It weighs 7 pounds and is 17 1/8 inches long.

SAW BLADES

Blades for reciprocating saws are made in a great variety of sizes and shapes. They vary in length from 2 1/2 to 18 inches and are made of high-speed or carbon steel. The material which is to be sawed determines the type of blade and kind of steel used in the blade. The manufacturers furnish carbon steel blades for cutting wood, fiberboard, asphalt, aluminum, magnesium, embedded nails, and other similar materials. The high-speed blades are used to cut metals of various thicknesses including conduit, steel pipe, channels, fiberboard, hard rubber, and other metals.

Each manufacturer's instruction manual furnishes a list of the types of saws which may be used and also the kinds of materials which each is designed to cut. Some manufacturers provide blades which only fit their saws. Other manufacturers make blades which fit most other saws.

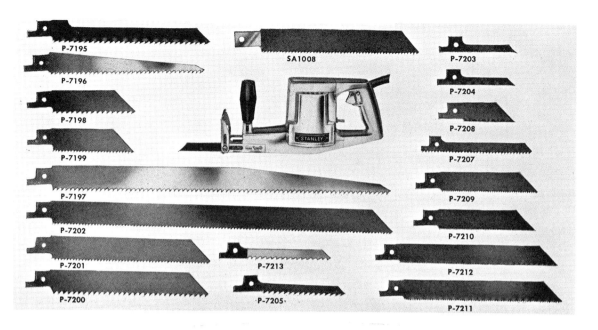

NUMBER	BLADE MATERIAL		100TH FORM			CUT				Teeth Per Inch	Length Inches	RECOMMENDED FOR CUTTING
	High Speed Steel	High Carbon Steel	Set	Wavy	Hollow Ground	Finish	Medium	Rough	Fast			
P-7195		X	X					X	X	6	6	For fast general rough-in, sawing in wood. Resists embedded nails
P-7196		X	X				X			7	6	General rough-in work in wood. will resist embedded nails
P-7197		X	X				X			7	12	
P-7198		X	X					X		6	3 1/2	All woods without nails. Fiberboard, "Builders Transite", asphalt, plaster, cast aluminum, magnesium, etc.
P-7200		X	X					X		6	6	
P-7199		X	X				X			10	3 1/2	
P-7201		X	X				X			10	6	Nails embedded woods. Plywood, asbestos and plaster.
P-7202		X	X				X			10	12	
P-7205		X	X				X		X	6	3 1/2	Scroll cutting in wood, composition materials, asbestos, etc. Can be used for pocket cuts.
P-7213	X				X	X			X	6	3 5/8	Fast smooth sawing of wood, decorative veneers, formica, plastics, fiberglass, etc. Can be used for pocket cuts.
P-7203	X		X				X			18	2 1/2	Cutting contours in sheet metals — heavier than 18 gauge
P-7204	X			X			X			24	2 1/2	Cutting contours in sheet metals — lighter than 18 gauge.
P-7207	X		X				X			10	3 5/8	Irregular contours in heavy gauge metals. "Builders Transite" and fiberboard.
P-7208	X			X			X			24	2 1/2	Metals lighter than 18 gauge sheet trim and tubing
P-7209	X		X				X			14	4	Metals heavier than 1/8" thick, angles, bar stock, "Builders Transite", hard rubber, fiber, etc.
P-7211	X		X				X			14	6	
P-7210	X		X				X			18	4	Metals heavier then 18 gauge — conduit pipe, steel pipe, tubing, channels, etc.
P-7212	X		X				X			18	6	
SA-1008		X	X				X			7	6	Flush cuts in nailed embedded wood

Fig. 6-7 Stanley blade chart

Sharp saws do faster and better work. Dull saws place a burden on the motor. Figure 6-7, page 85 shows a chart of types of saws, length, recommendations for types of materials which they will cut, and other information. This chart is typical of those provided by manufacturers.

OPERATING RECIPROCATING SAWS

Before operating these saws, be sure that the right type of blade is used. Check the manufacturer's instruction manual that lists which kind of saw blade to use on any type of material. For example: if using a Stanley saw, a carbon steel blade P7205-3 5/8 inches may be used for scroll cutting in wood or composition materials. A high-carbon steel blade P-7198-6 inch blade may be used for roughing-in work.

Be sure that the blade is pushed securely into the opening provided. Rock it lightly to be certain that it fits correctly. Then tighten the setscrew.

How to Plunge Cut Rectangular Openings

1. Carefully rest the saw on its shoe so that the blade will be in line with the mark for the opening.

2. Allow the blade to enter the wood. Gradually raise the angle of the saw until the blade enters the material and makes a kerf a little longer than the width of the blade.

3. The saw may then be held at an angle or in an upright position so that the rest of the cut may be completed. When making straight cuts, the procedure is similar to that of a handsaw. The saw may be held at any convenient angle, but at right angles to the surface when nearing a corner.

4. When a corner is reached, back up the saw, then make several cuts at an angle and up to the next line to be cut.

5. When enough material has been removed, turn the saw and cut along the new line. Cut the other sides in the same way. Figures 6-8 and 6-9 show types of rectangular cuts.

Fig. 6-8

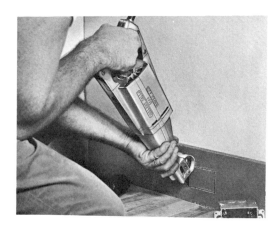

Fig. 6-9

How to Plunge Cut Curved Openings

The method used for these kinds of openings is practically the same as for rectangular openings. If a plunge cut is made, it must be started away from the outline and within the opening to be cut. When making these cuts, the saw must be held at right angles to the surface. Occasionally it is advisable to bore a hole in the space to be cut and then inset the saw blade. Figure 6-10 shows a circular opening being cut.

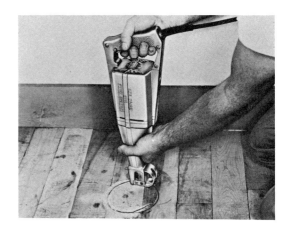

Fig. 6-10

How to Cut Straight or Curved Lines

Before starting the work, it is necessary to see that the line for the cut is marked clearly and that the material is firmly fastened to a bench or other equipment.

1. To start the cut in straight line work, set the shoe of the saw on the work.

2. Start the motor by depressing the switch trigger in the handle and move the blade into the work. Do not force the cutting.

3. Let the blade and saw do the work. Use only enough pressure to keep the saw cutting. Be sure to keep the shoe against the work at all times.

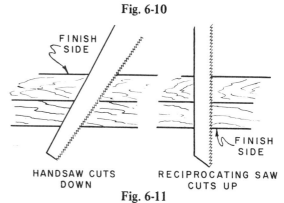

Fig. 6-11

In straight line cutting the saw is used very much like a handsaw, however, the blade cuts from the bottom side to the top side of the board instead of from the top to the bottom as with the handsaw. The good or finish side of the material should be placed face down during the cutting operation.

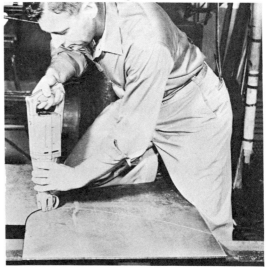

Fig. 6-12

On curved work, the procedure is the same as for line cutting except that the saw should be held at a right angle to the surface to be cut. Figure 6-12 indicates how a curved line may be cut.

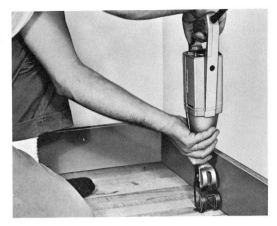

Fig. 6-13

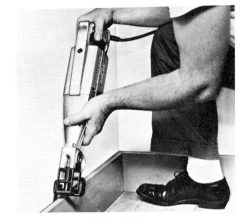

Fig. 6-14

FLUSH CUTTING

Cuts may be made flush against a wall, a floor, or any place where it is necessary to saw close to an obstruction. In order to make a flush cut with the Stanley saw, the position of the cutting edge of the blade must be changed to the direction of the cut. On the Rockwell, the blade carrier is swung out in order to clear the body of the saw. An extra attachment is required for the Millers Falls saw.

The procedure for making flush cuts is the same as for making cuts in openings. A plunge cut is made at the start of the operation. Sawing a double floor flush against a baseboard is shown in figure 6-13. Figure 6-14 shows how a baseboard may be removed.

SAWING METAL

In residential construction, the use of metals of many kinds has greatly increased. Few builders can construct a house without using metal cutting tools. Contours and straight line cutting can be done on metal, as well as on wood, with these saws. When

Fig. 6-15

Fig. 6-16

sawing metals, the general procedures as indicated for sawing lumber may be followed. When sawing metal pieces, it is important to fasten them securely in a vise or on a bench. Figures 6-15 and 6-16 show two types of metal-cutting jobs.

Care of Reciprocating Saws

These saws are lubricated at the factory. Usually they will not require additional lubrication for several weeks or for a designated number of hours of use. They should be lubricated as directed in the instruction manual.

Inlet and outlet passages should be kept clean to ensure a cool running motor. Accumulated dust should be blown out of the motor frame with an air jet.

Care should be taken not to drop these tools because a misalignment of parts may result. The saw should be checked periodically for loose parts and screws.

REVIEW QUESTIONS

A. Short Answer or Discussion

1. Compare the reciprocating saw with the sabre saw, pointing out similarities and differences.

2. What is the main use for which this saw is adapted?

3. Describe some distinguishing features which may appear on different models of reciprocating saws.

4. What range of blades are available in terms of blade length and teeth per inch?

5. Describe the cutting action of the reciprocating saw. How does this affect placement of the finish side of lumber when cutting with this saw?

6. How do the speed and length of stroke of this saw compare with that of the sabre saw?

7. At what angle should the blade be held to the work?

8. For what specific jobs is the hollow ground blade recommended?

B. Identification and Interpretation

1. In the cutaway view of the saw below, identify the lettered parts.

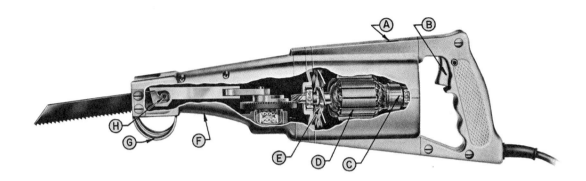

2. Where are the exhaust ports located on this saw?

3. List six specific jobs which are performed more easily with a reciprocating saw than with any other type of portable electric saw.

Unit 7 THE ELECTRIC DRILL

The electric hand drill is made in more types, capacities, and by more manufacturers than any other portable power tool. Figure 7-1 illustrates a lightweight, 1/4-inch, single speed, double-insulated drill with a universal-type, 115-volt ac motor. It has a double-reduction steel cut gear drive, a three-jaw geared chuck, and a trigger switch. The unique feature of this drill is that it is double-insulated and requires no grounding. Therefore, it is supplied with a two-conductor cord. This glass-filled nylon encased drill is an example of the double-insulation technique described in unit 1 as a possible future trend of portable power tools. Figure 7-2 shows a 1/4-inch, reversing, variable-speed drill. These drills are very popular and much more versatile than single-speed drills. They have a 4-amp, universal-type motor which operates on 115 volts ac. It has a 0-2 000 rpm range.

Figure 7-3, page 92, shows a heavy-duty, 1/2-inch, short-type drill designed to get into tight spots and ideal for use in construction. These types of drills may be mounted in drill stands for multiple drilling. Figure 7-3 (A), page 92, shows a stand designed for use with portable drills.

In the cutaway view of the conventional drill, figure 7-4, page 92, the parts listed may be identified.

Electric drills are designated by the maximum drill diameter that the chuck will hold. common sizes are 1/4 inch, 5/16 inch, 3/8 inch, 1/2 inch, 5/8 inch, 3/4 inch, and 1 inch. The chuck speed, which is fixed for each size drill, decreases as the size of the drill increases. The drill speed of a 1/4 inch drill, for instance, might be 1 000 rpm at no-load. The same type drill in 5/16-inch size is 1 000 rpm, no-load, and the 3/8-inch size of the same drill is 850 rpm, no-load.

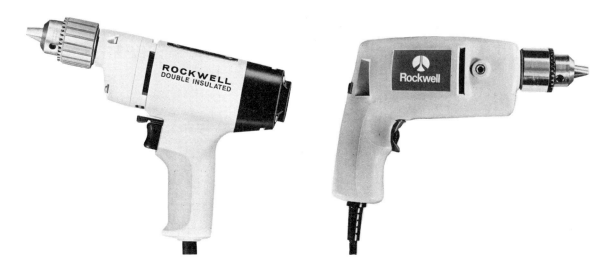

Fig. 7-1 1/4-inch double-insulated drill   **Fig. 7-2 1/4-inch reversible and variable-speed drill**

Fig. 7-3 Heavy-duty 1/2-inch drill

Fig. 7-3 (A) Drill stand

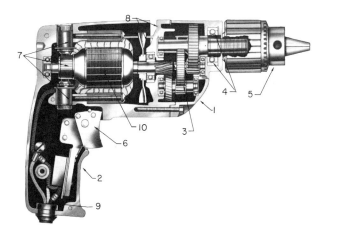

① Lightweight aluminum case
② Pistol-grip handle
③ Compound reduction gears
④ Spindle ball bearings
⑤ Three-jaw chuck
⑥ Trigger switch
⑦ Commutator and brushes
⑧ Cooling fan and air ports
⑨ Safety cord
⑩ Universal motor

Fig. 7-4 Cutaway of portable electric drill

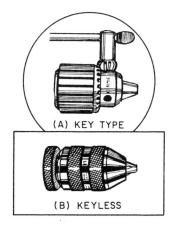

(A) KEY TYPE

(B) KEYLESS

Fig. 7-5 Types of chucks

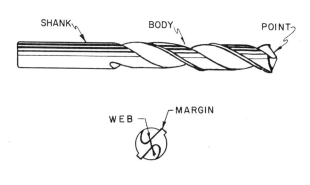

Fig. 7-6 Straight shank twist drill

PARTS OF THE ELECTRIC HAND DRILL

Chucks are made in different sizes to correspond to the capacity of the drills.

The chuck holds the drill with the hardened steel jaws which are tightened and released with a threaded sleeve. The sleeve is knurled so that it can be turned by hand. Some keyless chucks, figure 7-5 (B), are designed so that hand pressure alone is required to tighten them. The more common chucks have teeth on the lower edge, by which the final tightening pressure is applied with a key, figure 7-5 (A). A moderately firm pressure will tighten a good chuck.

The body of the drill houses the motor and a series of gears designed to give the drill the desired speed and power. The case is usually made of aluminum alloy or nylon for lightness of weight. Nylon cases are also nonconductive, reducing the danger of electrical shock. The bodies of drills are made in many shapes to adapt to the requirements of the job and to provide good balance for handling.

Handles are also made in many shapes. They are attached to the housing in several positions to provide ease of handling and control. The shape and location of the handle are very important considerations in the choice of a drill.

DRILLS AND BITS

Straight-Shank Twist Drill

The most commonly used drills for electric hand drills are straight-shank twist drills. Twist drills are made of carbon or high-speed steel. The latter are of better quality. Both may be used for drilling wood and metals. However, carbon drills do not hold up as well as high-speed drills, particularly when drilling metals.

The parts of a straight-shank twist drill include the shank, the body, web, margins, cutting lips, and the point, figure 7-6.

For drilling metal, cutting edges are generally sharpened to form an angle of 59 degrees with the centerline of the drill, figure 7-7. In other words, the edges form an included angle of 118 degrees. When drilling wood, an angle of 30 degrees with the centerline, (60 degrees included angle), (C), figure 7-8, page 94, is preferred. As a rule, the softer the material, the sharper the point of the drill is ground.

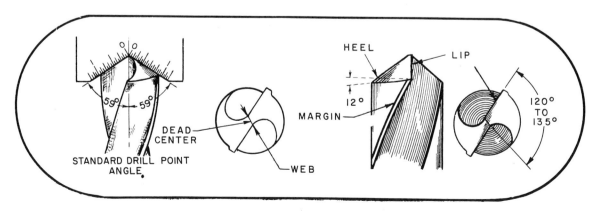

Fig. 7-7 Lip clearance

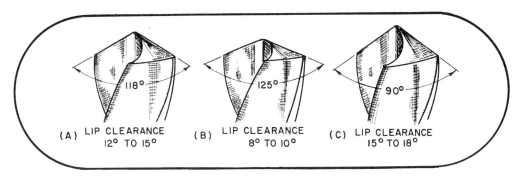

Fig. 7-8 Cutting angles of twist drills

Lip clearance allows the cutting edges of the drill to enter the material being drilled without interference. The average lip clearance of a twist drill is between 12 and 15 degrees, depending upon the hardness of the material to be drilled. Softer material leads to a greater clearance angle. Notice the relationship of the angles of the drill points to the lip clearance, figure 7-8. As the point becomes sharper, the lip clearance increases.

SYSTEMS OF DRILL SIZES FOR TWIST DRILLS

Drill sizes are designated under four systems: fractional, number, letter, and metric. The fractional size drills start from 1/64-inch with sizes varying in 1/64-inch graduations. The fractional sizes and the decimal equivalent for each may be found by referring to any table of decimal equivalents of an inch. The number size drills range from number 1 (measuring 0.228 inch) to number 80 (measuring 0.0135 inch). The letter size drills range from A to Z. Letter A drill is the smallest in the set (0.234 inch) and Z is the largest (0.413 inch). The millimeter sizes are made according to the metric system of measure. The sizes range from 0.4mm (0.0157 inch) to 50 mm (1.968 inch).

The sizes of twist drills are usually marked on the shank of small straight-shank drills and on the recess between the body and the shank of larger drills. The size of a twist drill can be measured (over the margins) with a micrometer caliper, or the drill may be gauged for size in a drill gauge. The following tables of drill sizes include all of the number and letter sizes of drills. They are arranged in order of size with the decimal equivalent opposite each drill size.

OTHER TYPES OF DRILLS AND BITS

Two differences distinguish drills and bits used with electric drills from those designed for a bit brace. They generally have no starting screw and have no tang. When a bit with a starting screw is to be used in a portable electric hand drill, a pilot hole the size of the starting screw is first drilled to eliminate its pulling effect. Otherwise, the drill would cut into the wood at too great a rate, tearing out a rough hole or stalling the drill.

The drills and bits used with the portable electric hand drill, aside from the straight-shank twist drill, are shown in the figures which follow.

Machine bits are used for conventional wood drilling operations and may not be used on metal. The point of this bit is unthreaded. The cutting lips are straight across so that a

Drill	Diameter in Inches	Drill	Diameter in Inches	Drill	Diameter in Inches	Drill	Diameter in Inches	Drill	Diameter in Inches
80	0.0135	55	0.0520	31	0.1200	8	0.1990	19/64	0.2969
79	0.0145	54	0.0550	1/8	0.1250	7	0.2010	N	0.3020
1/64	0.0156	53	0.0595	30	0.1285	13/64	0.2031	5/16	0.3125
78	0.0160	1/16	0.0625	29	0.1360	6	0.2040	O	0.3160
77	0.0180	52	0.0635	28	0.1405	5	0.2055	P	0.3230
76	0.0200	51	0.0670	9/64	0.1406	4	0.2090	21/64	0.3281
75	0.0210	50	0.0700	27	0.1440	3	0.2130	Q	0.3320
74	0.0225	49	0.0730	26	0.1470	7/32	0.2187	R	0.3390
73	0.0240	48	0.0760	25	0.1495	2	0.2210	11/32	0.3437
72	0.0250	5/64	0.0781	24	0.1520	1	0.2280	S	0.3480
71	0.0260	47	0.0785	23	0.1540	A	0.2344	T	0.3580
70	0.0280	46	0.0810	5/32	0.1562	15/64	0.2380	23/64	0.3594
69	0.0292	45	0.0820	22	0.1570	B	0.2420	U	0.3680
68	0.0310	44	0.0860	21	0.1590	C	0.2420	3/8	0.3750
1/32	0.0312	43	0.0890	20	0.1610	D	0.2460	V	0.3770
67	0.0320	42	0.0935	19	0.1660	E	0.2500	W	0.3860
66	0.0330	3/32	0.0937	18	0.1695	1/4	0.2500	25/64	0.3906
65	0.0350	41	0.0960	11/64	0.1719	F	0.2570	X	0.3970
64	0.0360	40	0.0980	17	0.1730	G	0.2610	Y	0.4040
63	0.0370	39	0.0995	16	0.1770	17/64	0.2656	13/32	0.4062
62	0.0380	38	0.1015	15	0.1800	H	0.2660	Z	0.4130
61	0.0390	37	0.1040	14	0.1820	I	0.2720	27/64	0.4219
60	0.0400	39	0.1065	13	0.1850	J	0.2770	7/16	0.4375
59	0.0410	7/64	0.1094	3/16	0.1875	K	0.2810	29/64	0.4531
58	0.0420	35	0.1100	12	0.1890	9/32	0.2812	15/32	0.4687
57	0.0430	34	0.1110	11	0.1910	L	0.2900	31/64	0.4844
56	0.0465	33	0.1130	10	0.1935	M	0.2950	1/2	0.5000
3/64	0.0469	32	0.1160	9	0.1960				

Twist Drill Sizes

Fig. 7-9 Hollow center auger bit

Fig. 7-10 Countersunk bit

Fig. 7-11 Combination bit

Fig. 7-12 Forstner bit

Fig. 7-13 Carbide-tipped bit

Fig. 7-14 Spade-type bit

flat-bottomed hole results. Sets of these drills have a standard size shank diameter, either 1/4 inch or 1/2 inch.

Countersinks provide the conical depression to receive the flathead wood or machine screws. The type shown may be used for countersinking either wood or metal.

The Forstner bit is used where large holes are to be drilled in wood or when the hole extends only part way through the stock. The Forstner bit leaves the bottom of the hole flat and smooth.

Carbide-tipped drills are used for drilling masonry or ceramics. They are available in a range of standard fractional sizes which meet the needs of sizes required for the installation of fastening devices used in masonry and ceramic materials.

Spade-type wood bits are a comparatively new type of bit used for boring holes in wood and other soft materials. The point is hollow ground to provide clearance and the shank is 1/4 inch in diameter so that the drills may be used in a 1/4-inch portable electric drill.

Combination bits make a counterbored and/or countersunk hole, shank hole and pilot hole, for driving flathead wood screws, all in one operation. Sizes selected are determined by the length of the screw to be driven and its gauge number.

Certain types of auger bits are made so that they may be used in an electric hand drill or in a brace. These type bits are supplied with a tapered square shank, and, in addition, that portion of the shank preceding the square tapered portion is ground with six equally spaced "flats". When used with a power drill the square tapered portion must be sawed off so the shank may be inserted in the chuck. Since there are three jaws in the chuck of a power drill, these will clamp on every other flat ground on the shank. The bit may still be used in a hand brace by clamping any two opposite corners of the flats in the grooves of the chuck.

Fig. 7-15 Auger bit

DRILL SPEEDS

Portable electric drills that do not have adjustable speeds are limited as to the drill size which may be used with each model. Generally, this is controlled by the chuck capacity of the drill. Electric drills with small chucks usually have a greater rpm than those having large chucks. If the twist drill fits the chuck, in most cases, it is suitable for use with that particular speed drill. However, there are drills, such as the spade type, which have a small shank and a large head. But these are used for cutting soft materials only where higher speeds are desirable.

Two general rules to keep in mind concerning drill speeds are: (1) the smaller the drill, the greater the speed that is needed for efficient cutting; (2) the harder the material being drilled, the lower the drill speed should be.

Lubricants or coolants aid in the rate and ease of cutting. Specific lubricants are recommended for different material.

Material	Coolant	Material	Coolant
Hard Steel	Turpentine	Brass	Paraffin
Machine Steel	Soluble Oil	Aluminum	Kerosene
Wrought Iron	Lard Oil	Wood	None

How to Select and Chuck Twist Drills

1. Select the proper size drill for the job.

2. Inspect the drill to see that it is properly sharpened.

3. Check the drill to see that it is straight and has no nicks or burrs on the shank.
   NOTE: A bent or burred drill may drill oversize and will be difficult to control during use.

4. Insert the drill in the drill chuck and tighten firmly with the chuck wrench, figure 7-16.

> CAUTION: Make certain that the drill switch will not be turned on accidently while the drill is being tightened in the chuck.

NOTE: The chuck wrench should be in good condition and should be held firmly into the chuck teeth while the chuck is being tightened to prevent the wrench from slipping and damaging either the chuck or the wrench.

Fig. 7-16 Tightening the key chuck

5. Check the drill to see that it runs true by starting the drill motor and observing the point.
   NOTE: If it does not run true, re-check for straightness, burrs, and proper chucking.

How to Use the Portable Electric Drill

1. Be sure the material to be drilled is held firmly in position, (clamped if necessary) so it cannot move when the drill is in operation.

2. Select the proper drill bit.

3. Chuck the drill and tighten it securely.

4. Connect the drill to the power outlet. Be sure the drill is properly grounded.

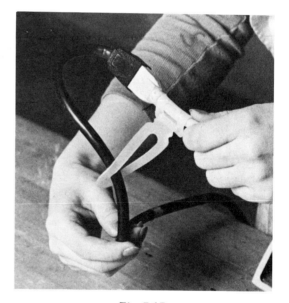

Fig. 7-17

> CAUTION: Extension cords should be connected so that they will not interfere with the operation or trip other workers. Inspect the condition of the cord and the attachment plug. The insulation must not be worn or torn with the wires exposed. Some manufacturers provide devices that keep the extension cord and the tool cord from separating, figure 7-17.

5. Test the hook up by pressing the trigger switch to see if the drill is operating properly and the drill bit is seated so it is running true. Release the switch.

6. When drilling metal, locate the starting point for the drill from a center-punch mark (A), a pilot hole previously drilled (B), or by "spotting" the drill by turning the chuck

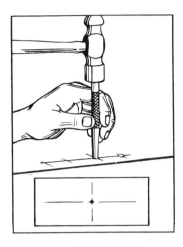
(A) CENTER-PUNCHED

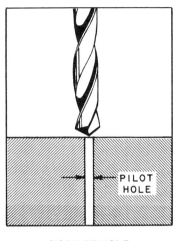
(B) PILOT HOLE

(C) SPOTTING

Fig. 7-18 Starting points for the drill

with the fingers (C), figure 7-18. When drilling wood, locate the starting point for the drill by making an impression with a scratch awl.

NOTE: When drilling large holes, drill a pilot hole first. The pilot should be slightly larger than the web of the larger drill, figure 7-18 (B).

7. With the switch off, place the drill point on the layout mark.

8. Adjust the drill to the proper position and angle.

9. Hold the drill at the correct angle to the surface being drilled.

10. Start the drill while applying slight pressure.

CAUTION: Hold the drill with one or both hands, as required by the type of drill and the kind of job. Brace the body well to avoid being injured when using heavy-duty drills.

NOTE: The pressure required will vary with the size of the drill and with the kind of material being drilled.

11. See that the drill is centered as soon as it is well started by removing and inspecting the impression.

12. If the drill is out of center, shift it to the desired location by one of the following methods:

   a. A small drill may be shifted slightly by tilting the drill in the opposite direction to that which the drill should be moved in, figure 7-19.

   b. A large drill may be shifted in metal by making one or more grooves in

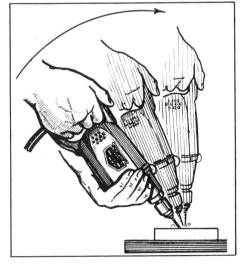
Fig. 7-19

HOLE DRILLED
INCORRECTLY

SHALLOW GROOVES
CHIPPED ON HEAVY SIDE

HOLE DRAWN
TO CENTER LOCATION

Fig. 7-20 Drawing the drill point

the impression with a cape chisel on the side of the center toward which the drill should be drawn, figure 7-20. The drill will cut toward the side where the chisel marks are made and help to bring the drill back to position.

13. Apply a suitable coolant with a brush or an oil can, if necessary. Refer to the chart on cutting oils given earlier in this unit.

14. Drill the hole to the desired depth. If the hole is to be drilled through the material, ease off on the pressure just as the drill breaks through.

CAUTION: Always make certain that the drill will not injure someone working on the other side of the work.

NOTE: It is good practice to clamp scrap stock on the back side of wood to be drilled so that when drill breaks through, it will not grab or splinter, but will leave a clean hole.

Fig. 7-21 Extension drills

DRILL ATTACHMENTS

Extension drills are ordinary twist drills that have been welded to a longer piece of drill rod. In some cases a small sleeve is used to join the drill and extension rod. Extension drills are used for drilling holes that are inaccessible to shorter drills, figure 7-21.

Ninety-degree angle drill attachments hold the drill at right angles, or 90 degrees, to the main driving shaft. This type has two bevel gears to transmit power from the drive shaft to the spindle. The gears and shaft are packed in grease and are enclosed in a steel casing. Ninety-degree angle drill attachments are equipped with either a standard drill chuck, figure 7-22, or a special collet chuck, figure 7-23.

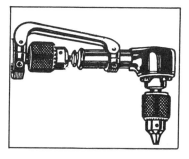

Fig. 7-22

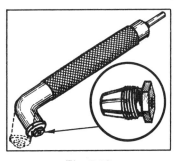

Fig. 7-23

Fig. 7-24 Hole saw with variety of saw blades

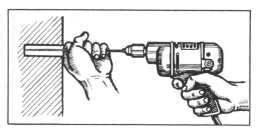

Fig. 7-25 Supporting extension drill

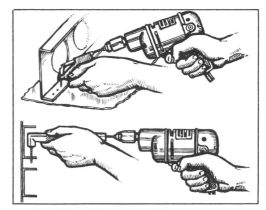

Fig. 7-26 Using angle drill attachments

Hole saws, figure 7-24, are available in sizes ranging from 5/8 inch to 4 inches. They are mounted on a mandrel which fits the portable drill chuck. The mandrel also holds a twist drill which drills a hole and serves as a guide for the hole saw.

The same general procedure is followed when using drill attachments as when using regular twist drills except for the special notations given for each.

1. Use a slow-speed drill.

2. Insert the extension drill into the chuck with great care.

3. Support the drill shank or the flexible shaft so that it cannot whip.

> **CAUTION:** If allowed to get out of control, the extension drill is very dangerous to the operator because of whipping. It should be inspected for alignment and proper centering in chuck before starting.

4. As the length of the rigid extension drill is increased, apply proportionately less pressure to it.

How to Use 45- and 90-degree Angle Drill Attachments

1. Lubricate the angle drive mechanism to prevent wear and overheating.

2. Select the proper size twist drill.

3. Install the drill and tighten the collet or chuck.

4. Hold the tool firmly so that it cannot rotate when power is applied.

How to Use the Hole Saw

1. Select a hole saw for the material to be cut.
   NOTE: Coarse-tooth saws are used for wood, fiber, cast-iron, and other coarse material. Fine-tooth saws are used for sheet metal, steel, porcelain, and other fine-grained material. Special saws are available for hard alloys and for cutting standard steel in production work.

2. Select a mandrel to fit the chuck of the drill and the hole saw to be used.
   NOTE: Some manufacturers supply mandrels to fit drills with less than 1/2-inch capacity. Other manufacturers supply mandrels only for 1/2-inch and larger drills. Each mandrel will fit the hole saws within a certain range of sizes.

3. Select a pilot drill to fit the mandrel.

4. Lay out the hole to be sawed and center punch the center in the usual manner as a guide for the pilot drill.

5. Assemble the hole saw and the pilot drill on the mandrel and secure the mandrel in the drill chuck.

6. Drill the pilot hole, keeping the drill perpendicular to the work.

7. Cut the hole with the hole saw, figure 7-27. Care must be exercised to apply pressure according to the material being cut, the coarseness of the saw, and the speed of the drill.

> CAUTION: The pressure should be decreased as the saw breaks through. The operator should hold the drill firmly and must be on the alert to back the saw off and shut off the drill if the saw catches as it breaks through.

Special Feature Drills

Hammer drills combine the features of both the hammer and the drill. They are mentioned here only to acquaint the student with their application.

Figure 7-28 shows a 1/2-inch hammer drill. It delivers 40 000 impacts per minute when the handle is twisted to actuate the collar and has an idle speed of 2 500 rpm. As a hammer drill it is used on concrete, brick, tile, and other similar materials.

Fig. 7-27 Using the hole saw

Fig. 7-28 A hammer drill

Fig. 7-29 Milwaukee magnum

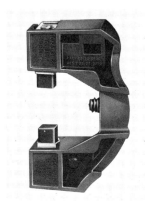

Fig. 7-30

Fig. 7-31

Fig. 7-32

Figure 7-29 shows a 1/2 inch capacity drill. Because of its larger drill size capacity, it has a 120 volt 4.5 amp motor which varies in speed from 0 - 350 rpm. The larger size cutting capacity requires lower rpm speeds.

In addition to its high performance capacities, this drill has some unique operating and maintenance features. Figure 7-30 shows the cartridge designed by the manufacturer which holds the carbon brushes along with a spare cartridge screw and spare brushes.

Figures 7-31 and 7-32 show operation features which make the drill convenient and safer to operate. The switch is a two-finger-lower pivot trigger that allows the operator to use the index finger in an in-line position against the side of the case. This position aids the operator to align the drill with the hole line. The forward-reverse switch is pocketed and positioned above the trigger to prevent switching the drill rotation by accident. The trigger switch lock control is also located above the trigger and is squeeze actuated. The action must be purposeful and positive. This particular drill may be obtained with detachable cords in various lengths. The lock feature prevents the cord from being pulled from the drill.

REVIEW QUESTIONS

A. Short Answer or Discussion

1. What is the distinctive feature of the 1/4-inch drill shown in figure 7-1?

2. How are electric drills designated?

3. How is drill speed affected by the size of the drill?

4. What type of chucks are available?

5. Describe three types of drill handles available.

6. How are twist drills sized and what systems are used to designate these sizes?

7. Describe two general rules relating to drill speeds.

8. What three ways are suggested for locating starting points when drilling metal? What way is suggested for drilling wood?

9. How can splintering on the back side of wood be avoided when drilling through it?

10. Describe three drill attachments and indicate their specific uses.

11. What precaution should be observed when using extension drills?

B. Identification and Interpretation

1. On the cutaway illustration, identify the lettered parts.

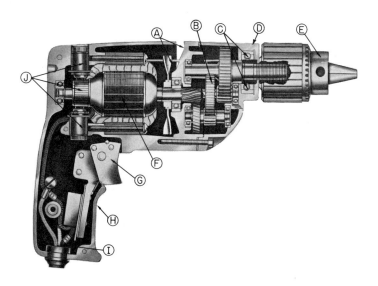

2. Identify each type of drill or bit illustrated and state the special use of each.

Unit 8 ELECTRIC POWER PLANES

The electric plane is becoming widely used to eliminate time-consuming hand plane operations. In addition to its speed, the power plane gives a much smoother and more accurate cut.

Figures 8-1 (A) and 8-1 (B) show a popular power planer. This model has a combination surface, edge, and bevel plane. It has a 10-amp, 115-volt ac-dc universal-type motor. It has an idle speed of 15 000 rpm with a 30 000 spm cutting capacity. It has a 1/8-inch depth capacity and a 3-inch width capacity. It weighs 15 pounds and is 18 inches long. This power plane is considered medium-sized and is used for production and heavy-duty work.

Figure 8-2, page 106, shows a lightweight power plane. This type plane is used to dress the edges of boards before finish sanding and will be discussed in unit 9.

The following chart gives the specifications of the power planes shown in figures 8-1 (A), 8-2, and 8-5.

Model	Amps	Horse-power	Speed RPM	Voltage	Width of Cut	Depth of Cut	Length	Weight
653	10	1.5	15 000	115	3″	1/8″	18″	15 lbs.
167	2.5	3/8	21 000	115	1 13/16″	1/64″	7 1/4″	3 3/4 lbs.
126	7	1.0	22 000	115	2 13/32″	3/32″	16″	9 1/4 lbs.

The cutter is mounted directly on the end of the motor shaft by means of a large thread and an accurately ground seat. The complete motor may easily be removed. It is interchangeable as a power unit when used with other equipment of the same manufacturer.

The cutter used in this machine is composed of a solid body upon which is ground two spiral cutting edges. When the edges become dull, the cutter body may be removed from the plane and sharpened. A grinding attachment is supplied with this plane, figure 8-3, page 106.

The depth of the cut is controlled by an eccentric. The location of the cutter, in relation to the shoe of the plane, is adjustable to allow for cutter wear. The front and rear shoes are always in alignment when the depth adjustment is at zero. A predetermined depth

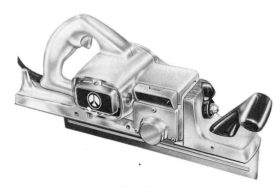

Fig. 8-1 (A) Power plane

Fig. 8-1 (B) Operating a power plane

Fig. 8-2 Power block plane

Fig. 8-3 Grinding attachment

Fig. 8-4 Plane adjustments

of cut may be taken throughout the length of a door or similar work. Variable depth of cuts may also be taken to a line by varying the depth adjustment while cutting. The apron of the plane is adjustable to make a bevel as well as right-angle cuts. Smooth, straight work can be done much faster than with a hand plane.

The power plane illustrated in figure 8-5 is a heavy-duty machine with a no-load speed of 22 000 rpm. Its width of cut is 2 13/32 inches and its maximum depth of cut is 3/32 inch.

The depth-adjustment lever is located at the front end of the plane. Graduations on this lever are in 64ths. The numbers, however, mark 32nds. Thus, number 1 gives a 1/32-inch cut and number 2 gives a 2/32-inch cut. A 1/64-inch cut is made by setting the lever halfway between 0 and 1.

The bevel adjustment sets the angle of

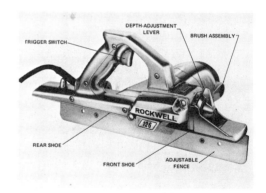

Fig. 8-5 Cutting side view of heavy-duty power plane

the apron to the plane shoe, figure 8-5. This adjustment is measured by two graduated hinges which are held by wing nuts. Both hinges must be lined up to the same angle before tightening the wing nuts.

An additional adjustment of this plane is an apron stop stud which is used where repeated cuts are made at the same angle.

The spiral cutter for this plane is sharpened with a special sharpening attachment, figure 8-6. The attachment will not handle carbide-tipped plane cutters because the cutter

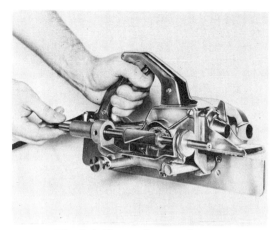

Fig. 8-6 Sharpening attachment

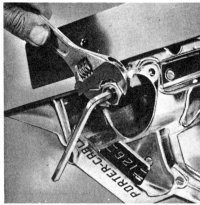

Fig. 8-7

is a straight blade, not spiral, and it is too hard. Therefore, carbide-tipped blades must be ground on a diamond-grit grinding wheel.

How to Assemble the Cutter

1. Make sure the power plane is disconnected at the power outlet.

2. Place the plane upside down on the bench so it rests on the handle and motor housing.

3. Remove the rear-cover retaining screw on the cutter housing and loosen the front one so the cover will swing forward.

4. Install the cutter on the cutter shaft by placing the slotted end of the cutter on the shaft first.

5. Place the nut on the end of the shaft.

6. Insert a hex wrench in the end of the shaft and hold it steady while tightening the nut with an open-end wrench, figure 8-7.

7. When the nut is securely tightened, put the cover back in place and tighten the cover retaining screws.

How to Set the Cutter

The cutter must be set to the "0" position so that the depth-adjustment lever will accurately gauge the depth of cut.

1. Set the depth-adjustment lever to the "0" position.

2. Place the plane upside down on the bench.

3. Turn the cutter adjusting lever toward the rear of the plane, figure 8-8, page 108.

4. Turn the cutter by hand until it lifts the straightedge.

5. Adjust the cutter lever until the tip of the cutter just touches the straightedge while it rests evenly on both shoes.
   NOTE: This adjustment must be made every time the cutter is sharpened.

How to Set the Vertical Fence

1. Loosen the angle screw.

2. With the try square, adjust the vertical fence to form a 90-degree angle with the shoe, figure 8-9.

3. Tighten the angle wing screw.

How to Adjust Depth of Cut

1. Swing the depth of cut lever located above the front of the shoe, figure 8-10.
   NOTE: It is not necessary to tighten or lock this lever which may be adjusted from a 0- to 3/32- inch cut.

How to Use the Power Plane

1. Position the hands as shown in figure 8-11.
   NOTE: The four fingers of the left hand should be wrapped underneath the motor and against the vertical fence. Keep the left thumb firmly on top of the front shoe.

2. Place the plane on the work with the cutter slightly back from the wood.

3. Make sure the electric cord cannot become tangled and is properly grounded.

4. Start the motor and begin to cut, keeping more pressure on the front shoe with the left hand than on the rear shoe with the right hand.

5. Keep a steady, even pressure down on the shoes and against the side of the vertical fence.
   NOTE: Depth of cut may be adjusted as you plane by controlling the depth of cut lever with the left thumb as the plane rides over the work.

6. When finishing a cut, use the right hand to keep greater pressure on the rear shoe than on the front. This prevents rounding or gouging the work.

Fig. 8-8

Fig. 8-9 Setting vertical fence at 90 degrees

Fig. 8-10 Adjusting for depth of cut

Fig. 8-11 Correct planing position

After removing preliminary stock, it is advisable to take a finish cut 1/32 inch to ensure a smooth surface that will require no sanding.

How to Cut a Bevel

1. Adjust the amount of bevel by loosening the two wing nuts on the vertical fence hinges and tilting the fence until the pointers on the hinges line up with the desired angle marking.

2. Tighten the wing nuts securely.

3. Proceed to cut in the same manner as for regular right-angle cuts. It may be necessary to make more than one pass, depending on the width of the bevel.

4. Keep the plane shoe and the fence pressed firmly against the work during the entire cut. Make each cut for the full length of the board.

5. To make settings for repeated cuts of the same angle, proceed as follows:

   a. Make the required settings of the fence and lock it in place with the two hinge wing nuts.

   b. Directly behind the front hinge of the vertical fence and on the underside of the motor housing is a headed pin which is held in place by a round head screw. With a screwdriver, turn the round head screw and release the stud.

   c. Move the stud until the head rests against the side of the fence.

   d. Tighten the round head screw. Now the fence can be adjusted to smaller angles and quickly reset to the original angle by simply moving it back against the stop stud.

How to Plane a Board to Fit

1. Mark the line carefully with a pencil and notice where most material must be removed.

2. To plane a concave curve, start the plane with the depth-adjusting lever set at "0" well behind the high spot.

3. As the plane advances, advance the lever to cut deeper.

4. When the high spot is passed, turn the lever back.

5. Work down the length of edge, working carefully to the pencil line.

6. To plane a convex curve, work the depth-adjusting lever in reverse.
   NOTE: A true fit can be accomplished by this method provided the bow or bend is not too great. Boards with several high spots along the edge can be smoothed by working down high spots first, cutting only 1/64 inch deep on each pass.

How to Sharpen the Plane Cutter

1. Extend the center support bar of the sharpening attachment out from the frame to its full length, figure 8-12, page 110, by loosening the setscrew, pulling the bar out to its full length, and tightening the setscrew.

Fig. 8-12 Sharpening attachment with extended center support bar

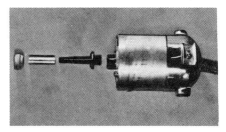

Fig. 8-13 Pull-apart showing motor, spindle, tubular sleeve, and wheel

2. Screw the spindle, figure 8-13, directly onto the motor chuck. Slip the tubular sleeve over the spindle. Then screw the grinding wheel (tapered side toward the motor) to the end of the spindle until it rests against the sleeve.

3. Attach the motor to the sharpening attachment by inserting the motor into the circular portion of the frame until the two lugs on the bottom of the motor slip over the two lugs provided in the sharpening attachment. Be sure that the switch is facing upward in a convenient position. Then lock the motor in place by turning it clockwise as far as it will go, figure 8-14.

Fig. 8-14 Inserting motor into sharpening attachment

4. To insert the plane cutter into the sharpening attachment:

   a. Remove the cutter arbor bearing by turning the knurled arbor knob until the spring retainers come out of their slots, figure 8-15.

   b. Draw the arbor clear of the frame so that the cutter retaining nut may be slipped from the arbor.

   c. Place the plane cutter on the arbor so that the slotted end engages the cross pin, figure 8-16.

   d. Replace and hand-tighten the knurled arbor nut.

Fig. 8-15 Cutting arbor is removed by turning knurled arbor knob

Fig. 8-16 Plane cutter, arbor bearing and knob in position before tightening

Fig. 8-17 Adjusting clearance between grinding wheel and plane cutter

Fig. 8-18 Cutter is passed across the face of grinding wheel

e. Replace the cutter arbor bearing by reversing the way it was removed.

5. To grind the cutter, move the arbor until the end of the plane cutter is opposite the grinding wheel. Be sure there is a small clearance between the grinding wheel surface and the cutter edge. This clearance may be adjusted by the knurled knob located at the front of the sharpening attachment, figure 8-17.

6. Start the motor. Begin feeding the cutter into the grinding wheel carefully until the first spark appears. Pass the cutting edge across the grinding wheel until the cut is completed, figure 8-18. Continue to feed the cutter into the grinding wheel until the sparks show along the full length of the cutter.

7. Draw the cutter back across the grinding wheel to the starting position. Note that the arbor automatically adjusts to follow the contour of the plane cutter.

8. After one edge of the cutter has been sharpened, turn the arbor in a semicircle until the pin engages in the spiral slot. Then grind the second cutting edge in the same manner as was done for the first. Never grind one edge of the cutter before making adjustments. Be sure that both edges have been ground while set at one adjustment. Only a very light grinding is necessary to restore the cutting edge to razor sharpness.

REVIEW QUESTIONS

A. Short Answer or Discussion

1. What are the advantages of power planes over conventional hand tool models?

2. Describe the possible adjustments and how they are made.

3. How are plane cutters sharpened?

4. How is the depth of cut adjusted and what are the minimum and maximum depths of cut on the power plane shown in figure 8-5?

5. What type of cutter can not be sharpened with the special attachment? Why?

6. What is the purpose of the apron stop stud?

7. How must the cutter be set so that the depth adjustment lever will accurately gauge the depth of cut?

8. What hand tool is used for the above adjustment?

9. How is the vertical fence set and what hand tool is used to verify the setting?

10. Describe the proper pressure to use at the beginning and end of cuts.

11. How can depth of cut be adjusted during planing?

12. Describe how to set the plane for a 30-degree bevel cut.

13. How would you set the plane to take a 2-inch wide rabbet cut?

14. Describe a situation where use of the apron stop stud would be applicable.

B. Completion

1. The number 2 on the depth adjustment lever of the heavy-duty power plane represents _____.

2. To make a 3/64-inch cut, set the depth adjustment lever _____ between 1 and 2.

3. The bevel adjustment requires setting _____ graduated hinges.

4. When placing a cutter on the cutter shaft, the _____ end is placed on the shaft first.

5. When the depth adjustment lever is set at "0", a _____ laid across the front and rear_____ should just touch the _____.

6. The special sharpening attachment handles blades of a _____ shape only.

7. It is good practice to take a finish cut of _____ inches to ensure a smooth surface that will not require sanding.

8. The accuracy of the bevel adjustment can be checked with a _____.

9. To plane a concave curve, the depth-adjustment lever is first set at _____.

10. The depth-adjustment lever is set at _____ when beginning to plane a convex curve.

C. Identification and Interpretation

1. On the plane illustrated, identify the lettered parts.

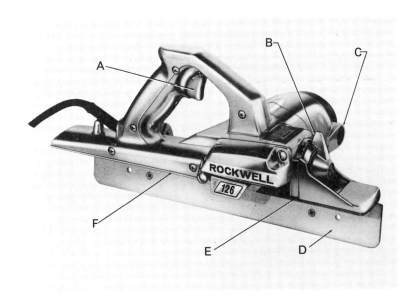

Unit 9 THE POWER BLOCK PLANE

The power block plane, figure 9-1, is used for surface and edge planing where it is necessary to remove only small amounts of material. It replaces the larger power plane in many instances because its size is more suited for use on small parts such as those found in cabinet construction.

Specific applications of this plane are: fitting doors to casings or correcting a sticking door, cleaning up rough rabbets or trimming rabbets which require clearance, planing the undercuts on mitered trim cuts, planing the edges of shingles, and beveling the edges of formica bonded to a wood base. Examples of two instances are shown in figures 9-2 and 9-3.

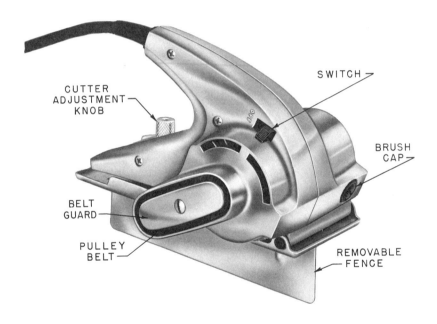

Fig. 9-1 Power block plane

Fig. 9-2 Planning edge of door

Fig. 9-3 Planing down rabbet cut on drawer front

CUTTERS AVAILABLE FOR THE POWER BLOCK PLANE

Both high-speed steel and carbide-tipped cutters are available for block planes. High-speed steel cutters are best suited for general planing, whereas carbide-tipped cutters are best used on plywood, hardboard, and other hard materials which quickly dull high-speed steel cutters.

Carbide-tipped plane cutters are designed to withstand the forces of normal cutting. However, carbide is a hard, brittle material which when subjected to bumps, shocks, and vibrations, can be easily damaged and have its effective cutting life shortened. To obtain maximum satisfactory service from carbide-tipped plane cutters:

1. Never subject the tip to shock loads. It might crack or shatter.

2. Let the plane get up to full speed before starting a cut.

3. Exert uniform pressure during the cutting operation.

4. Be careful not to hit nails or knots during the cutting operation. This might nick, crack, or knock the tip from the cutter body.

5. Remove the cutter for servicing at the slightest sign of a nick or crack.

6. Remove the cutter for servicing whenever a poor finish or the need for increased pressure during the cutting operation indicates the cutting edge is dull.

7. Clean and hone the carbide tips at frequent intervals to maintain keen cutting edges. Remove accumulations of wood dust and wood fluids. Hand hones in convenient sizes are available from abrasive manufacturers. Hone the plane cutter edges with light, smooth strokes. Brush out the hone occasionally with kerosene.

8. If the carbide-tipped edge (there may be more than one) is nicked, or if the cutting edge cannot be restored by honing, have an experienced mechanic regrind the cutter. Use a competent local grinding service, or return the cutter to the manufacturer of the machine.

SAFETY PRECAUTIONS

In operating this machine, the same basic instructions apply that are universally observed for all portable power tools. These include the following:

- Always make sure the plane switch is in the "off" position before connecting the plane to the power supply.

- Do not wear loose clothing that might become entangled with the fast-turning plane cutter.

- When a cut is finished, be careful not to come in contact with the cutter.

- Turn off the motor immediately upon completion of planing.

- Always disconnect the plane cord plug from the power outlet before making adjustments or replacing the cutter.

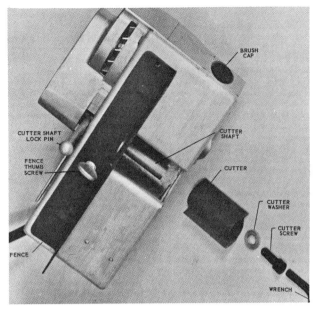

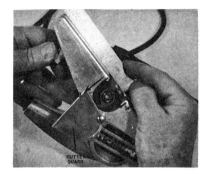

Fig. 9-4   **Fig. 9-5**

How to Install and Remove the Cutter

1. To install the cutter, insert the cutter-shaft lock pin as shown in figure 9-4.

2. Slip the cutter on the cutter shaft, making certain the counterbored end of the cutter is out or away from the plane.

3. Place the cutter washer on the cutter screw and insert the assembly into the counterbore of the cutter.

4. Insert the wrench into the screwhead and turn counterclockwise (the cutter has a left-hand thread) until it is tightened firmly.

5. Swing the cutter guard, figure 9-5, down to close the cutter well opening. This prevents bodily contact with the outer end of the cutter.

6. To remove the cutter, reverse the procedure outlined in steps 1 through 5.

How to Adjust the Cutter

NOTE: Each time a new or resharpened cutter is installed in the plane, it must be checked for correct cutting operation as described in the following procedure.

1. Loosen the cutter-adjustment lockscrew, figure 9-4, with a cutter wrench.

2. Lay a straightedge on the rear section of the base so it projects over the cutter well.

3. Turn the cutter through one complete revolution and note whethter the tops of the cutting edges touch the straightedge. Perform this operation carefully so that the cutting edges will not become nicked should they touch the straightedge.

4. If, when the cutter is turned, the tips of the cutting edges raise the straightedge from the surface of the rear section of the base, figure 9-6 (A), turn the cutter-adjustment knob slightly clockwise. This moves the cutter away from the straightedge.

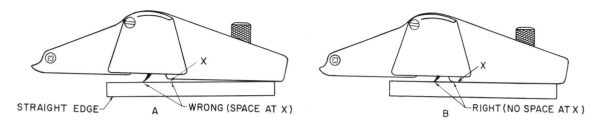

STRAIGHT EDGE⌐   A   ⌐WRONG (SPACE AT X)   B   ⌐RIGHT (NO SPACE AT X)

Fig. 9-6

5. Be sure the tips of the cutting edges still raise the straightedge. Readjust, if necessary, until the tips of the cutting edges just touch the straightedge while it is resting on the rear section of the base, figure 9-6 (B).

   NOTE: If the cutter is poorly adjusted as in figure 9-6 (A), the belt will break or the the belt cogs will shear off. When adjusted correctly as in figure 9-6 (B), the cutter will take a 1/64-inch cut.

6. If, when the cutter is turned, the tips of the cutting edges are below the straightedge, turn the cutter-adjustment knob slightly clockwise to move the cutter toward the straightedge.

7. Readjust, if necessary, until the tips of the cutting edges just touch the straightedge as the cutter is turned through one complete revolution.

8. Firmly tighten the cutter-adjustment lockscrew with the cutter wrench.

How to Adjust the Cutter for Rabbet Cuts

   NOTES: A cutter-adjusting shim is available for adjusting the cutter position for making rabbet cuts only. This shim is 5/8 inch O.D. x 7/16 inch I.D. x 0.010 inch thick. When making a rabbet cut, the outer (counterbored) end of the cutter should be flush with or extend slightly beyond the outer edge of the base. During the sharpening process, it is possible that the length of the cutting edges might be reduced slightly. To position the cutter so its outer end is flush or extends slightly beyond the outer edge of the base, the cutter-adjusting shim is used.

1. Install the shim on the cutter shaft.

2. Install the cutter on the cutter shaft with the counterbored end of the cutter out or away from the plane.

3. Check the end of the cutter shaft to make sure the outer end is flush with or extends slightly beyond the outer edge of the base.

4. If the cutter extends beyond the outer edge of the base, swing the cutter guard down so it closes the cutter well opening. Note whether the outer end of the cutter touches the guard. If it does, the shim should be removed.

5. If the cutter must be moved out farther to make it flush with or extend slightly beyond the outer edge of the base, install another shim next to the first shim.

6. Swing the cutter guard down so it closes the cutter well opening. If the outer end of the cutter touches the guard, remove one shim.

7. Insert the cutter shaft lock pin into the cutter shaft.

8. Install the cutter washer on the screw.

9. Insert the cutter washer-screw assembly in the counterbore in the outer end of the cutter and turn it counterclockwise into the cutter shaft.

10. Insert a wrench into the screwhead and tighten the screw firmly.

11. Remove the cutter shaft lock pin.

12. Swing the cutter guard up so its bottom edge is farthest from and parallel to the plane base.
    NOTE: Make certain the cutter guard is securely locked in the "up" position before making rabbet cuts. If necessary, tighten the cutter guard retaining screw to lock guard in the "up" position. Be extra careful not to contact the plane cutter while making rabbet cuts.

How to Install and Remove the Fence

1. To install the fence, position the fence on the plane base so the bosses on the fence nestle in the small holes in the base.

2. Insert the wingscrew through the hole in the fence and thread it into the plane base. Tighten the screw firmly by hand.

3. To remove the fence, remove the fence wingscrew and lift off the fence.

How to Use the Adapter Plate

NOTE: For making special cuts such as rabbet step and bevel cuts, wood block fences can be made to guide the plane. The wood fences are attached to the adapter plate by two small wood screws and the assembly is mounted on the plane base.

1. Cut a wood block (A, figure 9-7) about 8 1/8 inches long by 3/4 inch thick and wide enough so that when one edge of the block is flush with the right edge of the plane base, the distance from the other edge of the block to the left edge of the plane base will be equal to the width of the cut desired. Edges B and C should be parallel and square.

2. Lay the adapter plate (D) with the two small bosses (E) up on the wood block (A) so edge F is flush with either edge B or C of the wood block.

3. Screw two small wood screws (G) through the holes (H) into the wood block. The adapter plate assembly is shown in figure 9-8.

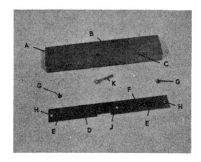

Fig. 9-7

Fig. 9-8

Fig. 9-9

Fig. 9-10

4. Using hole J, in the adapter plate, figure 9-8, spot drill a hole through the wood block. Use a drill bit that will provide a clearance hole for the adapter-plate assembly mounting screw (K).

5. Place the adapter-plate assembly on the plane base so the bosses (E) mate with the two holes in the plane base.

6. Insert the adapter-plate assembly mounting screw (K) figure 9-9, through the hole in the wood block and screw it into the tapped hole in the plane base. Tighten the screw firmly. The plane is now ready to make the cut of the selected width. The wood block acts as a fence to guide the plane along the edge of the work.

How to Use the Power Block Plane

1. Grasp the plane as shown in figure 9-10. The index or first finger is used to press the switch.

2. Determine the direction of the grain and position the plane to cut with the grain.

3. Start the plane. When the plane reaches full speed, rest the forward part of the base firmly on the surface to be planed and slowly move the plane forward so the blade contacts the surface.

4. Continue moving the plane slowly across the surface without forcing it — just fast enough to keep it cutting. Toward the end of the cut, apply greater pressure at the rear of the base so that the plane does not tilt or roll over the edge.

5. Upon completion of planing, lift the plane clear of the work before turning the switch off.

SHARPENING ATTACHMENT

A sharpening attachment is available which may be attached to the block plane for sharpening the spiral plane cutter. Straight steel and straight carbide-tipped cutters cannot be sharpened with the attachment. Directions for use of the sharpening attachment are provided by the manufacturer.

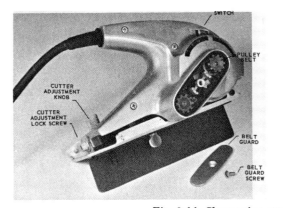

Fig. 9-11 Sharpening attachment

LETTER	PART NAME
A	BASE
B	SHAFT
C	RING — STOP
D	GRINDING WHEEL

CARE OF THE POWER BLOCK PLANE

Each time a job is finished, remove any accumulation of dust or wood chips from the plane. Be sure to disconnect the machine from the power circuit before cleaning it. The air passages can be cleared of dust and chips with compressed air.

If the wood being planed was somewhat green, sap-wood dust or sap-wood chips might have started to accumulate on the cutter and walls of the cutter well. This is easily removed immediately after

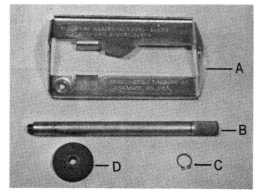

Fig. 9-12

you stop using the plane. Disconnect the plane from the power supply. Remove and wipe the cutter. Be careful not to cut yourself on the sharp edges of the cutter.

Keep a supply of sharp cutters on hand. As soon as the one on the plane shows signs of being dull, replace it with a properly sharpened cutter.

Should the pulley belt become damaged, it can be replaced easily in the following manner. Refer to figure 9-12. Make sure the plane cord is disconnected from the power supply.

1. Remove the belt-guard screw.

2. Remove the belt guard.

3. Remove the pulley belt.

4. Install the new pully belt by mating the belt cogs with the pulley grooves and evenly pressing the belt onto the pulleys.

5. Position the belt guard over the pulley well and install the belt-guard screw. Tighten the screw firmly.

For lubrication requirements, refer to the manufacturer's manual. Most parts are prelubricated and need not be lubricated for the life of the machine.

REVIEW QUESTIONS

A. Short Answer or Discussion

1. List a number of specific uses where the power block plane would be more advantageous than the large power plane.

2. Describe the types of plane cutters available and the best uses of each type.

3. How is the power block plane adjusted for depth of cut?

4. How is it adjusted for bevel cuts?

5. What accessory is available for adjusting the cutter to make rabbet cuts?

6. How is the fence removed for surface planing operations?

7. How are chips or sawdust removed?

8. How often should the plane be lubricated? How is it lubricated?

9. In what ways does the power block plane differ from the power planes discussed in unit 8?

10. Where should the straightedge be placed to adjust the cutter?

11. In a sketch, show how the straightedge should appear when the cutter is correctly adjusted.

12. What may happen if the cutter is adjusted incorrectly?

B. Completion

1. When making rabbet cuts be sure the cutter guard is securely locked in the _____ position.

2. To adjust the cutter it is necessary to loosen the _____ before it is possible to use the _____ .

3. Turning the cutter-adjustment knob _____ gives a greater cut; turning it _____ , a lesser cut.

4. The vertical fence _____ be adjusted for width of cut without using adapters.

5. The on-off switch is designed to be operated with the _____ .

C. Identification and Interpretation

1. Identify the lettered parts of the power block plane shown.

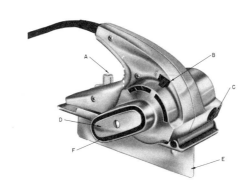

Unit 10 ELECTRIC ROUTER-SHAPER-POWER PLANE

The electric router is used freehand for controlled stock removal from surface areas. With its shaper table attachment, it molds ornamental edges on furniture and other woodworking projects. Finally, with its power plane attachment, it is used for the same purposes as the power plane described in unit 8. Thus, the electric router is perhaps the most versatile of all the portable power tools. Each of its uses will be discussed in this unit.

Figures 10-1 (A) and (B), page 124, show two routers which are typical of most models. They consist of motors containing chucks into which cutting bits are chucked. The motor slides into the base in a vertical position. The depth of cut is easily regulated by the depth-adjustment ring. The subbase rests on the workpiece.

Figure 10-1 (C), page 124, shows a manufactured plunge base router. This router has several notable features. The bit spins over the stock and is plunged vertically into the stock by drawing downward on the handles. The handles are attached to the motor unit rather than the router base. This feature permits installing the trigger switch into the handle. Other manufacturers produce routers with D-type handles which contain trigger switches.

The router illustrated has a chip shield as added eye protection and dust control. It also has a round base with a squared-off portion directly in front of the chip shield. This feature of the base makes the cutting bit more visible and therefore, easier to guide.

Routers are sized in terms of horsepower ratings (wattage) of their motors, ranging from 1/4 hp (186.5 watts) to 2 1/2 hp (1.87 kW) for heavy-duty production routers. The motors are highspeed, from 18 000 to 27 000 rpm.

ROUTER BITS

Router bits fall into two major classifications: bits with built-in shanks; and screw-type bits. The first type includes one-piece bits which have a shank built into the cutting head. Some also have a pilot or cylindrical tip built in below the cutting edge. The shank fits into the collet of the router motor. The screw-type bit has a threaded hole through the center of the cutting head. This type of bit requires the use of an arbor which is screwed into the top of the cutting head. When required, a separate pilot is screwed into the bottom of the cutting head. The pilot controls the horizontal depth of cut by riding along the edge of the work. Practically all jobs performed with the router are done by selection of the various cutters or bits which are available.

Straight bits are used for general stock removal, slotting, grooving, inlay work, background routing, and rabbeting.

Veining bits differ from straight bits in that they cut a radius into the wood. They are used principally for ornamentation.

Rabbetting bits cut a rabbet, or step-out into the edges of wood, as for constructing cupboard doors and drawer fronts.

Cove bits cut a concave radius into the edge of the workpiece.

Beading bits cut a convex radius.

Fig. 10-1 (A) Parts of the router

Fig. 10-1 (B) Router

Fig. 10-1 (C) Plunge base router

Fig. 10-1 (D) Router with "D" type handle

Other bits, such as *dovetail, chamfer, ogee,* and *coping,* have similar specific uses. There are many other specialized bits available, and manufacturers' catalogs should be consulted for the full range of bits.

How to Insert a Bit into the Collet

1. Select the correct bit for the job to be done. If the selected bit does not contain a built-in shank, a special arbor must be used. The threaded end of the arbor should then be tightly screwed by hand into the threaded hole on top of the bit.

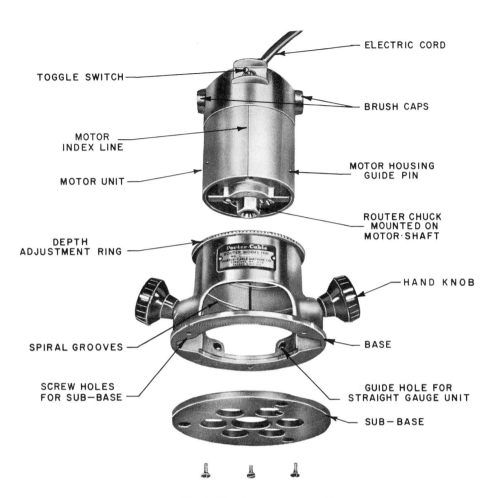

ELECTRIC CORD

TOGGLE SWITCH

BRUSH CAPS

MOTOR
INDEX LINE

MOTOR HOUSING
GUIDE PIN

MOTOR UNIT

ROUTER CHUCK
MOUNTED ON
MOTOR·SHAFT

DEPTH
ADJUSTMENT RING

HAND KNOB

SPIRAL GROOVES

BASE

SCREW HOLES
FOR SUB—BASE

GUIDE HOLE FOR
STRAIGHT GAUGE UNIT

SUB—BASE

Fig. 10-2 The router assembly

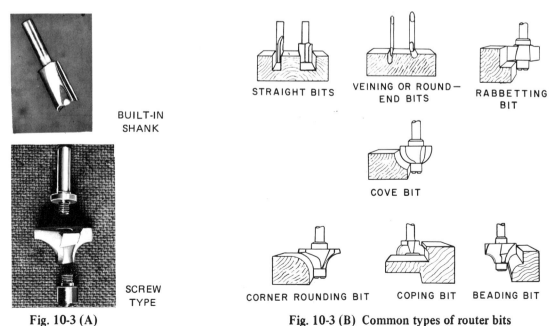

BUILT-IN
SHANK

STRAIGHT BITS

VEINING OR ROUND—
END BITS

RABBETTING
BIT

COVE BIT

SCREW
TYPE

CORNER ROUNDING BIT   COPING BIT   BEADING BIT

Fig. 10-3 (A)

Fig. 10-3 (B) Common types of router bits

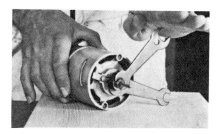

Fig. 10-4 Tightening bit and router collet

2. Screw the 1/4-inch collet into the threaded motor chuck as far as it will go without tightening. The bit (with arbor) should be inserted all the way into the collet and then backed out about 1/16 inch.

3. To tighten the bit in the chuck, lay the motor on the bench top with the chuck facing away from you, figure 10-4. Slip one wrench on the chuck so that the opposite end of the wrench rests on the bench to your left. This prevents the chuck from slipping when the collet is tightened with the other wrench. Reverse the procedure when removing the bit.

Fig. 10-5 Router base locking wing nut

Fig. 10-6 Inserting motor into base

How to Assemble the Motor into the Router Base

1. Loosen the locking wing nut on the router base, figure 10-5.

2. Pick up the motor with the right hand, positioning the thumb just to the right of the toggle switch.

Fig. 10-7 Adjusting for depth

3. Insert the motor into the base so that the spiral pins on the motor slip into the spiral grooves inside the base, figure 10-6.

4. Turn the motor clockwise until it fits rigidly in the base, then tighten the locking wing nut.
   NOTE: If the diameter of the bit is too large to fit through the subbase, remove the subbase by means of the three screws.

How to Adjust for Depth of Cut

1. Place the motor on a flat surface and loosen the locking wing nut. Turn the motor in the router base in a clockwise direction until the bit just touches the surface of the wood, figure 10-7.

Fig. 10-8 Aligning motor index line

Fig. 10-9 Freehand routing

CORNER ROUND   COVE   BEAD EDGE

Fig. 10-10

2. Lightly tighten the wing nut. Rotate the depth-adjustment ring until the zero line is exactly opposite the index line located on the motor housing, figure 10-8.

3. Loosen the wing nut. Tip the router so that the bit is away from the work and turn only the motor in a clockwise direction until the index line on the motor housing reaches the desired depth indicated on the ring.

4. After tightening the locking wing nut the router will be ready for use. If the depth is set at 1/4 inch, the cutting edge of the bit is exposed exactly 1/4 inch below the base of the router.
NOTE: It is advisable to make a sample cut on a scrap lumber before beginning a cut on a workpiece. This will show exactly how the cut will look and will enable checking of dimensions.

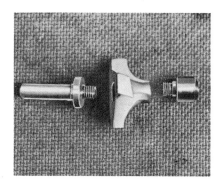

Fig. 10-11 Arbor, corner-round bit and pilot

Fig. 10-12 Corner-round cut

BASIC ROUTING CUTS

Freehand routing is commonly used to cut decorative edges on wood. This can also be done with the router edge guide which will be discussed later in this unit. Types of molding cuts vary from a simple corner round to the more decorative cove and bead edge, figure 10-10.

Probably the most widely used combination of cuts done by freehand routing are the rabbet and corner rounding cuts used on cupboard doors and drawer fronts. The 3/8-inch radius corner round is the most commonly used radius for cabinet work.

The corner-round bit requires an arbor. A pilot may also be used, figure 10-11, page 127. The purpose of the pilot is to act as a guide which rides against the edge of the workpiece. Without a pilot, the bit would move freely into the wood without any control. When no pilot is used, the edge guide, figure 10-14, page 129, may be used to serve the same purpose.

How to Cut a Corner Round

1. Be sure that the workpiece is firmly clamped to the bench with wood clamps or is otherwise secured.

2. Insert the corner-round bit into the router chuck.

    a. An arbor, bit and pilot are required. Screw the arbor into the top of the bit. Insert the arbor and bit into the collet of the motor. Tightly screw the pilot into the bottom of the bit.

3. Assemble the motor into the router base discussed earlier in this unit.

4. Adjust the router for depth of cut. The pilot should clear the work supporting surface. In order to do this, it may be necessary to elevate the workpiece on scrap lumber or have it hang over the bench.
   NOTE: For certain materials, it may be necessary to make several passes at gradually increased settings to attain the desired depth of cut.

5. Place the router with its base flat on the workpiece with the cutter ready to start cutting from the left corner.
   NOTE: Since the cutter rotates clockwise, more efficient cutting will be obtained if the router is moved from left to right as the operator faces the work.

6. Turn on the switch. Move the router cutter into the edge of the workpiece and proceed to cut from left to right while facing the work. The pilot rides against the edge of the workpiece.
   NOTE: Keep the cutting pressure constant, down and against the work. Do not crowd it to the extent that the motor speed slows excessively. Keep the base of the router flat. When making cuts on all four edges of a workpiece, make the first cut on the end of the board across the grain. Thus, if chipping occurs, it may be removed when making the next cut parallel with the grain.

7. When the cut is completed, shut off the switch and allow the cutter to stop revolving before laying the router aside. The router should be disconnected from the power source and laid on its side when not in use.

How to Cut a Rabbet

The rabbetting cut is made in exactly the same manner as the corner-rounding cut. If a combination such as the corner rounding and rabbetting of a cupboard door or drawer front is required, the workpiece is simply turned over after the corner-round cut is completed, and the rabbetting cut is made. A combination cutter is available that makes both cuts at the same time.

In place of the corner-rounding bit, a rabbetting bit is used, figure 10-13. When equipped with a pilot, the lateral depth of cut will be exactly 3/8 inch. Thus, the router must be adjusted to obtain a 3/8 inch vertical height.

The instructions for cutting a corner round apply with numerous other screw-type bits when doing freehand routing on the edges of work. In each case, it is necessary to use a pilot or edge guide.

Fig. 10-13 Rabbetting bit with arbor and pilot

THE ROUTER EDGE GUIDE

One of the most practical accessories for the router is the edge guide, figure 10-14. It is used to guide the router in a straight line along the edge of the board. It is particularly useful for cutting grooves on long pieces of lumber. The two rods on the edge guide simply slip into the two holes provided on the router base. The guide may then be moved in or out along the two rods to obtain the desired lateral depth of cut.

When cutting grooves on the edges of circular pieces, two wedge-shaped blocks of wood can be fastened to the face of the edge guide as shown in figure 10-15. The two wedges of wood will then follow the contour of the circular workpiece. As an alternative, the edge guide may be reversed on the rods, thus resulting in two-point contact when used on circular work.

Fig. 10-14 Router edge guide

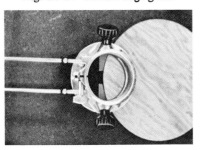

Fig. 10-15 Edge guide with wood blocks for circular work

GROOVING

The cutting of grooves or slots is a widely used router application. Generally, grooves are cut in the direction of the grain. An edge guide should be used to guide the router in a straight line parallel with the edge of the board. Straight bits for grooving are shown in figure 10-16. The distance from the groove to the edge of the board is determined by the edge guide setting.

Fig. 10-16 Straight grooving bits

Fig. 10-17 V grooving bit

Fig. 10-18 Grooving with edge guide

Many craftsmen use the V grooving bit, shown in figure 10-17, to obtain a plank-board effect on large sheets of plywood. Straight bits are used to groove the inside edges of drawers to receive the bottom piece.

How to Cut Grooves with the Router

1. Slide the two rods of the edge guide into the two holes provided on the router base.

2. Determine the desired distance from the edge of the groove to the edge of the workpiece. Move the edge guide in or out to match this distance.

3. Proceed as in the instructions for cutting a corner round, with the exception that a grooving bit will be used.

Fig. 10-19 Wooden T square

Fig. 10-20 T square guiding the router

DADOES

While dadoes are often cut on table or radial arm saws, the router is becoming increasingly used for this operation, especially on wide pieces of stock which are difficult to handle on the saw. Dadoing is similar to grooving except that the dado is cut across, rather than with, the grain.

Just as the edge guide is used for accurate grooving, a wooden T square, figure 10-19, is used for accurate dadoing. The T square guides the router in a straight line across the workpiece, figure 10-20.

How to Cut a Dado with the Router

1. Secure the wooden T square to the workpiece with a C clamp. With the base of the router butting against this cross-guide, align the cutter for the initial cut.

NOTE: Straight bits run about 13/16 inches maximum. If the width of the dado exceeds the width of the bit, more than one cut will be required and the T square is moved accordingly.

2. Proceed as in the instructions for cutting a corner round *except:*

   a. Use a straight bit with an arbor but without a pilot.

   b. Adjust for depth of dado by turning the motor in the base.

The basic cuts discussed include: shaping an edge such as a corner round cut, making a step-cut on an edge with a rabbet, cutting a groove, and cutting a dado. These are applied in making a wide variety of woodworking joints. For instance, the half-lap joint requires cutting rabbets; the cross-lap joint, cutting dadoes; slotting or mortising requires routing with a straight bit. Such specific applications of these basic cuts are fully explained in manufacturers' instructions. The student should refer to these instructions as required.

THE SHAPER TABLE ATTACHMENT

The router may be used as a stationary shaper unit when attached to a shaper table that is available as standard equipment. Many of the operations performed by freehand routing may also be done on the shaper table. This device is particularly useful for making cuts on small or narrow pieces of work.

In applications of the router for shaping, it is simply inverted and attached beneath the mounted steel table. Some tables include a feature that allows tilting of the motor for angle or bevel routing.

Because of the guiding fence on the shaper table, it is not necessary to use a pilot on the cutters as is the case with the portable router. The fence may be adjusted up to 3/32 inch to vary the lateral depth of cut when jointing. A guide is also available which enables the operator to shape or mold irregular pieces.

How to Prepare the Shaper Table for Use

NOTE: Figure 10-21 shows the major parts that make up the complete shaper table assembly, including the router motor and base.

1. Secure the router to the shaper table by fitting the router into the recess on the underside of the table so the base fits under the two lug clamps.

Fig. 10-21 Major shaper parts including table, router base, and motor

Fig. 10-22 Fitting router under table

Fig. 10-23 Aligning guide fence with spiral cutter

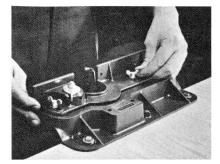

Fig. 10-24 Guide fence is locked to table by two wing nuts

NOTE: These two lug clamps are held to the underside of the table by two wingscrews with washers. Make sure that the wing locking nut on the router base faces the long straight edge (front of the shaper table).

2. After the base is secured, tighten the two lug clamps, figure 10-22, page 131.

3. Install the motor in the base as previously described, with the switch in a convenient position.

4. If small pieces are to be shaped, the center hole insert provided should be fitted in the table top to make the table opening smaller.

5. Fasten the complete shaper table assembly to the workbench. Depending on the bench top, fasten it by either three machine bolts and nuts or three lag screws through the holes along the back edge of the unit. The router should not touch the edge or side of the workbench. NOTE: The shaper table may be mounted on a piece of plywood so it may be moved from one job to another or stored away when not in use. When used in this fashion, the plywood support should be tightly clamped to the workbench.

Fig. 10-25 Shaper spindle

Fig. 10-26 Cutters and collars are locked on spindle with hex nut

6. Align and lock the guide fence to the table with the two wing nuts as shown in figures 10-23 and 10-24.

How to Install Cutters

NOTE: Although router bits may be used, the major portion of the work done with the shaper table involves the use of shaper cutters. A shaper spindle must always be used with cutters. These spindles, figure 10-25 are equipped with spacing collars and a locking hex nut.

1. Select the proper spindle, depending on the cutter used.

2. Screw the large threaded end of the shaper spindle directly into the motor unit and tighten.

3. Place the cutter or combination of cutters spaced with collars on the spindle and lock in place with a hex nut, figure 10-26.
NOTE: The arrangement of cutters and collars depends upon the type of cut desired. The shape of the cut may be varied by raising or lowering the router in the router base.

4. When changing bits or cutters, it is necessary that only the motor unit be removed, leaving the router base attached to the table.

How to Joint on the Shaper Table

NOTE: All jointing operations require either a shaper spindle and plane cutter, figure 10-27, or a plane cutter with a built-in threaded shank.

1. Install the cutter. If it is the combination type (spindle and cutter), install it as previously described. If it is one piece, screw the threaded shank directly into the motor chuck and tighten firmly with a hex wrench.

2. Align the fence with the cutter. To do this, proceed as follows:

   a. Make sure that the adjustable part of the shaper table fence (on the right side as you stand facing the table) is set at zero. That is, the depth adjustment thumb lever is all the way over to the right.

   b. Lay a straightedge along the left side of the fence, figure 10-28. While pivoting the complete fence on the right wing nut, adjust the fence so the straightedge just touches the cutting edge of the plane cutter.

   c. Tighten both fence wing nuts.

3. Adjust the fence for depth of cut. If 1/16 inch is to be removed from the board, hold the straightedge firmly against the left side of the fence, rotate the depth-adjustment thumb lever to the left until the adjustable part of the fence has been backed off 1/16 inch from the straightedge.

Fig. 10-27 Plane cutter

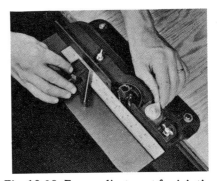

Fig. 10-28 Fence adjustment for jointing

Fig. 10-29 Jointing stock on shaper table

Fig. 10-30 Molding is ripped from larger stock

4. To make the cut, hold the board firmly against the face of the adjustable fence and feed steadily from right to left into the cutter and across the main fence, figure 10-29.

How to Make Molding and Shaping Cuts

1. Select and insert the suitable cutter or cutters, spaced as required.

2. Adjust the two sections of the fence into perfect alignment with the adjustable fence set at zero.
   NOTE: This alignment is maintained for all cuts except jointing.

3. Set the fence for depth cut by moving the entire fence forward or backward.

4. Shape and rip the molding from a large piece of stock as shown in figure 10-30.
   NOTE: Long pieces of narrow stock are not as easily handled for shaping because they tend to bend or give as they are fed through the cutter.

How to Shape Circular or Irregular Pieces

1. Remove the entire fence from the surface of the shaper table.

2. Insert the two straight support posts into the table and secure them from beneath with hex nuts, figure 10-31.

3. Slip the circular guide bracket over the two posts. Lower the bracket until the cylindrical tube reaches a position just above the cutting edge mounted on the arbor. Then tighten the circular bracket wingscrew.

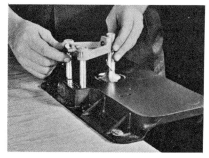

Fig. 10-31 Attaching circular guide bracket

Fig. 10-32 Shaping a round piece of wood

NOTES: The circular tube acts as a guide against which the workpiece rests. It permits cutting circular workpieces as well as irregularly shaped wood. Care should be taken to see that the circular tube does not touch the edge of the cutting head. Never attempt to raise the motor in the base while the circular guide is in position.

4. Proceed to shape the edge as illustrated in figure 10-32.

ROUTER BIT SHARPENING ATTACHMENT

Special attachments are available for the sharpening of router bits and cutters. A typical example of such a sharpener is shown in figure 10-33. The sharpening attachment ensures not only sharp cutting edges, but balanced edges to permit uniform stock removal by each edge of the bit. The attachment is adjustable for either two- or three-fluted bits or cutters and for any angle which the cutting face may have.

The sharpening attachment consists of a tripod to support the router and a holding fixture in which bits and cutters are inserted, figure 10-34.

The holding fixture, figure 10-35, has a 1/2-inch arbor hole into which bits with a 1/2-inch diameter shank may be fastened directly. For 1/4-inch shanks, a split sleeve or bushing is used. An arbor with a 3/8-inch shank for smooth-hole cutters is also furnished. The cutter slips on the end of the arbor and is held in place by a special screw that expands the arbor inside the hole of the cutter. Special allen wrenches are provided for these screws.

The holding fixture is adjustable at four points.

1. Setscrew A, figure 10-35, locks the bit or cutter in correct relation to the grinding wheel.

2. The indexing collar, B, brings each cutting edge of a two-fluted or three-fluted cutter into position and holds

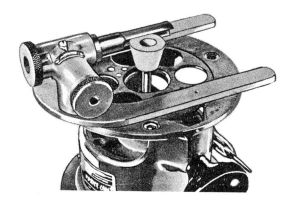
Fig. 10-33 Router bit sharpener

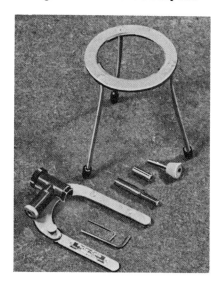
Fig. 10-34 Component parts

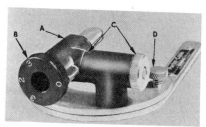
Fig. 10-35 Adjustments

Fig. 10-36 Inserting motor

Fig. 10-37 Spindle housing and barrel with graduations

it there while grinding. It will always return to the same edge and to the same position each time the spindle is rotated.

3. On shear-cut bits and cutters, the face of the cutting edge is at an angle to the shank and not parallel to it. Angle adjustment, C, is provided to adjust for this.

4. The vertical feedscrew, D, lowers the bit or cutter on the grinding wheel surface, providing control of the amount of material that is to be ground away.

How to Attach the Sharpener

1. Remove the motor from the router base.

2. Insert the grinding wheel shank into the router collet about 1/2 inch and tighten.

3. Replace the motor into the base.

4. Invert the router and slip the tripod over the head of the motor as shown.

5. Rotate the router base from above the ring so that it falls in place, figure 10-36.

How to Sharpen a Two-Fluted Straight Bit

1. Check the sharpening fixture for the angle of adjustment. The centerline on the spindle should match the centerline on the barrel, figure 10-37.

2. Insert the bit into an adapter.

3. Insert the adapter and the bit into the spindle.

4. Tighten them in the spindle with the small setscrew using an allen wrench.

5. Place the grinding fixture on the inverted motor base.

6. Hold the base and turn the motor upward until the cutting edge of the bit rests flat on the top of the grinding wheel, figure 10-38.

7. Make necessary adjustments so that the two flutes will be sharpened in correct relationship to each other. To do this, proceed as follows:

Fig. 10-38 Checking cutter position against grinding wheel

Fig. 10-39 Tightening expansion screw to hold cutter on arbor

    a. Set the zero mark over the spring housing, figure 10-38, until the locking pin clicks into place.

    b. Rotate the cutter until the numeral 2 clicks in place.
    NOTE: This is the locking position for the opposite cutting edge since the cutter has been rotated halfway around.

    c. Check the position of the cutting edge against the wheel, figure 10-38.

8. Turn feedscrew D (figure 10-35) to the right, lifting the bit clear of the grinding wheel. This allows for some downward feed when grinding begins.

9. Keep a firm grip on the router and turn on the motor.

10. Begin stroking the bit across the grinding wheel while gradually lowering the bit by means of the feedscrew.

11. After one edge has been sharpened, rotate the opposite edge into position.

12. Proceed to grind down the second edge.
NOTE: Do not attempt to make any adjustments when sharpening the second edge after the first edge has been sharpened. Both edges on a bit should be sharpened at the same setting.

How to Sharpen Straight Fluted Cutters

NOTE: Assume the cutter has three flutes as shown in figure 10-39.

1. As described for straight fluted bits, check the sharpening fixture for angle of adjustment. The centerline on the spindle should match the centerline on the barrel, figure 10-39.

2. Lock the required size arbor in the spindle.

3. Slip the cutter over the arbor at the outer end where the expansion takes place.

4. Tighten the expansion screw as shown in figure 10-39.

5. Make the necessary adjustments so that the three flutes will be sharpened in correct relationship to each other. The first edge to be ground should be set so that it is indexed at zero.

6. Grind the first edge in the same manner as was described for two-fluted bits.

Fig. 10-40

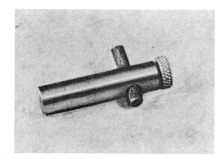

Fig. 10-41 Holding fixture and abrasive stone

7. Turn the index collar until the first numeral 3 clicks into place then sharpen the second edge.

8. Turn the collar to the second numeral 3 and sharpen the third edge.

How to Sharpen Form Cutters

NOTE: Assume the cutting edge of the cutter is located at approximately a 45-degree angle to the arbor, figure 10-40.

1. Relocate the barrel on the base to the hole at the left of the base, figure 10-40.

2. Swing the spindle so that the cutter hangs over the center of the horseshoe base and tighten.

3. Turn the motor up until the cutter lies flat on the grinding wheel (with the spindle angle adjustment loose).

4. Lock the spindle angle adjustment.

5. With the index collar set at zero, lock the arbor in the spindle and sharpen the cutter as previously described for straight fluted cutters and bits.

How to Dress the Abrasive Grinding Wheel

NOTE: It is advisable to dress the wheel when it begins to glaze and take on a glossy appearance, or when the grinding surface no longer appears to be flat. Before sharpening bits and cutters, wipe them free of wood dust which may clog the abrasive pores and reduce grinding effectiveness.

1. Place the abrasive stone holder, figure 10-41, in the spindle.

2. With the abrasive stone in a vertical position, secure the holder with the allen setscrew.

3. Set the vertical feedscrew at the upper position to allow for downfeed.

4. Raise the motor until the grinding wheel nearly touches the abrasive stick.

5. Start the motor and begin to pass the abrasive stick across the wheel, lowering the feedscrew until it begins cutting the wheel, figure 10-42.

6. Continue to do this until the wheel is flat across the top.

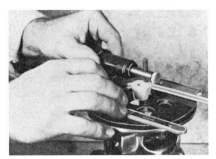

Fig. 10-42 Dressing the abrasive wheel

Fig. 10-43 Tightening plane cutter on spindle

ELECTRIC PLANE ATTACHMENT

The router may be used as an electric plane when incorporated into an electric plane attachment. Such an attachment is standard equipment available for various models of routers.

Fig. 10-44 Inserting motor into plane attachment

How to Set Up the Plane

Before inserting the motor into the power plane attachment, it is necessary to insert the spindle and spiral cutter into the motor chuck.

1. Insert the spindle and tighten it directly into the motor chuck.

2. Slip the spiral cutter onto the spindle with the slotted end toward the motor chuck.

3. Screw on the hex nut with the chamfered slide toward the cutter and tighten it using two wrenches as shown in figure 10-43.

    The motor with cutter is now ready to be inserted into the power plane attachment.

4. Hold the plane upside down by its handle with your left hand, figure 10-43.
    NOTE: Be sure the wing nut on the plane attachment is loosened.

5. With the right hand, insert the motor into the plane attachment, making sure the spiral ways fit easily into the spiral grooves of the attachment.
    NOTE: The motor must be inserted in such a way that, when in planing position, the toggle switch faces upward.

6. When the inner end of the spiral cutter is just within the vertical fence of the plane, tighten the locking wing nut.

USING THE ROUTER – PLANE

After the plane attachment has been properly set up, it is used in the same manner as the self-contained power plane discussed in unit 8. The procedures for aligning the cutter, setting the vertical fence, adjusting the depth of cut, bevel cutting, and proper positions for use of the plane are given in detail in unit 8 and should be referred to for the router-plane use.

Fig. 10-45 Hinge butt templet section

ROUTER ACCESSORIES

Special devices are manufactured for use with the router to handle specific jobs in construction work and in millwork and furniture industries. In the latter fields, dovetail templets and special veneer-trimming accessories are widely used. In construction work, door and jamb butt templets, lock face templets, lock mortisers, and stair routing templets are used to speed production over hand tool methods.

THE HINGE BUTT TEMPLET

The router is widely used in the construction field with a specially designed templet for routing out hinge butts on doors and jambs. Once the hinge butt templet has been adjusted for a single door, any number of doors and jambs of the same size may be routed simply be moving the templet from one door edge to the next. Figure 10-45 shows a hinge butt templet section and figure 10-46 shows the complete hinge butt templet and frame assembly. Figure 10-47 shows how a hinge butt templet is used with a router.

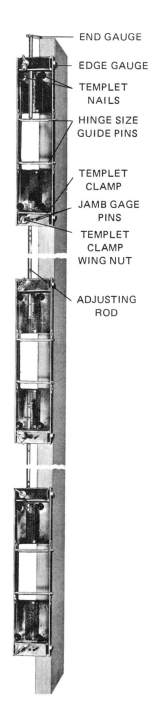

END GAUGE

EDGE GAUGE

TEMPLET NAILS

HINGE SIZE GUIDE PINS

TEMPLET CLAMP

JAMB GAGE PINS

TEMPLET CLAMP WING NUT

ADJUSTING ROD

Fig. 10-46 Complete templet and frame assembly

The templet determines the size and position of the butt recess on the edge of the door and jamb. The frame assembly is used to lock the complete templet to the door and to locate the three butt recesses on the door and jamb.

How to Use the Hinge Butt Templet

NOTE: Assume that a templet is to be used for a right-hand door, 6 feet 8 inches long, and 3-inch hinges are to be used.

1. Insert the six guide pins in the three templet sections (2 pins to a section), figure 10-48.

   NOTE: Holes marked 3 are for 3-inch hinges; holes between 3 and 4 are for 3 1/2-inch hinges; holes marked 4 are for 4-inch hinges; and remaining unmarked holes are for 4 1/2-inch hinges. Always keep the slots in the ends of these guide pins in a horizontal position parallel to the templet.

2. Select the templet section with reads "End Gauge Setting for Right-Hand Door and Jambs" on the information plate.

3. Insert the gauge through the templet clamp on the "End Gauge Setting" end of the templet section until it touches the guide pin.

4. Tighten the templet wing nut.

   NOTE: The end gauge automatically provides proper clearance between the top of the door and the jamb.

5. Lay this templet section on the door with the end gauge plate hooked tightly over the top of the door and the two edge gauges which protrude below the bottom of the templet section butted tightly against the face of the door. See figure 10-49.

6. Drive in the templet nails to secure this section to the door.

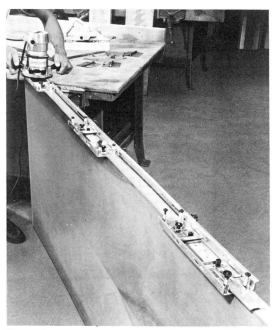

Fig. 10-47 Hinge butt templet being used with router

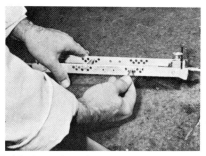

Fig. 10-48 Locating size guide pins in hinge butt templet

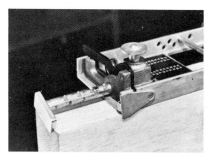

Fig. 10-49 Position of end gauge on top of door

7. Take one of the adjusting rods and insert the end marked with eight closely spaced notches and the words "Hinge Length Setting" through the templet clamp of the section with is already nailed to the door.

Fig. 10-50 Insert adjusting rod into templet section

Fig. 10-51 Router on templet, ready to begin cutting

8. Locate the end of this rod at the 3-inch mark on the "Hinge Length Setting" information plate.

9. Seat clamp into two rod notches and tighten the clamping wing nut.

10. Take the templet section which has the two information plates reading "Door Size Setting" and fit the clamp of this templet section onto the other end of the first adjusting rod until the end of the rod is in line with the 6 feet 8 inches-mark on the information plate.

11. Seat the clamp into two rod notches and tighten the clamp wing nut.

12. Butt the templet section edge gauges tightly against the face of the door and drive in the templet nails.

13. Take the remaining adjusting rod and insert the end which has five widely spaced notches and on which is stamped "Door Size Setting" into the clamp of the templet section just nailed to the door.
    NOTE: The end of this rod lines up with the 6 feet 8 inches mark on the other information plate.

14. Seat the clamp into two rod notches and tighten the wing nut.

15. Slide the remaining templet section onto the second adjusting rod until the end of the rod is in line with the 3 mark of the "Hinge Length Setting" information plate.

16. Seat the clamp into two rod notches and tighten the clamp wing nut.

17. Butt the edges of this section tightly against the face of the door and drive in the templet nails. The door is now ready to be routed for hinges.

How to Rout the Hinge Butt

1. Attach the templet guide designated for use with the hinge butt templet to the router base.

2. Install the bit specified for butt routing into the collet and motor.

3. Adjust the motor in the base until the bit is just touching the edge of the door while the router is resting on a templet section.

4. From that point, lower the bit to cut the thickness of the hinges (about 1/8 inch for the average hinge).

5. With the router in position on one of the templet sections so the bit is clear of the door, figure 10-51, turn on the motor.

6. Slide the router into the door along the right-hand guide pin for about 1/2 inch.

7. Pull the router back from the door and take a light cut of about 1/4 inch along the edge of the door, working from right to left, until the left-hand guide pin is reached.

8. Move the router into the door along the left-hand guide pin to the back of the templet.

9. Move the router along the back of the templet until it rests against the right guide pin.

10. Bring the router toward you, passing over the first cut.

11. Slide the router over the templet to remove all of the remaining stock.

12. Repeat this operation on the remaining templet sections.
    NOTE: Mortises may be prepared for either square or round corner hinges. If square corner hinges are to be used, the butt corners are squared with a corner chisel that is available for the router.

Fig. 10-52 View showing hinge butt after routing

Fig. 10-53 Claw hammer is used to remove templet

How to Rout the Jamb

1. Without disturbing the settings, remove the complete templet assembly from from the door by pulling the templet nails with a claw hammer, figure 10-53.

2. Loosen the wing nut holding the end gauge and rotate the end gauge until it is parallel with the bottom of the templet.

3. Tighten the wing nut.

4. Slide the edge of the templet (the edge without the edge gauges) over the face

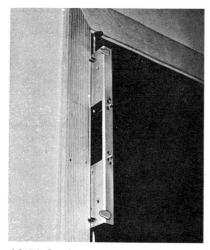

Fig. 10-54 Jamb gauge pins position templet

of the jamb until the first row of six jamb gauge pins which stick out underneath each templet section are aligned against the edge of the jamb, figure 10-54, page 143.

NOTE: This row of jamb pins is used for hanging 1 3/8 inch thick doors. The second row is for 1 3/4 inch thick doors.

5. Butt the end gauge against the top of the jamb, figure 10-54, and drive the templet nails into the jamb.

6. Proceed to rout the jamb in the same manner as for door mortises previously explained, using the same router settings.

NOTE: To rout door frames or jambs with door stops already in place, simply position the edge of the templet (without edge gauges) against the rabbetted edge or door stop and proceed in the same manner.

THE LOCK MORTISER

The lock mortiser utilizes the motor of the router to mortise for a box lock quickly and accurately. The width of the cut is determined by the size of the cutter used. A crank raises and lowers the cutter as it is removing stock. An adjustment on this crank determines the limits of vertical motion of the cutter. A sectional rod attachment is hung from the top of the door to locate the mortises at a uniform height on other doors. The height of the mortises may also be set from the floor.

This particular machine is also supplied with cutters for boring straight holes for cylinder bolt locks. The feed is automatic on the straight boring operations. When boring straight holes, the crank is set at zero so that the machine does not work up and down when the crank is turned.

How to Use the Lock Mortiser

1. Assemble the mortiser as shown in figure 10-55. Push the shaft forward and clear of the motor carriage. Snap the motor in place with the oiler pointing up, and turn the motor to the left until it stops. Be sure that the chuck face and shoulder on the shaft are clean. Screw the shaft into the chuck up to the shoulder.

2. Be sure the proper size cutter is on the shaft.

3. To set the length of cut on the crank, loosen the nut on the crank pin and turn the knurled screw in the center of the crank until the desired length is reached. Then tighten the nut.

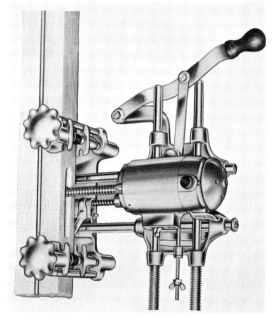

Fig. 10-55 Lock mortiser

4. Measure the length of the lock body and mark the door for this length plus 1/4 inch. This will be the location of the cut.

5. Place the mortiser on the door with the cutter at the top end of the stroke. Clamp it in position with the cutter at the top of the mortise.

6. Set the collar on the rod at the bottom of the mortiser to the desired depth. This depth should be the full depth of the lock plus about 1/8 inch.

7. Turn the crank to see if the stroke is correct. Turn on the motor switch and press the button at the side of the feed box at the bottom of the machine.

8. Turn the crank until the full depth of the cut is reached. The feed will then automatically stop. Pull the motor carriage and motor back to the original position.

9. Connect the height rod and set it through the holes in the clamps in the mortiser, either resting it on the floor or hooking it over the top of the door. Use the setscrews to lock the rod in the clamps. The mortiser is now adjusted to make the cut on additional doors.

10. Release the two clamps, fasten the mortiser on the next door, and repeat step 8.

LOCK FACE TEMPLET

Figure 10-56 shows a templet that may be attached to the door after the mortise for the lock has been cut. This templet locates the cut for the lock faceplate.

Practically all doors are beveled on the closing edge. The lock faceplate, therefore, must be flush with the beveled edge of the door. The clamps at each end of this templet are on swivels, so that when the templet is laid flat against the beveled edge of the door, the clamps automatically swivel to fasten on the sides of the door. This swiveling action allows the templet to lie flat against the beveled edge of the door. The cut can then be made parallel to this edge.

The side guide plates of this templet are tied together so that when the templet size is changed, both plates move apart or together simultaneously. Thus, the cut for the lock faceplate is always in the center of the door edge.

How to Use the Lock Face Templet

1. Loosen the screw that holds the width adjustment. Pull on the crossbar to widen both edge gauges so that the setting will be exactly in the center of the edge of the door. Set these two bars 1/8 inch farther apart than the required cut and tighten the screw securely.

2. Loosen the screw that holds the end block, slide the block to provide a templet opening 1/8 inch longer than the required length of the cut, and tighten the screw.

3. Lay the templet flat on the edge of the door with the two wingscrews on the right side. Tighten these screws.

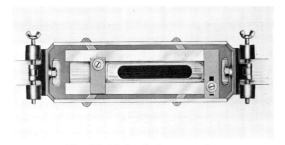

Fig. 10-56 Lock face templet

4. When tightening these screws with the fingers, the clamps will automatically swing on the pivots in the amount necessary to compensate for the bevel on the edge of the door. This will make the lock-face cut parallel with the edge.

5. To make a gauge to set the templet in the proper location over the mortise, cut a piece of wood to about 3/4 inch thick and 2 inches wide. To this piece, nail another piece 3/4 inch thick, 1 inch wide and 1/8 inch longer than the desired face cut. After the templet is clamped on the door, this gauge should be removed.

6. Lay the router flat on the templet face, and turn the depth-adjusting knob until the bit just touches the edge of the door. Turn the graduated dial to zero. Then turn the knurled knob to the required depth, and lock the sleeve in the base so that the motor cannot shift. Use a 5/8-inch bit with 5/16-inch bit arbor.

7. Make the cut, starting at about the center on the left side. Move the router to the top, then to the right, down to the bottom, over to the left, and then back to the starting point.

8. Square the corners with the special corner chisel.

9. Always keep the bit sharp when doing this operation. A grinder for this purpose comes with the lock mortiser.

The side guide plates of this templet are tied together so that when the templet size is changed, both plates move apart or together simultaneously. Thus, the cut for the lock faceplate is always in the center of the door edge.

STAIR ROUTING TEMPLET

Figure 10-57 shows a templet used for guiding the router when routing out stair stringers for treads and risers. The templet is adjustable to different pitches of stairs, different thicknesses of treads and risers, different nosing location, and different allowances for wedges. It is reversible for either right- or left-hand stringers without disturbing the setup.

To use this templet, it is first necessary to lay out the treads and risers for two complete stairs. The templet will be set to this layout and locked into position. After the templet is set, it may be used to cut all the treads and risers without further adjustments. Only pitch lines are required for the balance of the stair layout. Assume we are to lay out a stair casing with a tread of 9 inches and a riser of 8 inches.

How to Use the Stair Templet

1. Draw a line up 2 inches from the bottom of the stringer. (Approximately 2 inches on a 12-inch stringer; 1 1/2 inches on an 11-inch stringer; and 1-inch on a 10-inch stringer.

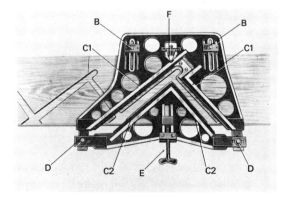

Fig. 10-57 Stair routing templet

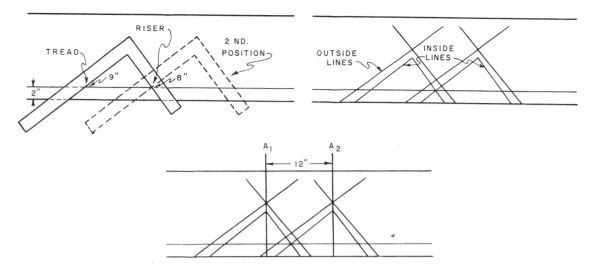

Fig. 10-58 Preliminary layouts for use of the stair templet

2. Place the square so that the left side of the square meets the line at 9 inches (tread), the right side at 8 inches (rise). Draw these lines for both stairs.

3. Draw the inside lines, making the necessary allowances for the shims to be used with the treads. Shims usually have a taper of 3/8 inch to every foot of length. Assuming that 1 1/8-inch stock is to be used for the tread and 3/4-inch stock for the riser, the front of the tread will be 1 1/8 inches and the back 1 3/8 inches while the front of the riser will be 3/4 inch and the back will be 1 inch.

4. Draw the two vertical pitch lines (A_1 and A_2), figure 10-58, and measure the distance between the two. In this case it is 12 inches, so the next pitch lines will be drawn 12 inches apart to locate the templet for the rest of the stringer.

5. Place the templet on the stringer so that the bolt heads, B, are on top and loosen all four of these with the wrench.

6. Place the locating gauges in the top section of the templet at points C1. Place the templet so that these gauges just touch the outside lines that have been drawn. Move the two guide bars, B, down until they are firmly against the stringer and then lock the bolts.

7. Place the locating gauges in the holes provided for them in the bottom section of the templet, points C2. Again, line them up so that they barely touch the lines. Now lock the two bolts, D, that lock the top and bottom sections of the templet. Remove the gauge blocks.

8. Lock the templet to the stringer with the screw shaft, E. This will keep the templet from moving when the routing cut is being made. Turn the screw shaft in a clockwise direction until the templet is seated securely.

9. Before making the cut, remove the guide blocks in the lower section. Set the locating pointer, F, directly over the vertical line that was previously drawn, and lock it in this position. For all further cuts, it is only necessary to align this pointer over the pitch lines previously drawn.

10. It is always best to make a trial cut and templet adjustment on a scrap piece of stair stringer in order to get the proper setting before attempting to cut the finish stringer.

REVIEW QUESTIONS

A. Short Answer or Discussion

1. Describe the procedure for setting the router to make a cut 1/4 inch deep.

2. How is the router adapted for cutting straight grooves a specified distance from the edge of a straight board?

3. What is required to enable the router to cut grooves on edges of circular pieces?

4. What are the two types of router bits? Which requires the use of an arbor?

5. For what purpose is a pilot used with certain bits?

6. When making cuts on all four edges of a workpiece, where should the first cut be made? Why?

7. What device is recommended for accurate dadoing?

8. How does cutting dado differ from cutting a corner round so far as the bit is concerned?

9. When using shaping cutters, how are they installed in the router motor unit?

10. How is depth of cut adjusted when jointing on the shaper table?

11. What are the commonly used templets for construction work?

12. When routing a hinge butt, what is the usual depth of cut?

13. In setting the collar on the lock mortiser rod for depth of cut, how deep should it be set?

14. How does use of the lock face templet assure that the cut will always be in the center of the door edge?

15. What adjustments can be made in using the stair routing templet?

B. Completion

1. The component of the router which is used also for shaper and planer operations is the _____ .

2. The variety of router cuts is obtained from the great assortment of _____ available.

3. The motor is locked in position in the base by means of _____ .

4. The most commonly used freehand cuts are the _____ and _____ cuts.

5. When adjusting the router for depth of cut with a pilot being used, the pilot should clear _____ .

6. The router is adjusted for a 3/8-inch cut when the _____ on the motor housing is aligned with the 3/8-inch indication on the _____ .

7. The fence on the shaper table may be adjusted to _____ inches for jointing.

8. For all shaping operations except jointing, the two sections of the fence should be _____ .

C. Identification and Interpretation

1. Identify the lettered parts of the router illustrated.

2. Describe the router bits shown.

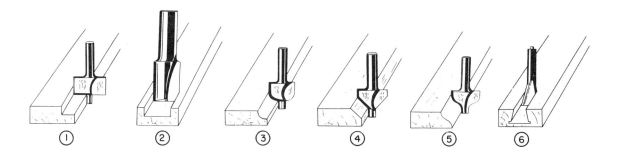

Unit 11 FLOOR
AND DISC SANDERS

Floor (drum) and disc (edge) sanders are primarily used by the carpenter to remove old finishes and smooth the surface after the finish has been removed. The floor sander is used to sand large floor areas. The disc sander is used for any close sanding, such as long edges, near walls, and in corners.

FLOOR (DRUM) SANDERS

Floor sanding machines are made in various sizes and weights and are equipped with motors from 1 to 5 horsepower (746 watts to 3.73 kilowatts). Drum widths range from 7 to 12 inches. The heavy-duty type (weighing about 230 pounds) is used for sanding large floor areas such as those found in commercial buildings. Heavy-duty sanders are not recommended for sanding residential floors, because the ceilings may crack from the weight and vibration. The light-duty type is preferred for general floor sanding, figure 11-1.

The motor on the heavy-duty type is usually provided with a voltage change switch which allows the sander to be operated on either 110 or 220 volts.

A dust collector bag is provided on all types of floor sanders to protect the operator from dust and to reduce the necessary cleaning in preparation for finishing.

Controls for operating the machines are conveniently located on the handle. The pressure of the sanding drum on the floor is controlled on the larger machines by a ratchet that keeps an even pressure on the floor when the machine is in motion.

SELECTION OF ABRASIVES FOR FLOOR SANDING

Since floor sanding involves the heavy removal of material, the coated abrasive product selected should be exceptionally durable. Silicon carbide abrasives having a backing of strong paper or a combination of paper and cloth are most suitable. The backing should be flexible so that it will readily fit around a drum and may be bent into the slot of the drum without cracking.

Coated abrasives (with paper and combination backings) are available in rolls, sheets, and discs. Sheets may be obtained cut to fit the various size drums found on different machines. These forms of coated abrasives may be obtained in a range of grit sizes. The grit selected will depend upon the condition

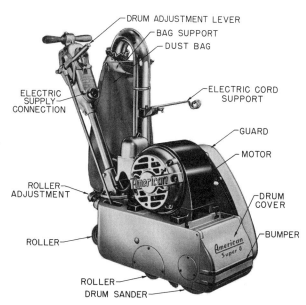

Fig. 11-1 Light-duty sanding machine

RECOMMENDED ABRASIVES FOR VARIOUS SURFACES

KIND OF FLOOR	OPERATION	FLOOR CONDITIONS	GRIT
Oak, maple, and close-grained hardwood floors	Roughing	Ordinary floors	2
		Well laid floors	2
		Very uneven floors	2 1/2
		Very hard floors	2 1/2
	Finishing	Ordinary finish	1
		Fine finish	1/2
		Extra fine finish	0
		Rough finish	2
Soft wood floors	Roughing	Ordinary floors	3
		Pine floors — average amount of pitch	3
		Pine floors — much pitch	3
		Very uneven floors	3
	Finishing	Ordinary finish	1
		Fine finish	1/2
Parquet floors		Roughing	2 1/2
		Semi finish	1/2
		Finishing	0
Cork tile floors		Roughing	1 1/2
		Semi finish	1/2
		Finishing	0
Resurfacing old floors — soft and hard woods	Removing varnish paints, etc.	Ordinary conditions	3 1/2-4
		Extra heavy coat, paint or varnish	4 1/2
	Roughing	Ordinary floors	1 1/2-2
	Finishing	Ordinary finish	1/2
		Fine finish	0
		Rough finish	1

of the floor and the type of wood to be sanded. Most manufacturers of abrasives and floor sanding equipment prepare charts which recommend the grade of abrasives to be used for various surfaces. An example of such a chart is shown above.

Both closed-coat and open-coat abrasives are used for sanding floors. In general, the closed-coat, silicon carbide, paper-backed abrasives are used for sanding new floors or old floors where the paint and varnish have been removed. The open-coat, combination-backed, silicon carbide abrasives are used for the first cut on old floors for the removal of paint, varnish, and shellac and for surfacing floors that are uneven.

When open-grit paper is required, it is sometimes advisable to use a medium-grit paper in preference to a coarse grit. It may take less time and effort to make two light passes over the floor than to use a coarse grit and make one pass leaving heavy abrasions on the surface which require extensive finish sanding later.

How to Prepare the Floor Prior to Sanding

1. Sweep the floor clean.

2. Scrape off foreign substances such as resin, chewing gum, etc.

3. Nail down any loose boards.

4. Set all facenails and other metal fasteners so that they are below the surface of the floor.

5. Remove the baseboard shoe to avoid damaging it with the sander. Replace it upon completion of sanding.

How to Install the Abrasive Sheet on the Drum

1. Be sure the electric lead is not plugged in.

2. Select an appropriate type abrasive sheet (refer to the abrasive chart).
   NOTE: If it is necessary to cut a sheet from a roll, use the old belt as a pattern. The tang of a file or a screwdriver can be used to mark the sheet. Break the sheet off along the scored mark. If an old abrasive belt is not available, prepare a templet from cardboard.

3. Flex both ends of the sheet by pulling the smooth side across an edge as shown in figure 11-2 (A). Applying it to a rounded edge is preferred as then, the abrasive is less apt to crack.
   NOTE: The steps which follow apply to a particular type floor sander. However, they basically apply to all types of floor sanders.

4. Tilt the machine back so that the handle rests on the floor.

5. Raise the drum guard and rotate the drum to a position so that the slot may be opened with the wrench provided for this purpose, figure 11-2 (B). In this case, the drum is aligned with a mark on the machine so that the wrench can be properly inserted.

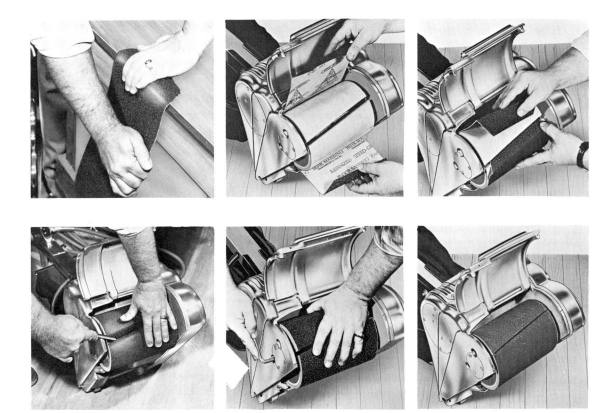

Fig. 11-2

6. Open the slot about 1/2 inch and then remove the wrench.

7. Roll the paper around the drum, figure 11-2 (C). Insert equal lengths of both ends into the slot, lining up both edges of the paper with the edges of the drum.

8. Push the paper into the full width of the slot as far as possible, figure 11-2 (D). The paper must fit very tightly around the drum and into the full width of the drum slot, especially at the slot corners.

9. Align the drum for inserting the wrench. With fingers spread, fold the paper firmly in place with one hand and tighten the paper in place by turning the wrench clockwise, figure 11-2 (E).
    NOTE: Turn the wrench until the drum jaws are firmly closed. The sound of paper being drawn between the tension springs is not necessarily an indication that the drum jaws are closed completely tight.

10. Inspect the paper. If it is loose, reopen the drum and repeat steps 5 through 9. The completed installation should appear as shown in figure 11-2 (F).

    NOTE: Before using the sanding machine, the following items should be checked.

    • The electric current to which the sanding machine is to be connected must correspond to the specifications on the motor nameplate.

    • Be sure the machine switch is in the "off" position before plugging in the lead.

    • When possible, plug into an outlet which is on a separate circuit having a 20-ampere fuse. If this is not possible, be sure any other outlets on the circuit are not in use when the machine is plugged in. When neither of these situations is possible, it may be necessary to connect directly to the sevice panel in order to avoid blowing the fuse.

    • Be sure the dust bag is securely attached to the dust pipe, that the abrasive paper is snug on the sanding drum and that the extension cord is properly supported in the wire support and that it is in a trailing position behind the machine. A good way to keep the extension cord out of the way during the operation of the machine is to place it over the operator's shoulder.

1. Start the motor and roll the machine on its wheels to a point five or six feet out from the corner along the right hand wall of the room. The drum should be pointed in the direction of the far wall.

2. Start the machine with the drum clear of the floor. This may be done by tilting the machine backward. After the drum has attained its full speed, gradually lower it to contact the floor and push the machine forward slowly.
    NOTE: This method of bringing the drum into contact with the surface is particularly necessary to feather sanding cuts where they stop or overlap each other during the floor sanding operation. Practice raising and lowering the drum several times before starting the motor so that you acquire the skill to raise and lower the drum in a smooth movement.

    On some machines, raising and lowering the drum can be accomplished by adjusting the rollers.

3. Sand with the grain unless the boards are cupped (concave shaped) or otherwise uneven; then, it is permissible to sand at a 45-degree angle or directly across the grain on the first cut only.

    NOTE: When sanding, move very slowly (take short steps) and steadily forward keeping the machine in motion when the drum is in contact with the floor.

4. Before the machine gets too close to the opposite baseboard, gradually raise the drum to taper off the cut. Start the machine back over the same cut, and lower the drum as the machine moves, backing up until the machine reaches the starting point.

5. Move the machine to the left the width of the drum, and start forward with the next cut. When half of the room has been sanded in this manner, turn the machine around and do the other half. Lap the cuts a foot or so in the middle of the room. To prevent gouges, raise the drum at the end of each cut while the machine is still in motion.

    NOTE: If there are areas of the floor surface that have not been touched by the above sanding, do not try to sand down these areas only, but repeat the process over the entire room.

Empty the dust bag after every hour of operation or when the dust bag is full. Always empty the dust bag upon completion of using the machine even though it may contain only a little dust. Never leave the dust in the bag overnight because oil, grease, or chemicals in the wood dust can create spontaneous combustion. Never empty the dust bag into an open fire, an incinerator, or a furnace. Wood dust is explosive under such conditions.

How to Take the Finish Cut

1. When the rough cut has been taken over the full area of the room and the edges have been rough sanded with a floor edger, replace the abrasive belt on the drum with a finer one (generally two grades finer refer to the chart) and proceed as in making the

first cut. However, the operator may move the machine over the floor with a little more speed and with less pressure of the sanding drum on the floor. NOTE: All the finish sanding must be done by sanding with the grain. The edges are then finish sanded with the disc or edge sander.

FLOOR EDGE (DISC) SANDER

Several types of disc sanders are used by the carpenter. On type, figure 11-3, most often referred to as a floor edge sander, is used for blending edges with the center of the floor, sanding stair treads, landings, closets, etc. that cannot be done with a floor drum sander.

Fig. 11-3 Edge sander

This machine is made in sizes from 3/4 to 1 3/4 horsepower (560 watts to 1.3 kilowatts) and has disc sanding surfaces from 6 to 8 inches in diameter to which artificial-type coated abrasives are generally applied. It is provided with a bag that catches the dust as the machine is being used. Rollers on the base of the sander support it and on some machines may be adjusted to control the depth of cut.

The abrasive sheet used on the edger is in the shape of a disc. The disc may be purchased already cut to shape or may be cut out from a roll or sheet of abrasive paper.

As with the floor sander, a silicon carbide abrasive with a strong paper or combination backing is most efficient. The same grit sizes as those for drum sanders are available, either closed- or open-coated. Again, closed types are used on unfinished floors and open types for removing old finishes.

How to Cut an Abrasive Disc for the Floor Edger

NOTE: Cutting out discs is sometimes necessary when no ready-made discs are on hand.

1. Select the appropriate type of abrasive. It may be in sheet or roll form.

2. If an abrasive disc cutter is available, place the sheet on the cutter with the abrasive side up. Pound the sheet on the edge of the cutter with a wood mallet (or a block of wood and hammer) until the disc is cut out.

3. An alternate method for cutting out the disc is to scribe the desired diameter on the smooth side of the abrasive sheet with a pair of steel dividers until the disc can be easily pressed out. Punch a hole the size of the setscrew provided to fasten the disc to the sander.

How to Install the Abrasive Disc on the Floor Edger

NOTE: The following procedures apply to a particular make of machine. However, they basically apply to most makes of machines.

1. Set the machine on its top and loosen the locknut with the wrench provided. The edger locknut has a *left-hand* thread; therefore, loosening must be done in a *clockwise* direction.

Fig. 11-4

2. Pull out the lockscrew and metal clamp and remove the old disc.

3. Insert the screw with the clamp as shown in figure 11-4 (A) through the hole in the sandpaper and into the threaded hole in the machine, (B). Tighten in a *counterclockwise* direction with the wrench, (C). Before final tightening, be sure the sandpaper disc is centered.

4. Complete the tightening. Turn the machine over to its normal sanding position. It is now ready for sanding.

How to Use the Floor Edger

NOTE: Edging should be done after each sanding of the body of the floor. That is, after the floor body has been rough sanded, the edges are rough sanded, etc.

1. Install an abrasive disc one grade finer or the same grit size as was used on the drum sander in taking the roughing cut. One grit finer is preferred.

2. Tilt the machine or adjust the rollers (depending on the type of machine) so that the disc clears the floor.

3. Hold the machine firmly and turn on the switch. Wait until the machine attains its full speed before lowering the disc to begin sanding.

4. With a firm grip on the handles, lower the disc to a cutting position and move the machine back and forth in a slow sweeping motion (about 18-inch sweeps) away from the baseboard and toward the finished sanded areas. Operate with the weight of the machine only on the disc, otherwise pronounced rotary marks will show on the floor. Do not allow the rollers to tip.

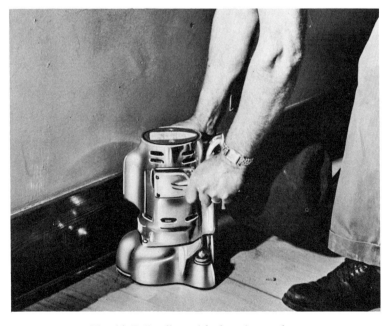

Fig. 11-5 Sanding with the edge sander

5. Do not rest the machine in one place while the disc is turning. As soon as one area is sanded smooth and clean, move the machine to the next area and continue until the edges of the room are finished.

   NOTE: When it is necessary to stop the machine, raise the disc clear of the floor before turning the switch to the off position.

   NOTE: Empty the dust bag after every hour of operation or when the dust bag is half full.

6. After finish sanding has been completed with the drum sander, do the finish edging. Again, with a finer abrasive than was used on the other parts of the floor.

7. To check for laps or scallops where the sanding operation lapped, clean the floor with a vacuum cleaner and look across the foor surface from several angles. If any laps or scallops are detected, sand them out by hand with a sanding block and fine sandpaper or with an orbital sander.

8. Finish the extreme corners of the room by hand with a hand scraper or with a finishing (oscillating) sander.

PORTABLE DISC SANDER

The portable disc sander is a tool designed to operate a wide assortment of disc and spindle attachments. However, the items covered herein will deal primarily with those used by the carpenter. The basic machine and its standard equipment are illustrated in figure 11-6.

Note that the trigger switch is located under the handle. To reduce operator fatigue on long jobs, a lock button on the left side of the handle holds the trigger in the "on" position. To shut off the machine, the trigger is pulled and released immediately.

The rubber-covered guide-grip may be threaded into either side of the machine for either right- or left-hand operation, and may be removed entirely for use in confined areas.

On the shaft of the machine, a fiber washer is provided which serves to reduce friction between the bearing face and any attachments that are applied. It enables the attachments

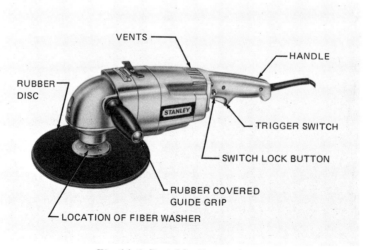

Fig. 11-6 Portable disc sander

to be loosened easily when a change is required. The fiber washer should never be removed from the shaft except for replacement.

How to Use the Portable Disc Sander for Sanding

NOTE: Sanding performed by the carpenter with this tool is primarily for the removal of old finishes — paint, varnish, etc.

1. Select an appropriate type abrasive disc. For roughing, very coarse open-grain abrasive discs (silicon carbide or aluminum oxide) are used. These are designed for paint removal and for work on wood or other coarse materials where the grit might load up quickly. Use intermediate abrasives for the intermediate stage, then with fine grit discs prepare the surface for the finish coat.

2. Install the rubber backup pad by threading it onto the shaft and tightening it securely *by hand.*

3. Install the abrasive disc. Installation involves the following steps:

    a. Slip the disc over the shaft and fit it snugly against the backup pad so that enough threads are exposed for attaching the retaining nut.

    b. Screw the retaining nut onto the shaft so that it forces the abrasive disc back against the pad.

    c. Insert the spanner wrench prongs (provided with the sander) in the depressions on the retaining nut, then insert the hex wrench (also provided with the sander) in the shaft socket.

    d. Hold the shaft with the hex wrench and tighten the retaining nut with the spanner wrench.

Fig. 11-7

4. Start the machine and, when it has attained full speed, apply it to the surface to be sanded. For best results, tip the machine slightly with just enough pressure to bend the disc, figure 11-7. Grasp the control handle firmly and operate the sander freely without forced effort. The sander should be used with long, sweeping motions, back and forth, advancing along the surface to produce smooth, continuous coverage. NOTE: Always hold the sander in a natural comfortable position. Heavy pressure will slow the cutting action, reduce abrasive life, and gouge the surface. Do not hold the sander in one spot or use a circular motion as this, too, will result in irregular surfaces. If sanding is to be prolonged, lock the switch in the on position by means of switch lock button.

5. When sanding is completed, lift the machine clear of the surface and stop the machine.

Fig. 11-8

How to Use the Portable Disc Sander as a Stationary Grinder

NOTE: A bench stand is available to which the sander may be attached figure 11-8. The stand is first screwed securely to the bench and then the sander is fastened to it.

1. Secure the sander to the bench stand. To do this, proceed as follows:

    a. Remove the guide grip.

    b. Turn the sander on its side with the shaft toward the edge of the worktable and set the flat side in the cradle of the bench stand.

    c. Thread the large thumbscrew under the bench stand into the threaded hole in the side of the sander. Turn this screw finger-tight only.

2. Install the wheel adapter. The wheel adapter is used to attach any wheel which does not thread directly onto the machine shaft, except for an abrasive cutting wheel which has a special cup-shaped metal hub for an adapter. To install the wheel adapter proceed as follows:

    a. Thread it onto the shaft.

    b. Insert the hex wrench in the end of the shaft, and tighten the adapter ring by inserting the spindle wrench in the depressions on the collar of the ring.

    c. Slide the abrasive wheel onto the shaft and screw on the retaining nut. Tighten it by inserting one spindle wrench in the adapter ring and the other spindle wrench in the collar of the retaining nut. Hold the adapter ring while turning the retaining nut.

    d. To remove the assembly, simply reverse this procedure.

3. Stand clear of the wheel and turn the switch on. Lock the switch in the on position by means of the switch lock button.

4. Proceed to grind. Stand clear of the wheel to avoid flying particles. Be sure to wear safety goggles.

How to Use the Portable Disc Sander for Cutting with an Abrasive Cutting Wheel

NOTE: For this particular machine a 7-inch abrasive wheel and a special cup-shaped metal adapter are available.

1. Turn the metal hub onto the shaft and tighten it by hand.

2. Then thread on the retaining nut and tighten it with the spanner wrench while the shaft is held stationary as previously described.

3. Turn on the sander and proceed to cut as illustrated in figure 11-9. Support the sander with both hands so that it is not allowed to tilt once the cut has been started. Feed the wheel slowly into the material. Be sure that the material being cut is held securely.

How to Use the Portable Disc Sander for Sanding Clapboards with a Paint Remover Attachment

NOTE: A paint remover attachment is used with the portable disc sander primarily for removing old paint from clapboard siding. The function of the attachment is to control the depth and scope of sanding.

Fig. 11-9

1. Install the paint remover attachment. The procedure for installation described as follows applies to one particular machine used as an example.

    a. Thread the rubber-covered auxiliary handle in the left side of the sander.

    b. Remove the abrasive disc retaining nut and abrasive disc (if one is on the machine).

    c. Set the sander-polisher on a bench so it rests on the motor frame with the handle and rubber-covered auxiliary handle with the pad facing up.

    d. Hold down on the handle with the left hand and, with the heel of the right hand, hit the right edge of the pad a smart blow upward and away from you. This will loosen it. Unscrew and remove the pad.

    e. Remove the three screws around the arbor.

    f. Place the paint remover attachment on gear housing cover with button-headed guide screws pointing up. Attach firmly to the sander with the three roundhead screws furnished with the attachment, figure 11-10 (B).

    g. Thread the paint remover pad onto the arbor, figure 11-10 (C).

2. Select and install the abrasive disc. Center it on the paint remover pad and screw the abrasive disc retaining nut, furnished with the remover, onto the arbor. Tighten it firmly with the large hex wrench to hold the abrasive disc in place.

    NOTE: For thick coats of paint, abrasive discs with the larger grits should be used. If the paint is fresh, it can be expected that the discs will load up more than when older paint is being removed. Carbide discs do not tend to load to the same extent as paper discs. They have longer life than paper discs because any loading may be removed with a small penknife or other pointed tool. Paint solvent may also be used to clean discs that have become loaded. Use abrasive discs having open coats for all paint removal operations.

3. Adjust the paint remover guide screws. For most applications, the button-headed guide screws should be so positioned that when a straightedge is laid on them, the pad just clears the straightedge, figure 11-11, page 162. In this position, the pad rim will not rub on the clapboard edge on which the screws ride.

    NOTE: The screws may be adjusted to keep the pad edge farther away from the overlapping clapboard if desired. To change the position of the screws, loosen the locknuts, adjust the screws to desired positions and tighten the locknuts.

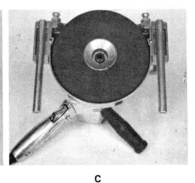

A   B   C

Fig. 11-10

4. Adjust the paint remover side rails. There are two knobs for controlling the distance the side rails extend above or below the pad. In the following instructions, the right knob is the one on the same side of the motor frame as the metal handle. The right side rail is the one controlled by this knob. To lower the right side rail, turn the right control knob toward the front of the machine. To raise the right side rail, turn the right control knob toward the rear of the machine. To lower the left side rail, turn the left control knob toward the rear of the machine. To raise the left side rail, turn the left control knob toward the front of the machine.

   NOTE: The distance of the rails above and below the pad edge determine the depth of cut. For most applications, satisfactory operation will result when one side rail is adjusted so it is 1/32 inch above and the other rail 1/32 inch below the pad edge, figure 11-12. For removing very thin coats of paint, it is sometimes desirable to reduce the depth of cut. To do this, the rail that is above the pad should be moved down. Try several positions on a piece of scrap lumber until you find the location best suited for the job. Do not change the position of the rail that is 1/32 inch below the pad edge.

5. *To sand small areas,* proceed as follows:

   a. Start the motor and bring the button-headed guide screws into contact with the edge of the clapboard above the one to be sanded.

   b. Bring the abrasive disc in contact with the clapboard and move the machine back and forth from left to right until the paint has been removed, figure 11-13.

   c. To sand close to the edge of the board above, tilt the machine forward.

   d. To sand the lower part of wide clapboards, simply move the machine down and up, back and forth from left to right, and in circles.

   e. To spot sand from a ladder, make sure the ladder is firmly anchored and close enough to the house so you won't have to reach too far. Work with one arm outside of one of the legs and the other between the rungs of the ladder, figure 11-14.

6. *To sand large areas,* sanding is done in the same manner as for small areas, but the operator moves from left to right or right to left to cover the entire surface.

7. *To sand up to window or door frames,* adjust the paint remover attachment as follows:

   a. If the window or door frame is to your left, the left rail of the paint remover should be adjusted so it is higher than the edge of the pad. The right rail should be adjusted so it is lower than the edge of the pad.

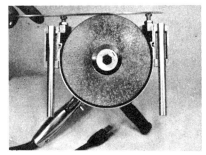

Fig. 11-11

Fig. 11-12

Fig. 11-13

Fig. 11-14

Fig. 11-15

b. If the window or door frame is to your right, then the right rail should be higher than the pad and the left rail lower than the pad.

8. *To remove paint from porches,* proceed as follows:

 a. Raise one rail above and lower the other rail below the pad edge.

 b. Move the machine from left to right, back and forth in circular paths, or any combination of these, figure 11-15.

9. *To sand floor edging,* the guide screws are adjusted up to the baseboard.

10. *To sand masonry,* install a #24 or #36 grit carbide disc. Paper or cloth discs are not suitable for this operation. Sanding is done in the same manner as for wood. In this case, it is necessary that the operator wear a dust mask to keep the dust from entering the nose and mouth.

CAUTION: In all cases, safety goggles should be worn when using the paint remover attachment.

REVIEW QUESTIONS

A. Short Answer or Discussion

1. Why are heavy-duty floor sanders not recommended for sanding residential floors?

2. What factors are important in selecting the coated abrasives for floor sanding?

3. What preparations should be made to the floor prior to sanding?

4. How should the extension cord be kept out of the way when sanding?

5. In what direction should the first cut be made?

6. What two precautions should be observed in regard to the dust bag?

7. How can gouging the floor be avoided?

8. In what direction should finish sanding be done?

9. Should the floor be given both first and finish cuts with the floor sander before the edges are sanded? Explain.

10. If you use a #2 grit on the drum sander (first cut), what grit would you use for the edge sander (first cut)?

11. How is the floor checked for laps or scallops after finish sanding is completed?

12. What is the major use of the portable disc sander?

13. How should the portable disc sander be applied to the surface?

14. Describe two uses of the portable disc sander other than sanding.

15. What is the function of the paint remover attachment used with the portable disc sander?

B. Completion

1. _____ should be worn when using the portable disc sander to remove paint.

2. The extreme corners of the floor should be finished with _____, _____, or _____.

3. Applying too much weight to the machine in edge sanding may result in _____ on the floor.

4. Drum widths of floor sanding machines range from _____ to _____ inches.

5. On some types of edge sander, the _____ may be adjusted to control depth of cut.

6. For paint removal operation, abrasives having _____ coats should be selected.

7. To sand masonry with the portable disc sander, a _____ disc should be used and a _____ should be worn.

8. Before plugging in the lead of the floor sander, be sure the _____ is in the _____ position.

9. A _____ fuse should be installed on the circuit in which the floor sander is used.

10. Tapering off the sanding cut is called _____.

C. Identification and Interpretation

1. Complete the following chart indicating the machines you would use and the coated abrasive you would select for each of the operations listed.

JOB		MACHINE	ABRASIVE
A.	Rough cut old uneven residential oak floor.		
B.	Finish cut new parquet floor.		
C.	Remove old paint from cedar siding.		
D.	Rough cut pine flooring in a small closet.		
E.	Sand masonry steps.		

Unit 12 PORTABLE BELT AND FINISHING SANDERS

The surfacing of lumber for interior trim has always been a laborious job for the carpenter. Some of this work was formerly done with the smooth plane and by hand sanding. The better class of trim was surfaced with a cabinet scraper. Today, this type of work is often done with portable sanding machines. Floor sanding machines are almost always used to make floors ready for finishing.

The portable sanders used by the carpenter may be classified into four general groups: belt sanders, finishing sanders (orbital and oscillating), disc sanders, and floor sanders. Each type has features which make it very useful for particular kinds of work.

PORTABLE BELT SANDER

The portable belt sander is the most useful of the portable sanders for general woodworking. It may be used for chamfering; rounding edges; smoothing rough boards; and finesurfacing wood, metal, and other materials. With abrasive belts of the appropriate type, it may also be used for removing old finishes (paint, varnish, etc.) and for sharpening edge tools. Figure 12-1 shows a typical belt sander with an identification of its components.

Belt sanders are equipped with 115- or 230-volt, ac/dc motors having from 3/4 to 1 1/4 horsepower (559.5 to 932.5 watts). Power is transmitted from the motor to the rear rubber-covered traction wheel through a set of reduction gears. The traction wheel in turn drives the continuous abrasive belt. Forward wheel (idler pulley) serves as a rotating support for the belt and, by means of a belt-centering adjusting screw, also functions to center or track the belt.

The size of a belt sander is often designated by the width of the belt that it takes. Belt widths may be 2, 3, or 4 inches. The weight of the machine generally increases with the width of the belt from 8 to 25 pounds. Those with 2-inch belts are identified by some manufacturers as standard-duty machines. The 3-inch belt size sanders are called heavy-duty, and the 4-inch belt size are called super heavy-duty.

Belt lengths vary with each type of machine (from 21 to 27 inches long) and must be ordered to suit the particular machine.

The professional-type belt sanders include a dust bag attachment which takes up the dust as it is produced in much the same manner as an ordinary vacuum cleaner. The heavy-duty portable belt sander (3-inch belt width, weight about 14 pounds) with a dust bag attachment is the one most preferred for general woodworking.

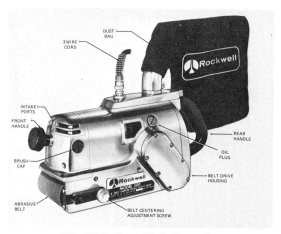

Fig. 12-1 Portable belt sander

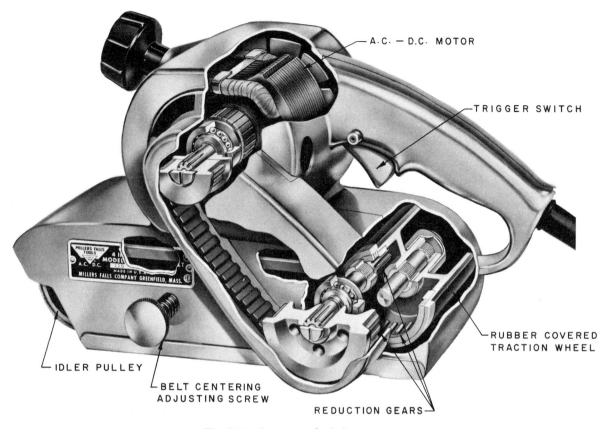

Fig. 12-2 Cutaway of a belt sander

SELECTION OF ABRASIVE BELT

The principal abrasive materials used on belts for machine sanding are aluminum oxide and silicon carbide. The first is not as hard as the second, but is tougher and more suited for woods and soft (nonferrous) metals. Silicon carbide is extremely hard and best suited for surfacing stone, marble, and glass.

MANU-FACTURER	TYPE OF ABRASIVE AND TRADE NAMES FOR PAPERS & CLOTHS				TRADE NAMES FOR COATING		
	Aluminum Oxide Cabinet or Finishing Paper	Garnet Cabinet or Finishing Paper	Aluminum Oxide Metal Working Cloth	Silicon Carbide Paper	Water-proof Paper	Electro-Coated	Open Coat
Armour	Garalun	H. T. Garnet	Alundum	Crystolon	Rub-wet	Electro-Coated	Amour-ite
Behr Manning	Adalox	Garnet	Metalite	Durite	Speed-wet	Light-ning	Open Kote
Carbor-undum	Cabinet or Finishing Paper-Alo	Cabinet or Finishing Paper-Garnet	Metal Cloth	Abrasive Cloth or Paper	Water-proof	Electro-Coated	Open
Minnesota Mining & Manu-facturing	Produc-tion	Garnet	Three-M-Ite	Tri-M-Ite	Wet or Dry	Elek-Tro-Cut	Cutrite

Abrasives are classed as open-coated or closed-coated, meaning that the grits are spaced apart or close together. Closed coatings provide hard, fast, cutting action for hardwoods and dense metals. The open coatings are more suited to soft materials and painted surfaces.

Information identifying the type of abrasive used on the belt, its grade, etc. is found stamped on the inside of the belt, along with a large arrow which is used as reference for installing the belt. When the belt is properly installed, the arrow should point in the direction of rotation.

The correct type of abrasive belt to use can be determined from charts provided by manufacturers of sanding machines and coated abrasives.

ABRASIVE CHART

MATERIAL	ROUGHING	FINISHING	FINE FINISHING
OAK, WALNUT	2 1/2, 2, OR 1 1/2	1/2 OR 1	2/0, 3/0, OR 4/0
MAPLE, BIRCH	2 1/2, 2, 1 1/2, OR 1	1/2 OR 1	2/0, 3/0, OR 4/0
MAHOGANY, GUM	2 1/2, 2, OR 1 1/2	1/2 OR 1	2/0 OR 3/0
CYPRESS	2 1/2, 2, OR 1 1/2	1/2 OR 1	2/0
FIR, WHITE PINE	1 1/2 OR 1	1/2 OR 1/0	2/0
YELLOW PINE	2 OR 1 1/2 (OPEN)	1/2	1/0

SAFE OPERATION OF A BELT SANDER

Any power tool can be dangerous if safety precautions are not followed. Loose clothing that might become entangled between the abrasive belt and the sander frame should not be worn. The sander should be kept away from the body while the abrasive belt is in motion. The sander cord plug should always be disconnected from the power source before changing belts, and it should be properly grounded when in operation.

In addition, a check should be made to see that the machine is adequately lubricated. For this purpose, maintenance instructions provided with the machine should be referred to.

How to Install the Belt

1. Select the proper abrasive grit for the job by consulting an abrasive chart.
   NOTE: Be sure that the right size belt is selected.

2. Lay the sander on its left side and retract the idler (forward) pulley. This decreases the span between the forward and rear pulleys, thus permitting the belt to be easily slipped into place.
   NOTE: For some machines, this is done by turning the tension release lever located between the front and rear pulleys counterclockwise and locking it under a catch on the plate. Other machines are equipped with a flat slotted spring for this purpose. To release the belt tension on these machines, the front pulley is pressed back until the slot drops over the retaining pin.

3. Hold the abrasive belt so the arrow that is pointed on the inside is at the top and pointing toward the front of the machine. Now slip the belt over the rear pulley and then over the front pulley, figure 12-3 (A).

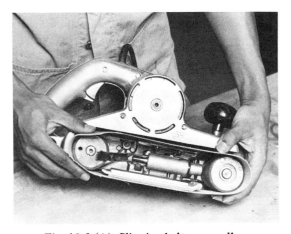

Fig. 12-3 (A) **Slipping belt over pulleys**

Fig. 12-3 (B) **Moving tension lever to restore belt tension**

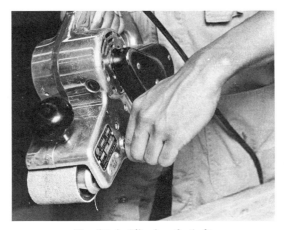

Fig. 12-4 **Aligning the belt**

4. Position the belt so outer edge is flush with the outer ends of the pulleys.

5. Release the lever from its catch to restore belt tension, figure 12-3 (B). On machines equipped with the flat, slotted spring, lift the rear end of spring until the slot clears the retaining pin.

How to Track the Belt

1. With the right hand on the rear handle, tilt the sander back so the belt will run free.

2. Start the motor and adjust the belt-aligning screw located on the left front side of the machine, figure 12-4. Turn the screw to the right or left until the belt runs in the center of the pulleys. Do not let the belt rub on the belt guide block or frame of the sander because damage will result.
   NOTE: Be careful not to bump the belt-aligning screw during the sanding operation. If this or the plate on the end of the idler pulley should become bent, the belt will not track properly and may run off the pulleys or rub against the belt guide block and frame.

GENERAL PROCEDURES FOR USING THE SANDER

1. Firmly fasten the item to be sanded. The sander exerts a tremendous pulling force and fastening should be done accordingly. Usually a stop placed at the rear of the article provides the necessary resistance to this force.

2. Check to see that the sander switch is in the off position before connecting it to the power circuit.

3. Start the motor before the sander is placed on the suface and check to see that the belt is tracking on center. Make any necessary adjustments.

4. Carefully place the moving belt on the surface. Let the rear part of the belt touch first and level the machine as it is moved forward. Do not press down on the machine; its own weight produces the necessary sanding action.
NOTE: Excessive pressure on the belt causes the motor to overheat and the abrasive belt to become clogged.

5. Immediately upon contact with the surface, guide the machine over the surface with overlapping strokes in a direction parallel with the grain.

6. Keep the machine flat on the work surface and work over a fairly wide area to obtain an even surface. Do not let the machine tilt or the edge of the belt will make a deep cut into the surface. Do not pause in any one spot during the sanding operation because the belt will quickly remove the material at that place, making the surface uneven. When running out to the end of a board, be careful that the front of the machine does not drop. This will cause rounding of the edge.

7. Upon completion of sanding, lift the machine off the work and stop the motor.
NOTE: Always lift the sander off the work before starting or stopping the motor because the effects of starting and stopping them become a gradual process and result in less strain on the motor and driving mechanism.

8. Change to belts with successively finer grits and sand entirely with the grain until the maximum smoothness has been attained.

How to Surface a Wide Board

1. Install a number 2 1/2-grit (coarse) abrasive belt.

2. With the belt positioned diagonally across the grain, move the machine in the direction of the grain, figure 12-5. Care must be taken that the belt is not pushed off the pulleys of the machine.

3. Overlap the strokes well and cover the entire surface, working from both sides of the board, that is, once with the sander angled to the left and once angled to the right.

4. Smooth the surface by guiding the machine back and forth with the grain.

5. Change the belt to a number 1 1/2- or 1-grit and follow the same procedure.

6. Finish off by thoroughly working over the grain lengthwise.

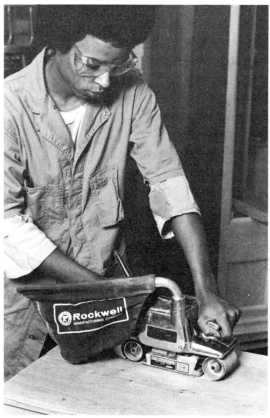

Fig. 12-5 Surfacing a board

Fig. 12-6 Machine adjusted for curved surface

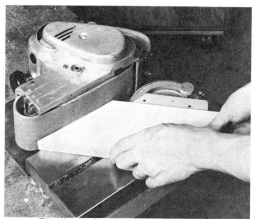

Fig. 12-7 Sanding to a given angle

7. Do the final sanding with a number 2/0- or 3/0-grit belt and work entirely back and forth with the grain, figure 12-5.
   NOTE: Always finish work by sanding with the grain.

How to Sand Convex-Curved Surfaces

NOTE: A flexible pad is specifically made for sanding convex-curved surfaces. It is fastened to the base in place of the regular shoe by screws at the front end. The pad has a soft rubber base which permits the belt to conform to curved and irregular surfaces, figure 12-6.

1. Proceed to sand with the grain, carefully guiding the machine to the curved surface. Use a uniform movement with a minimum of pressure.
   NOTE: Observe the same techniques and precautions as previously described for belt sanding.

How to Sand Small Pieces, Concave Edges, and Miter Joints

1. Secure the machine to a bench or stand it on its side. Check with a try square to see that the face of the belt is square with the bench surface, and adjust it accordingly by shimming.
   NOTE: Stands may be made or purchased specifically for use with the belt sander positioned on its side.

2. Apply the edge to be sanded to the moving belt. Use the sanding shoe for straight work, and the front pulley as a spindle sander for curved work, figure 12-7.

How to Grind Edge Tools

1. Install a metal cutting (silicon carbide) belt on the sander.

2. Position it on its side so that the belt is in a vertical position.

3. Prepare a support for resting the tool. The sander should be positioned as close to this support as possible without rubbing against it.

4. Grind the tool by placing it against the moving belt.

How to Remove Old Paint and Varnish with a Belt Sander

NOTE: Two problems are common to such work. One is loading (clogging) the abrasive with the material being removed, and the other is overheating the paint or varnish by working too long in one place. By following steps 1 through 3 these problems can generally be overcome.

1. Install a spaced grain (open-coat) abrasive belt.
2. Lower the sander at the far end of the work and pull back with a fairly quick stroke. Use a single stroke action.
3. Raise the machine and do the same in a different location.
4. A piece of felt about 1/4 inch thick can be inserted under the shoe for spot sanding and for working on stubborn areas, particularly when such areas are low (concave).

SPECIAL SANDING PROCEDURES

Ordinarily, the sanding stroke is back and forth. Some materials and some types of operations, however, require a different technique.

In spot sanding, use the machine with only the front pulley touching the surface. This is especially required in smoothing excess plaster or cement between building blocks, or in removing excess glue from wood joints.

On metals, slate, marble, or plastic materials, there is no grain, so the sanding may be done in different directions.

When sanding up to a baseboard or edge of a housed panel, attach a flat piece of thin metal to the front of the machine to prevent damaging the edge of the vertical section. The strip can be held under the front knob on the sander, figure 12-8.

When sanding door edges or other thin pieces, hold the machine level on the surface. Rocking from side to side will produce rounded corners and an uneven edge.

For sanding lengthy work on walls or other vertical surfaces, the sander can be counterbalanced with a length of sashcord, two small pulleys, a light wood frame, and a weight. This weight can be the same as or slightly less than the weight of the sander.

The frame consists of two pieces leaned against the wall with a third piece nailed across their top ends. The two pulleys are located so the weight on one end of the cord will be out of the way, but will balance the sander fastened to the other end. When starting vertical work, angle the

Fig. 12-8 Guard attached to machine to protect vertical edge

machine so you can see the belt make contact with the material. As the belt touches, level the machine and make the stroke away and to the left. This movement will offset any tendency to cut heavily into the work at the start of the stroke.

MAINTENANCE INSTRUCTIONS FOR BELT SANDERS

Cleaning the Sander

For the most satisfactory service from the sander, keep the air ports, motor housing, frame, and pulley assemblies clean and free from dust and dirt. Remove the belt and use a small paintbrush to remove the dust accumulations around the pulley assemblies and frame. The motor is cooled by air being drawn in at the front of the motor housing and being expelled through the side ports. Keep these ports free of dust accumulations for a cooler running motor. Keep the handle and switch clean. Cleanliness is the best way to prevent trouble. Empty the dust bag on the dustless models when it is not more than half full. Occasionally turn the bag inside out and brush accumulations from the lining with a soft brush. This will permit the bag to "breathe" better.

Belt-Guide Block, Drive Pulley

The belt-guide block is a hardened steel bar located on the frame between the pulleys and in line with the upper edge of the belt. It is attached to the frame with screws. This block is used to protect the frame when tracking the belt. Do not allow the belt to ride across the face of the block in operation. The belt should be tracked so the edge just passes the face of the block. When the block becomes worn or grooved, replace it with a new one.

The rubber-covered drive pulley at the rear of the machine is crowned or tapered from the center to either side to make the belt run true and in line with the idler pulley at the front of the machine. After considerable use, the crown will wear away and the belt will begin to run off the side of the pulley and cut into the frame. When the crown is worn to this extent, replace the drive pulley with a new one. This action can be checked each time the belt is replaced and tracked. After the belt is tracked to the front pulley, watch it for a few seconds to see that it runs true and stays in place on the back pulley. Avoid getting oil and grease on the outer surface of the wheels since poor belt traction will result.

Lubrication

The chain case, gear chamber, and other parts require lubrication periodically. Specific directions for lubrication are provided with each sander and should be referred to, to determine when and where lubrication is required.

SUMMARY OF MACHINE CARE

Make a habit of regular and thorough inspection of all parts of the sander. When wear, dirt, loose parts, or other damage is noticed, correct it right away.

Occasionally check the ground connection to the sander frame to be sure it is not loose. Check the lubricant in the gear chamber daily if the machine is used frequently and always before operation if used less often. The life of the gears depends upon maintaining proper lubricant level and using only that lubricant specified in the parts list for the specific machine.

FINISHING SANDERS (ORBITAL, OSCILLATING)

Finishing sanders are generally used for fine sanding where only a small amount of material must be removed to obtain the desired finish. On occasion they are used for rough sanding and for removing old finishes. Specific applications of this machine are: sanding interior trim and cabinet work; leveling wallboard and plywood joints; rubbing down finishing coats; and for places where belt sanders would be too heavy or cumbersome to use.

A finishing sander may be identified as either an orbital or oscillating type. The sanding pad motion on the orbital type is circular (moving in a 3/16- or 1/4-inch orbit) and on the oscillating type is a slight back-and-forth arcing (vibrating) movement. Of the two types, the orbital type is preferred for general finishing work because of its faster cutting action. The oscillating type is usually used for rubbing down finish coats. Either type produces a finish by sanding with or across the grain. This characteristic is particularly desirable when finishing joints such as the miter, where sanding must be done both with and against the grain.

Finishing sanders are light in weight (3 to 8 pounds). The heavier types are generally identified as heavy-duty finishing sanders, figure 12-9. Both the heavy- and light-duty models may be operated with one or both hands. Figure 12-10 shows a light-duty finishing sander in use. This sander is designed for use with only one hand.

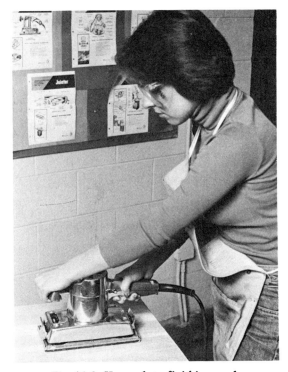

Fig. 12-9 Heavy-duty finishing sander

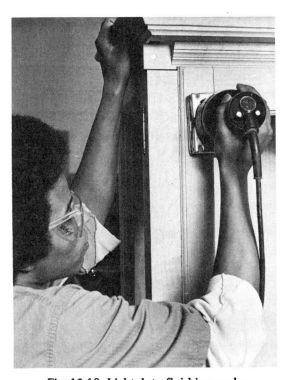

Fig. 12-10 Light-duty finishing sander

SELECTION AND INSTALLATION OF ABRASIVES

Selecting the proper coated abrasive, either coarse, fine, open-coated, etc., as with the belt sander, depends upon the type of sanding to be done. In general, the artificial abrasives (silicon carbide, and aluminum oxide) are preferred. However, garnet (a natural abrasive) is very often used for sanding soft wood and removing old finishes. The coarse grit sizes remove the most material, yet the finer grit sizes produce the best finishes. A table of abrasives to use with the finishing sander for various types of sanding operations follows.

KIND OF MATERIAL	MATERIAL REMOVAL		MATERIAL REMOVAL WITH FAIR FINISH		FINE FINISH	
	GRIT	SIZE OF GRIT	GRIT	SIZE OF GRIT	GRIT	SIZE OF GRIT
Soft Wood Soft Wallboard	Cabinet Paper (Garnet)	2-1	Cabinet Paper (Garnet)	1/2-2/0	Finishing Paper (Garnet)	3/0-5/0
Plastics	Cabinet Paper (Aluminum Oxide)	60-100	Wet Paper "C" Weight (Silicon Carbide)	120-220	Wet Paper "A" Weight (Silicon Carbide)	240-600
Hard Wood Hard Compositions Wallboards, Etc.	Cabinet Paper (Aluminum Oxide)	36-50	Cabinet Paper (Aluminum Oxide)	60-100	Finishing Paper (Aluminum Oxide)	120-180
Soft Metals	Metal Working Cloth (Aluminum Oxide)	36-60	Cabinet Paper (Aluminum Oxide)	80-120	Wet Paper (Silicon Carbide)	150-320
Hard Metals	Metal Working Cloth (Aluminum Oxide)	40-60	Metal Working Cloth (Aluminum Oxide)	80-120	Metal Working Cloth in Oil (Aluminum Oxide)	150-320 or crocus
Hard Brittle Minerals and Compositions	Cabinet Paper (Aluminum Oxide)	50-80	Finishing Paper (Aluminum Oxide)	100-180	Wet Paper "A" Weight (Silicon Carbide)	220-320
Hard Tough Minerals and Compositions	Metal Working Cloth (Aluminum Oxide)		Metal Working Cloth (Aluminum Oxide)	80-120	Finishing Paper (Aluminum Oxide)	150-320
Paints and Varnishes	Cabinet Paper (Opencoat Garnet)	2 1/2-1 1/2			Wet Paper "A" Weight (Silicon Carbide)	240-400

ABRASIVE RECOMMENDATIONS FOR FINISHING SANDERS

The strip of abrasive is usually attached at each end of the pad by some type of spring or friction device which secures the sandpaper. When different grades of abrasives are required for a job, extra pads can be obtained for applying the different grades. Most machines are designed so that the pads can be easily interchanged, enabling the rapid application of the different grades of abrasives needed to do a job.

How to Use the Finishing Sander

1. Select the correct abrasive by referring to the preceeding chart. See page 167 for comparable trade names for abrasives.

   NOTE: Start the work with an abrasive grit just coarse enough to remove the high spots and excessive roughness. Follow with a second sanding using a grit one or two grades finer. Continue with progressively finer grits until the desired finish is obtained. Do not go from a coarse grit to a very fine grit in one step. By doing so, it will be impossible to remove swirl marks that might have been made by the coarse grit abrasive. Use the finest grits practical for the roughing operation and then finish with continually finer grits as outlined above.

2. Cut, do not tear, the abrasive sheet to size.

   NOTE: Sheets already cut to size may be purchased.

3. Make sure the sander is disconnected from the power circuit before attaching the abrasive sheet.

4. Slip one end of the abrasive strip under the front or rear clamping device on the pad holder and fasten, figure 12-11.

5. Fold the abrasive sheet straight over the pad and attach the free end under the fastening device at the opposite end of the pad holder. Fasten it so that the sheet is stretched tightly over the pad surface, figure 12-12.

6. Start the sander above the work and set it down on the work evenly. Move it slowly back and forth in wide overlapping arcs.

   NOTE: Sanding is usually done by guiding the sander over the work surface with one hand. The normal weight of the machine is sufficient for proper sanding. Do not put additional pressure on the machine. This will only slow down the speed of the pad, reduce the sanding efficiency, and put an additional burden on the motor. It might also cause the sander to jump on the work.

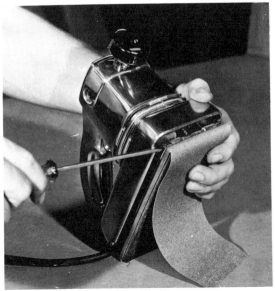

Fig. 12-11

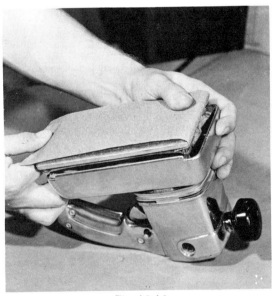

Fig. 12-12

7. When sanding is completed, lift the sander off the work before stopping the motor.

How to Use the Finishing Sander for Removing Paint and Varnish

1. Select and install a coarse, open-coat abrasive to avoid clogging the abrasive surface.

2. Start the machine before applying it to the surface. Keep it moving over new areas to avoid heating and softening the material being removed. Try to work the entire surface down at the same time by working in wide overlapping arcs. Do not concentrate on small areas.
   NOTE: If liquid removers or heaters are used to speed the removal, be sure the surface is cool and dry and the excess material has been scraped away before applying the sander.

How to Use the Finishing Sander to Smooth Wallboard and Taped Joints

1. Select and install a 50-grit open- or closed-coat sandpaper.

2. Start the machine before applying it to the surface. Apply it level to the surface and work it evenly. Use an overlapping circular movement and work in all directions while smoothing the featheredge down to the level of the surrounding surface. Be careful not to abrade into the paper covering the wallboard.

3. When using a sander with a dust bag attachment be sure to use the special dust bag for dry-wall sanding. The regular dust bag is not suitable for this application since the fine plaster dust quickly clogs the dust bag pores, preventing it from breathing.

How to Use the Finishing Sander for Rubbing and Polishing

1. For rubbing, install a felt rubbing pad. For polishing, install a polishing pad.

2. When polishing, apply rouge to the pad or apply paste wax to the surface which is to be polished.

3. Apply the pads to the surface in the same manner as described for sanding.

MAINTENANCE OF THE FINISHING SANDER

Maintenance of electrical components is discussed in unit 1. Lubrication should be done as specified by the operating instructions. This usually includes lubricating the motor bearing every two or three months and the transmission every two weeks if the sander is used continuously, and at proportionately longer intervals if the machine is used less frequently.

Repairing the Pad

If the sander bounces while sanding, the felt pad is probably not bearing evenly on the surface of the work. To correct this, place a sheet of 150-grit open-coat abrasive paper face up on the work table and run the sander pad on the abrasive until the felt is again smooth and level, figure 12-13, page 178. Jumping movement of the sander may also indicate that the machine is not being held correctly or that too much pressure is being applied. This is especially true when sanding raw wood. Hold the machine lightly and evenly. Do not apply any more pressure than the weight of the hand and arm. Let the machine do the work.

Cleaning the Underside of the Pad Assembly

To clean the underside of the pad assembly, the pad must first be removed. The procedure for removal varies with each machine. When doing this, follow the operating instructions.

Fig. 12-13

General Care and Cleaning

Be careful not to drop or bump the machine. It may throw the parts out of line, causing improper movement, overheating, or excessive wear.

After working on plaster, metals, or other materials having abrasive properties, the dust should be blown from all parts of the machine to prevent it from working into the bearings and motor parts and causing failure.

If the machine is provided with a dust bag, empty the bag when it is about half filled. At frequent intervals, remove the dust bag entirely from the machine, turn it inside out and brush away the dust that is clinging to the inner surface. The bag will breathe better and the vacuum system will operate more efficiently. When leveling plaster material, be sure to use the special dry-wall dust bag.

In some machines, a dust filter is incorporated in the grill on the front of the sander. The grill may be opened to install and remove the filter. Do not operate the sander with a clogged filter. Never operate it without any filter. The filter will clog, and require periodic cleaning. To clean it, merely tap the filter to loosen and shake out the dust. Do not use an air jet to blow out dust as this will damage the filter. In reinstalling the filter, be sure that it is completely seated in the filter opening. Also make sure the grill is closed. Failure to install the filter correctly will permit passage of air containing abrasive laden dust to get into the machine and cause damage to the motor. If the sander is operated with a clogged filter, the flow of air through the motor is decreased and the sander will overheat.

Form a regular habit of cleaning and inspecting the sander. Replace worn parts and tighten any loose screws as soon as they are noticed.

REVIEW QUESTIONS

A. Short Answer or Discussion

1. Why is the portable belt sander considered the most useful of all types of sanders?

2. Describe the power train of a portable belt sander.

3. What provision is made for belt tracking?

4. In what sizes are belt sanders available, and what determines the size?

5. What are the specific advantages of each of the two most common artificial abrasives?

6. What harmful results may occur from excessive pressure on the belt of the sander?

7. What precautions must be observed in the use of the portable belt sander?

8. What are the differences in direction of sanding between rough surfacing and final sanding?

9. How is the sander adapted for curved surfaces?

10. What technique avoids damage to the belt when sanding up to a vertical surface?

11. Describe the two basic types of finishing sanders.

12. What natural abrasive is commonly used with finishing sanders and for what purposes is it used?

13. Why is it harmful to change from a coarse to a very fine grit abrasive in one step?

14. Describe two precautions to observe when sanding taped joints in wallboard.

15. List three possible reasons for a sander to jump during operation.

B. Completion
1. When using a finishing sander for dry wall sanding, the _____ should not be used.

2. The _____ sander is usually used in wide overlapping arcs.

3. In spot sanding, the belt sander should be used with only the _____ touching the surface.

4. Two problems which may be encountered in using the belt sander to remove old paint are: _____ and _____.

5. To grind edge tools with the belt sander, a _____ belt should be installed.

6. In placing the operating belt sander on the surface to be sanded, the _____ end should touch first.

7. The belt sander is centered by means of the _____.

8. In placing a belt on the sander, the _____ on the inside of the belt should be positioned at the _____ and pointing toward the _____ of the machine.

9. Belt tension is controlled for installing or removing the belt by the _____.

C. Identification and Interpretation

1. Identify the lettered parts of the sander illustrated below.

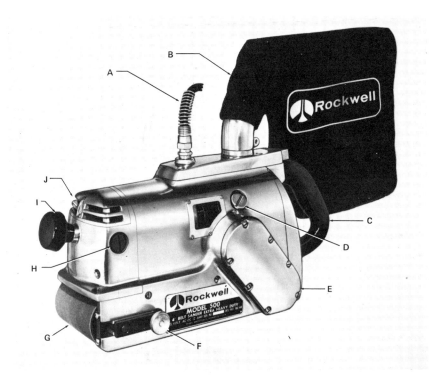

Unit 13 STAPLERS

Manual processes of driving fasteners to secure material together are being replaced by automatic devices. There are many reasons why these machines have gained popularity in the construction field. They reduce the cost of the fastening job, lessen the amount of manual labor involved, and provide a more efficient method of fastening materials together.

This unit will be concerned with stapler and stapler-nailer devices.

STAPLERS

Perhaps the first automatic fastening device to gain acceptance was the spring stapler. This used staples instead of nails or tacks to secure insulation bats or other light materials to wood framed surfaces when closely spaced nailing was required. The use of the stapler allows the staples to be set and driven with one hand, leaving the other hand free to support and adjust the material being secured, figure 13-1.

Different types of staplers and tackers have been developed to accommodate various types of fasteners. Some are actuated by spring power, others by air pressure, the air being supplied from cylinders of compressed carbon dioxide or from portable air compressors. Both types are controlled by trigger action.

Spring-Actuated Staplers

Figure 13-2 shows a pistol grip gun tacker actuated by a spring lever. This machine is designed to drive staples in close corners and is lightweight to provide easy handling in overhead or hard-to-reach places.

Fig. 13-1 Stapling insulation

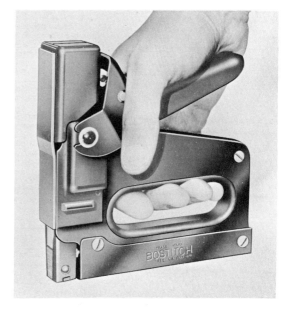

Fig. 13-2 Spring-actuated stapler

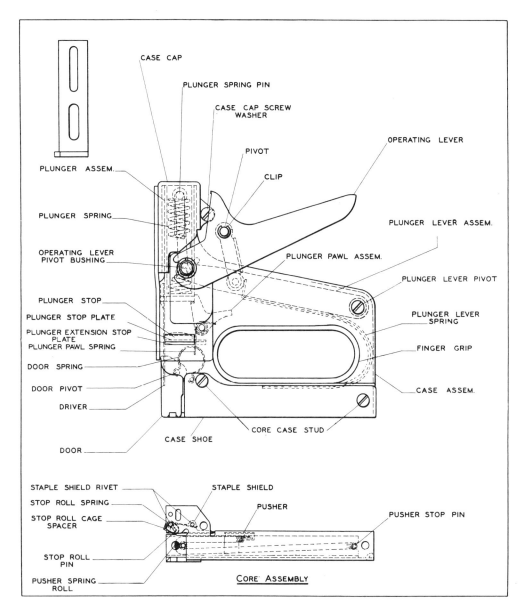

Fig. 13-3 Stapler parts

Figure 13-3 illustrates the parts of a typical pistol-grip stapler. Different models of this stapler require different sized staples. No staples other than the sizes designated should be used in any particular model. The list below gives some examples of models and their required staple sizes.

Model	Required Staple	Lengths
T 5-6 Tacker	Bostitch STCr 2619	1/4'', 5/32'', 3/8'', 1/2''
T 5-8 Tacker	Bostitch STCr 5019	1/4'', 5/32'', 3/8'', 1/2'', 9/16''
T 5-12 Tacker	Bostitch STCr 2115	1/4'', STCr 019 3/8'', 1/2''

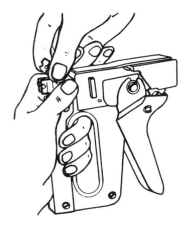

Fig. 13-4 **Open the door**

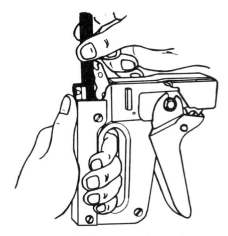

Fig. 13-5 **Insert the staples**

Fig. 13-6 **Keep the pressure at the point where the staples are driven**

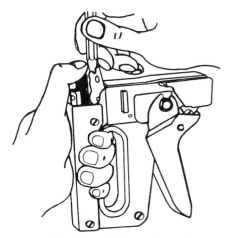

Fig. 13-7 **Release the staples**

How to Use the Spring-Actuated Tacker

1. To load, slide the loading door upward until it unlocks, then swing it open as shown in figure 13-4.

2. Slide a stick of staples onto the core against the pressure of the pusher, figure 13-5, and close the door. The tacker is now ready to operate.
    NOTE: For tackers with an "out turn door", slide the spring on the door to the right or left, then swing the door open and proceed the same as for a standard tacker.

3. To operate, place the tacker with the front end by the point where the staple is to be driven. Grasp the lever with the fingers through the opening in the finger grip and press the operating lever downward until the trigger is released. Lift the heel of the tacker slightly from the work so that all downward pressure is at the door as the staple is driven, figure 13-6.
    NOTE: Do not try to operate the tacker while the door is open.

4. To remove the staples, hold the tacker as if to load and open the door. Then, with the thumb or forefinger of the left hand over the end of the core (so that the staples will

not fly out when released), press the lower end of the driver inward, using a small screwdriver or pencil, figure 13-7, page 183. The staples will be automatically ejected against the fingers of the left hand.

5. To clear the tacker of fouled staples, grasp the tacker with the left hand, holding the door closed with the thumb and index finger, figure 13-8. Caution: Keep the fingers away from the bottom of the door. With the right hand, pull the operating lever so that it is spread open to its fullest extent. If an attempt is made to open the door before spreading the lever apart as described above, there is danger that the driver will become wedged in the door and snap or bend. The door can now be tapped lightly, figure 13-9, and will open up, readily exposing the channel and allow any jammed staples to be withdraw.

Heavy-Duty Spring-Actuated Staplers

Spring-actuated staplers are also made in heavier types and are designed with a hammer-like form and a trigger. These staplers are used extensively by carpenters and material appliers for securing all types of building papers, insulation foils, thin plywood, and many other coverings that used to be secured by flathead nails.

Figure 13-10 shows a stapler scientifically balanced to deliver a powerful blow with a natural swing of the arm. It drives staples, 3/4 inch long and made of 1/16-inch diameter wire, flattened for easy driving. Each staple has a holding capacity equivalent to two, 3/4- x 1/16-inch wire nails. The staple points diverge as they are driven, thus providing greater holding power. The stapler weighs two pounds and four ounces and loads 50 staples.

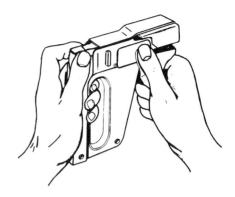

Fig. 13-8 Spread the operating lever open

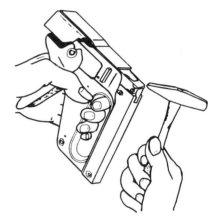

Fig. 13-9   Tap the door lightly to expose the channel

Fig. 13-10

Fig. 13-11

Another type of stapler used for conventional fastening is shown in figure 13-11.

When heavy tacking is required, a rubber mallet may be used in conjunction with the stapler as shown in figure 13-12.

Air-Actuated Staplers

Staplers which are actuated by compressed air depend on the air pressure to ensure penetration of the staples. It is important that the compressor line pressure be maintained at the manufacturer's recommendations. Figure 13-13 shows a general installation and control system that would be satisfactory for operation of this type of stapler.

Figure 13-14, page 186, illustrates a compressed air-actuated stapler that operates on 70 pounds air pressure per square inch (psi). It is used to drive staples into soft woods. For harder materials, the pressure may be increased to provide penetration. The maximum pressure for this type of stapler is 120 psi.

Staples for this air stapler come in a round cartridge. The staples feed through this cartridge in a ribbon-like form.

Fig. 13-12 Using a rubber mallet with hammer-type stapler

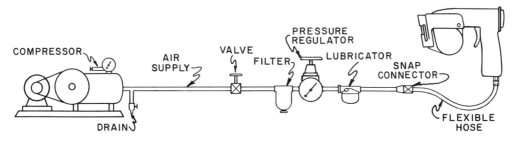

Fig. 13-13 Control system for an air-actuated stapler

Fig. 13-14 An air-actuated stapler, round cartridge

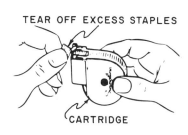

Fig. 13-15

Fig. 13-16

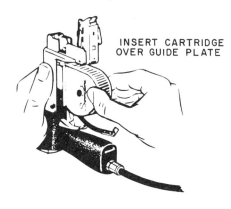

Fig. 13-17

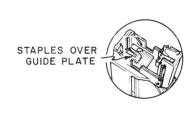

Fig. 13-18

How to Operate the Air-Actuated Stapler

1. To load, make sure that the staple belt does not protrude beyond the edge of the cartridge. To tear off any excess, hold the cartridge firmly in one hand over the name stamped on the cartridge. With the other hand, tear off the excess with a quick, sharp stroke, figure 13-15.

2. Release the swingcase by grasping the notched edge of the latch, on both sides, and slide the latch all the way back in the direction of the arrow. Then swing it out to open the case, figure 13-16.

3. To insert the cartridge, hold the stapler in one hand as shown in figure 13-17 and the cartridge in the other, with the feed pawls and the flat side of the cartridge up. Insert the cartridge so the staples cover the guide plate, figure 13-18.

4. To lock the cartridge in the stapler, push the cartridge in as far as it will go. Partially close the swingcase, but do not latch it. Insert the hook on the holding strap into the square hold at the back of the swingcase, figure 13-19. Slide the swingcase all the way down until it clicks, figure 13-20. The stapler should now be ready for operation when properly hooked to a line.

5. To drive the staples, press the trigger; then release it to provide for driving additional staples.

> **CAUTION:** Never point the stapler at any person or at finished materials. Remember that this stapler acts as a gun and become dangerous if not properly handled. Never force the swingcase or swing latch with any tool other than the fingers.

6. To change the cartridge, slide the latch all the way back as shown in figure 13-16; swing out the swingcase and slide out the cartridge.

If the stapler is improperly loaded or misfires, a jam may occur. Carefully go through the complete unloading process again. Then press the trigger twice without replacing the cartridge. Clean out the loose or jammed staples and reload.

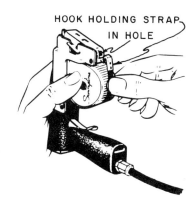

Fig. 13-19

Fig. 13-20

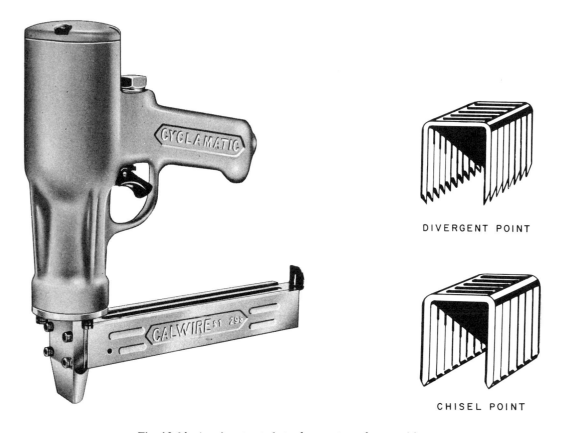

Fig. 13-21 An air-actuated stapler, rectangular cartridge

Air-Actuated Stapler (Rectangular Cartridge Type)

Other styles of air-actuated staplers are available which have a rectangular type cartridge for feeding the staples. These may be purchased in various sizes to accommodate a range of staple sizes. For example, the stapler illustrated in figure 13-21 accommodates and drives a 3/4-inch to 7/8-inch staple.

Staples for this machine may be obtained with a chisel or divergent point, may be plain steel or galvanized, and may be rosin coated.

The stationary system (compressor) used with this machine is illustrated in figure 13-22, page 190. Note that provision is made for attaching two staplers to the compressor thus permitting the use of two staplers on the job from one system.

The stationary system (filter, regulator, and lubricator unit) should be installed as close to the working location as possible, preferably within 15 feet. It should be conveniently located for easy draining adjustment and filling with oil. A snap-in type hose connection is best for connecting the stapling air hose to this unit. The air hose must have at least a 3/8-inch diameter.

Pneumatic staplers have many applications in construction work. They may be used for securing plywood, hardboard, particle board, gypsum lath, and gypsum board to supporting members.

STANDARDS FOR SELECTION OF STAPLES

The selection of the proper type staple for specific jobs is necessary to ensure good workmanship, and to comply with local building codes. Tables for selection of staples for fastening various types of materials have been prepared by the Federal Housing Authority, F.H.A. Bulletin No. UM-25a. An excerpt from this Bulletin follows showing the type of tables and data on power-driven wire staples which this publication provides. The Bulletin may be obtained from the Architectural Standards Division, Federal Housing Authority, Washington 25, DC.

F. H. A. BULLETIN No. UM·25a
POWER DRIVEN GALVANIZED WIRE STAPLES

Section I - General

This Bulletin sets forth specifications and conditions of use for machine-driven staples made from galvanized steel wire which are protected from the weather for fastening the following materials listed in tables: sheathing, sub-flooring, underlayment, gypsum lath, asphalt and wood shingles, tin caps for built-up roofing.

Section II - Description

Staples may be either chisel-point, divergent point or divergent-chisel-point type and shall be specified by gauge, overall length and overall crown width. In general, staples should penetrate the member receiving the point approximately 2/3 of their length and have a minimum overall length member not less than those shown in the tables below for a particular use. Both legs of each staple must penetrate the framing member.

Section IV - Condition of Use

This Bulletin covers requirements for power driven galvanized wire staples and does not apply to hand actuated hammer driven staples. Staples driven by mallet type portable driving machines where the penetration and seating of the staples are fully controlled by the driving machine itself rather than the force of the mallet blow are considered power driven.

(g) Plywood Subflooring (See MPS for Maximum Spacing of Framing Members)

Thickness of Plywood	Gauge of Staple	Minimum Crown of Staple	Minimum Length of Staple	Spacing on Supports at Edges of Sheet	Intermediate Members
1/2 in.	16	3/8 in.	1-1/2 in.	3 in.	6 in.
1/2 in.	14	3/8 in.	1-1/2 in.	4 in.	8 in.
5/8 in.	16	3/8 in.	1-5/8 in.	3 in.	6 in.
5/8 in.	14	3/8 in.	1-5/8 in.	4 in.	8 in.
3/4 in.	16	3/8 in.	1-3/4 in.	3 in.	6 in.
3/4 in.	14	3/8 in.	1-3/4 in.	4 in.	8 in.

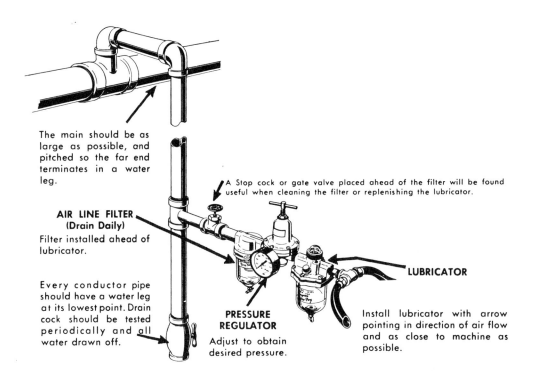

The main should be as large as possible, and pitched so the far end terminates in a water leg.

A Stop cock or gate valve placed ahead of the filter will be found useful when cleaning the filter or replenishing the lubricator.

AIR LINE FILTER
(Drain Daily)
Filter installed ahead of lubricator.

Every conductor pipe should have a water leg at its lowest point. Drain cock should be tested periodically and all water drawn off.

PRESSURE
REGULATOR
Adjust to obtain desired pressure.

LUBRICATOR

Install lubricator with arrow pointing in direction of air flow and as close to machine as possible.

Fig. 13-22 A stationary compressor system

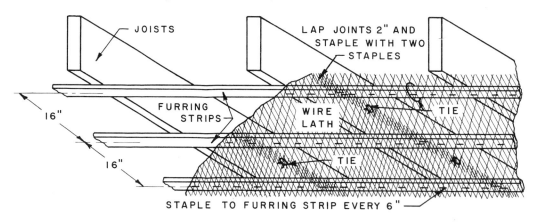

JOISTS

LAP JOINTS 2" AND STAPLE WITH TWO STAPLES

FURRING STRIPS

WIRE LATH

TIE

16"

16"

TIE

STAPLE TO FURRING STRIP EVERY 6"

Fig. 13-23 Approved stapling specifications for metal lath

REVIEW QUESTIONS

A. Short Answer or Discussion

1. What are the two general kinds of staplers and how do they differ?

2. What determines the amount of penetration of staples driven by air-actuated staplers?

3. What advantages does the use of staplers have over hammer and nail methods?

4. Describe two different types of pneumatic staplers and state the major way in which they differ.

5. In the order in which they are connected, describe the basic components of a pneumatic stapler system and give the function of each component.

6. What publication outlines requirements governing the selection of power-driven staples for various construction applications?

7. Does the above publication cover hammer-driven staples? Explain.

8. How far should staples generally penetrate the member receiving them?

9. What types of points are available on staples?

10. How are staples specified?

B. Completion

1. For heavy tacking, a _____ is often used in conjunction with a hammer-type stapler.

2. The compressed air in a pneumatic system is kept clean by the _____.

3. When power-driven staples are used to fasten subflooring to joists, _____ of each staple must penetrate the framing member.

4. Air pressure in pneumatic systems is adjusted by the _____.

5. Sixteen-gauge staples used to secure 3/4-inch plywood subflooring must be spaced _____ inches at the edges of each sheet and every _____ inches on intermediate framing members.

C. Identification and Interpretation

1. Identify the types of staples illustrated.

2. Sketch a block diagram of a pneumatic stapler system.

Unit 14 NAILING MACHINES

Nailing machines are primarily designed to increase the speed with which nails can be driven. As a result, many types of these machines are being used in construction. Many other equally important advantages result from the use of nailing machines. The possibility of flying nails and injury to fingers while driving nails is practically eliminated. The convenience of nailing has decreased strain on the operators' knees, legs, and back. In terms of efficient nailing, they have provided a means of driving a nail so that it will perform its maximum function without damage to the nail or material. In terms of performance, nailing machines easily provide a tight, undamaged, and properly nailed floor in a minimum of time.

These time- and labor-saving devices are available in several types, each designed for specific uses. Different types provide for nailing or tongue-and-groove flooring, prefinished hardwood flooring, unfinished flooring, subflooring, sheathing, and decking.

MANUAL-TYPE NAILING MACHINES

Figure 14-1 illustrates a machine designed primarily for draw nailing tongue-and-groove hardwood flooring. It uses a barbed-type nail and has a capacity of approximately 150 nails.

Basically, the machine positions the nail for the thickness of flooring being laid. It is adjustable to accommodate either 25/32-inch or 33/32-inch tongue-and-groove flooring.

The operator places the machine in position on the flooring board and drives the joint up snug, using the rubber-capped end of the hammer. Then, striking the ram head with the metal end of the hammer, the operator drives the nail at the correct angle and sets it. The ram head returns automatically to its outermost position and the next nail drops into position ready for nailing.

The model shown in figure 14-1 is constructed with a lightweight magnesium case. It can be adapted for face nailing by attaching a face nailing shear plate and shoe in place of the tongue-and-groove shoe assembly shown.

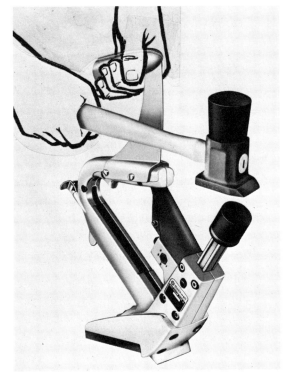

Fig. 14-1 Nailing machine used on flooring

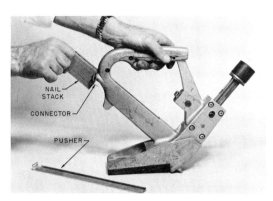

Fig. 14-2 Loading the nailer

How to Load the Nailer

1. Unhook the connector from the pusher.

2. Remove the pusher.

3. Insert the nail stack in the rail with the heads as shown in figure 14-2.

4. Install the pusher in the rail.

5. Hook the connector in the slot of the pusher.

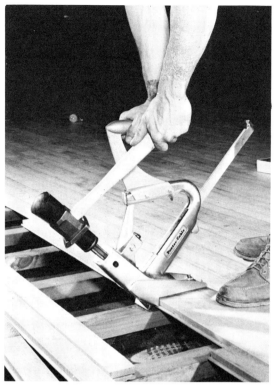

Fig. 14-3 Position for tongue-and-groove nailing

How to Nail Tongue-and-Groove Flooring

1. Butt the grooved edge of the first board against the wall and nail in place in the conventional manner.

2. Place the groove of the second board over the tongue of the first board and drive the second board snug, using the rubber end of the hammer head.

3. Place the groove of the third board over the tongue of the second board and, as in step 2, drive it snug.

4. Position the nailer on the tongue of the third board as shown in figure 14-3.

5. Strike the ram head of the nailer with the metal end of the hammer to drive the nail. When the nail has been completely driven, the ram will return to its original position, farthest from the nailer body.
   NOTE: If the ram fails to return to its original position, the nail has not been completely driven.

6. Continue to strike the ram head until the ram returns to its original position. This usually requires two blows. Take care not to drive one nail on top of another because damage to the nailer may result.

7. Slide the nailer along the tongue of the board to the next location for nailing. Repeat steps 5 and 6.

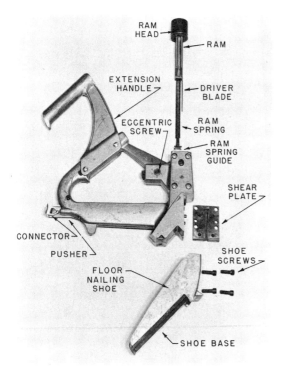

Fig. 14-4 Nailer parts

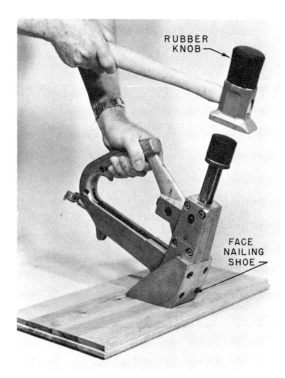

Fig. 14-5 Position for face nailing

8. Continue to nail the flooring in this manner for as long as space allows. Install and nail remaining boards in the conventional manner.

How to Face Nail

Face nailing requires the attachment of a face-nailing shear plate and shoe to the basic machine.

1. Unscrew the two ram stop screws and remove the ram and driver blade, figure 14-4.

> **CAUTION:** This must be done to avoid damage to the driver blade and shear plate.

2. Remove the four shoe screws using a 7/32-hex wrench. Then remove shoe base assembly.

3. Remove the shear plate assembly, figure 14-4.

4. Install the face nailing shear plate assembly, making certain that the grooved face of the assembly is placed next to the nailer body.

5. Place the face nailing shoe on the nailer body as shown in figure 14-5.

6. Install and firmly tighten the four shoe screws.

7. Position the nailer on the board as shown in figure 14-5.

8. Nail following the same procedures given for tongue-and-groove nailing.

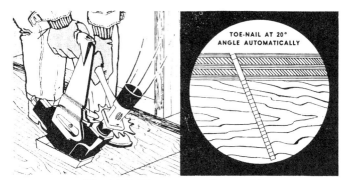

Fig. 14-6 The power nailer machine

Figure 14-6 shows a power nailer model. This type of floor nailing machine is equipped with a magnetic hopper-type feed. The nails are set and driven with a plunger of nonmagnetic stellite which is an extremely hard cobalt steel. This type of nailer is adjustable so that nails from brad size to common flooring size, or nails used to secure plywood, wallboard, or metal lath may be used. The magnetic field keeps the nails in true alignment until they reach the nonmagnetic stellite, which releases them so that they may be driven by the power provided by the operator. This machine is operated in the same manner as the nailing machine previously described.

PNEUMATIC NAILING MACHINES

Pneumatic or air-actuated nailing machines are basically the same as air-actuated staplers. The compressor system described in unit 13 for air-actuated staplers is the same system used for air-actuated nailers.

An additional system called a portable filter lubricator system is also available. In this system, a filter-lube assembly is attached to the operator's person. This accessory makes it possible to work some distance from the compressor site, figure 4-7.

Figure 14-8, page 196, shows a pneumatic nailing machine. This machine is portable, operated by compressed air, and similar in operation to that of the compressed air-operated stapler. It is used for face nailing boards on large areas such as flat and pitched decks or roofs, sidewall sheathing, and subflooring.

The nailer shown in figure 14-8 drives T nails, V nails, corrugated fasteners, and staples. T nails are available in a variety of shank diameters and in lengths up to 2 3/8 inches. They are used in the same types of jobs as conventional nails.

V nails are a headless finishing type nail and are available in various shank diameters and in lengths up to 1 1/8 inch. They are used primarily as sash pins in sash, window, door, and frame construction.

Fig. 14-7 Portable system

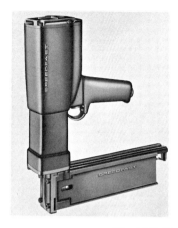
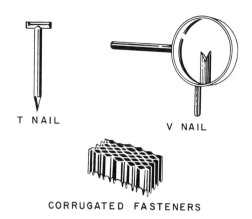

Fig. 14-8 Pneumatic nailing machine and fasteners

They are also used for cabinet work and, in general, may be used wherever a finishing nail is employed.

Another type of pneumatic nailing machine employs a "walking stick" accessory. Such a device is illustrated in figure 14-9. The entire unit weighs about 30 pounds and is guided to the nailing position by the foot of the operator which fits into a stirrup on the machine.

This machine has the capacity of nailing a minimum of 5 000 square feet per day of 1-inch x 6-inch boards, nailed 12 inches on center. The machine is provided with a boxlike hopper from which the nails, about 600, are fed automatically by gravity.

Fig. 14-9 Using a walking stick

SAFETY PRECAUTIONS

Any air-actuated device must be handled with extreme caution since the pressure employed to drive the nails ranges from 40 to 90 pounds per square inch. Since this pressure is enough to drive nails through hardwood, it follows that careless use of the machine can result in painful accidents. The air supply to the machine should never be opened until the nailer is in position to be used. The nailer itself should always be placed squarely on the surface to be nailed so there is no danger of the nails richocheting off the surface. Disconnect the gun from the air supply when not in use for extended periods of time.

How to Prepare and Test the Nailer

CAUTION: Do not open the air supply until steps 1-4 are completed.

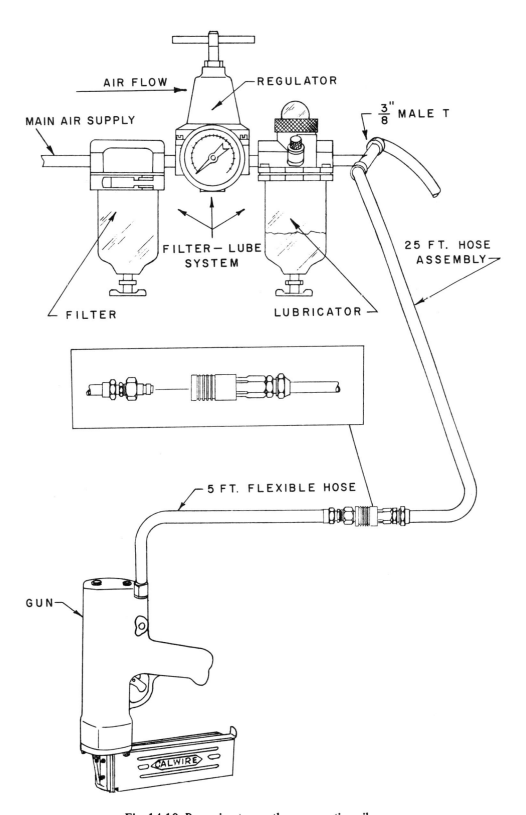

Fig. 14-10 Preparing to use the pneumatic nailer

Refer to figure 14-10, page 197, for the following steps.

1. Screw the 3/8-inch male hose fitting of the 25-foot how assembly into the 3/8-inch male T.

2. Screw the 5-foot flex pigtail into the gun.

3. Connect the pigtail and the hose by pulling back the sleeve on the coupler body, located on the end of the 25-foot hose, and inserting the coupler nipple, located on the end of the 5-foot hose, into the coupler body.

4. Fill the lubricator half full with oil as recommended by the manufacturer.

5. Open the compressor air valve to supply the system with air, and adjust the regulator to 90 pounds pressure.

> **CAUTION:** Never use more than 90 pounds of pressure.

6. Test fire the nailer by driving nails into a scrap block of wood. Be sure the nailer is placed squarely against the driving surface.

How to Use the Walking Stick Attachment

1. Connect and test the nailer as described above.

2. Load the hopper with the proper size nails and guide the machine to the location in which the nail is to be driven.

3. To drive the nail, hold the machine firmly on the surface by pressing the right foot in the stirrup. Lift the handle upward. This feeds one nail into the metering device and then drops it into a driving chamber as the handle is lowered. By pressing the trigger, a nail is driven home (completely driven).

4. The machine can be adjusted to drive nails flush or below the surface. The speed with which the nails can be driven depends upon the training of the operator.

REVIEW QUESTIONS

A. Short Answer or Discussion

1. What are the advantages of nailing machines over usual nailing methods? What are the disadvantages?

2. Describe the "automatic" features of manual-type nailers.

3. How is the nailing machine adapted for nailing plywood sheathing?

4. Why can the nailing machine not be used when laying the first and last few boards in tongue-and-groove flooring?

5. When does the nailing ram return to its outermost position?

6. What principle is employed in the power nailer model described?

7. How do pneumatic nailing systems differ from pneumatic stapling systems?

8. What type of nails does the pneumatic nailing machine use for finish nailing?

9. Describe the device for face nailing large flat or slightly pitched areas.

10. State the safety precautions which apply to any air-actuated device.

11. What precautions must be observed in the preparation of a pneumatic nailer for operation?

12. How is the pneumatic nailer tested to assure proper operation and what precaution should be used in such testing?

B. Completion

1. The nailing machine in figure 14-1 uses a _____ type nail.

2. The power nailer machine has a _____ hopper feed.

3. To snug up tongue-and-groove flooring prior to nailing, the _____ end of the hammer is used. The _____ end of the hammer is used to strike the _____, driving home the nail.

4. To use pneumatic nailers some distance from the compressor, a _____ is used.

5. The nailing machine in figure 14-8 drives _____, _____, corrugated _____, and _____.

6. The _____ device is guided to position for nailing by the _____ of the operator.

7. The air supply to a pneumatic nailer should never be _____ until the nailer is in position to be used.

8. The pneumatic nailer must always be placed _____ on the surface for nailing to avoid _____ of the nail.

Unit 15 POWDER-ACTUATED DRIVERS

As the name implies, the principle involved in actuating this driver is similar to that used in firing a gun. Cartridges of various weights of propellant powder are inserted in the cartridge chamber of the driver. The explosion of the cartridge actuates the driver.

Powder-actuated systems consist of three basic units: the tool or driver, the powder charge, and a fastener. Fasteners, or drivepins as they are commonly called, are of three main types: *threaded,* for direct fastening of an object to concrete or steel; *headed,* for bolting an object after the drivepin has been driven; and *eyelet,* for making attachments with wire. Figure 15-1 illustrates these three types of drivepins.

Figure 15-2 illustrates a typical lightweight powder-actuated driver. With its interchangeable barrels, it is used to drive 1/4-inch and 3/8-inch drivepins into concrete or steel. Drivers are available with the capacity to drive a pointed steel stud through a structural steel plate 3/4 inch thick, or into hard concrete so that a pull of several tons is necessary to remove the stud. Safe handling, obviously, is of extreme importance with this type of equipment.

Penetration of the drivepin is determined by the amount of space between the pin and the cartridge: the closer the cartridge is to the pin, the greater the penetration will be. A power positioning rod is used to gauge the placement of the cartridge in the barrel. The manufacturer's instructions should be followed although the maxim, "more rod, less penetration," applies.

DRIVEPINS

Drivepins are made of special high-alloy steels that are heat-treated to maximum strength and plated for corrosion resistance. Those designed for driving into concrete have long shanks and are available in different shank and head diameters, thread sizes and lengths to meet specific job requirements. Drivepins for steel have short knurled shanks and are similarly available in various shank diameters, thread and head sizes. All drivepins have plastic guides on the shanks to hold them in the tool barrel and to help guide them straight when fired.

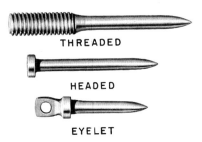

THREADED

HEADED

EYELET

Fig. 15-1 Types of drivepins

Fig. 15-2 Lightweight powder-actuated driver

The chart which follows gives a general idea of the range of uses and types of drivepins available. It is representative only, however, and is not intended to show the complete range manufacturered.

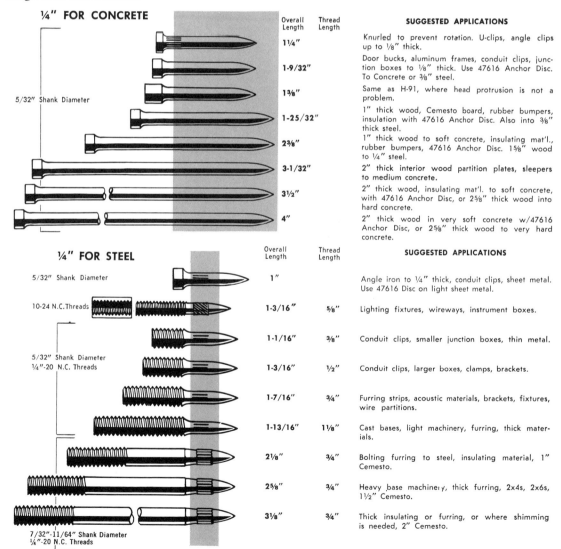

¼" FOR CONCRETE

5/32" Shank Diameter

Overall Length	Thread Length	SUGGESTED APPLICATIONS
1¼"		Knurled to prevent rotation. U-clips, angle clips up to ⅛" thick.
1-9/32"		Door bucks, aluminum frames, conduit clips, junction boxes to ⅛" thick. Use 47616 Anchor Disc. To Concrete or ⅜" steel.
1⅜"		Same as H-91, where head protrusion is not a problem.
1-25/32"		1" thick wood, Cemesto board, rubber bumpers, insulation with 47616 Anchor Disc. Also into ⅜" thick steel.
2⅜"		1" thick wood to soft concrete, insulating mat'l., rubber bumpers, 47616 Anchor Disc. 1⅝" wood to ¼" steel.
3-1/32"		2" thick interior wood partition plates, sleepers to medium concrete.
3½"		2" thick wood, insulating mat'l. to soft concrete, with 47616 Anchor Disc, or 2⅝" thick wood into hard concrete.
4"		2" thick wood in very soft concrete w/47616 Anchor Disc, or 2⅝" thick wood to very hard concrete.

¼" FOR STEEL

5/32" Shank Diameter

10-24 N.C.Threads

5/32" Shank Diameter
¼"-20 N.C. Threads

Overall Length	Thread Length	SUGGESTED APPLICATIONS
1"		Angle iron to ¼" thick, conduit clips, sheet metal. Use 47616 Disc on light sheet metal.
1-3/16"	⅝"	Lighting fixtures, wireways, instrument boxes.
1-1/16"	⅜"	Conduit clips, smaller junction boxes, thin metal.
1-3/16"	½"	Conduit clips, larger boxes, clamps, brackets.
1-7/16"	¾"	Furring strips, acoustic materials, brackets, fixtures, wire partitions.
1-13/16"	1⅛"	Cast bases, light machinery, furring, thick materials.
2⅛"	¾"	Bolting furring to steel, insulating material, 1" Cemesto.
2⅝"	¾"	Heavy base machinery, thick furring, 2x4s, 2x6s, 1½" Cemesto.
3⅛"	¾"	Thick insulating or furring, or where shimming is needed, 2" Cemesto.

7/32"-11/64" Shank Diameter
¼"-20 N.C. Threads

THE GRAY BLOCKS INDICATE THE PENETRATION REQUIRED FOR BEST HOLDING POWER

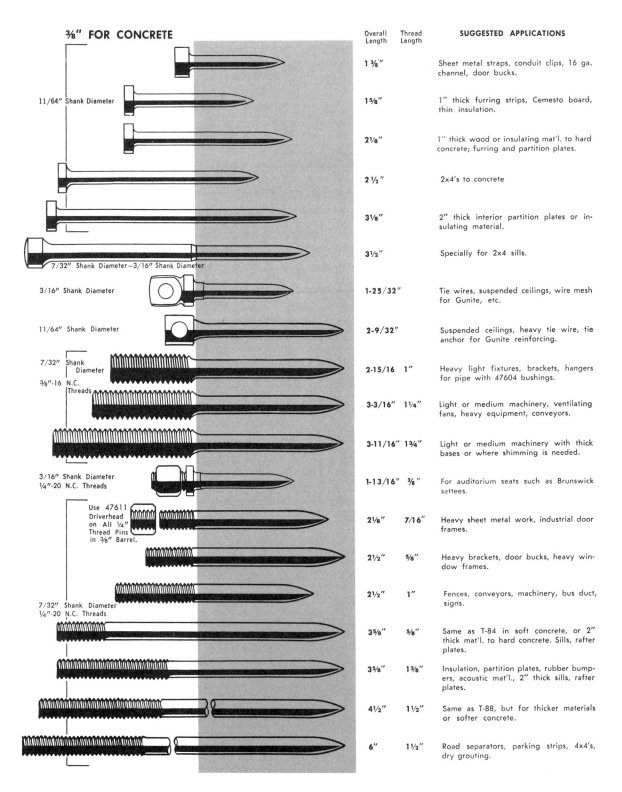

3⁄8" FOR CONCRETE

	Overall Length	Thread Length	SUGGESTED APPLICATIONS
11/64" Shank Diameter	1 3⁄8"		Sheet metal straps, conduit clips, 16 ga. channel, door bucks.
	1 5⁄8"		1" thick furring strips, Cemesto board, thin insulation.
	2 1⁄8"		1" thick wood or insulating mat'l. to hard concrete; furring and partition plates.
	2 1⁄2"		2x4's to concrete
	3 1⁄8"		2" thick interior partition plates or insulating material.
7/32" Shank Diameter—3/16" Shank Diameter	3 1⁄2"		Specially for 2x4 sills.
3/16" Shank Diameter	1-25/32"		Tie wires, suspended ceilings, wire mesh for Gunite, etc.
11/64" Shank Diameter	2-9/32"		Suspended ceilings, heavy tie wire, tie anchor for Gunite reinforcing.
7/32" Shank Diameter 3⁄8"-16 N.C. Threads	2-15/16"	1"	Heavy light fixtures, brackets, hangers for pipe with 47604 bushings.
	3-3/16"	1 1⁄4"	Light or medium machinery, ventilating fans, heavy equipment, conveyors.
	3-11/16"	1 3⁄4"	Light or medium machinery with thick bases or where shimming is needed.
3/16" Shank Diameter 1⁄4"-20 N.C. Threads	1-13/16"	3⁄8"	For auditorium seats such as Brunswick settees.
Use 47611 Driverhead on All 1⁄4" Thread Pins in 3⁄8" Barrel.	2 1⁄8"	7/16"	Heavy sheet metal work, industrial door frames.
	2 1⁄2"	5⁄8"	Heavy brackets, door bucks, heavy window frames.
	2 1⁄2"	1"	Fences, conveyors, machinery, bus duct, signs.
7/32" Shank Diameter 1⁄4"-20 N.C. Threads	3 5⁄8"	5⁄8"	Same as T-84 in soft concrete, or 2" thick mat'l. to hard concrete. Sills, rafter plates.
	3 5⁄8"	1 3⁄8"	Insulation, partition plates, rubber bumpers, acoustic mat'l., 2" thick sills, rafter plates.
	4 1⁄2"	1 1⁄2"	Same as T-88, but for thicker materials or softer concrete.
	6"	1 1⁄2"	Road separators, parking strips, 4x4's, dry grouting.

THE GRAY BLOCKS INDICATE THE PENETRATION REQUIRED FOR BEST HOLDING POWER

GUARDS FOR SPECIAL WORK

Accessory guards are available for use with powder-actuated drivers to facilitate special fastening jobs. These include guards for door bucks, conduit clips, lathing channel, hanger straps, angle iron, and many applications.

Couplings and bushings are also available to connect threaded rods or tie wires to the drivepins. Manufacturers' literature should be consulted for such needs.

BASIC RULES FOR USING POWDER-ACTUATED TOOLS*

1. Know the material to be penetrated. If a common nail can be hammered into the base material, do not use a powder-actuated tool.

2. Select the proper fastener for the job. Consider only the section of the fastener that is imbedded under the work surface of the material, since the section above the work surface of the material will be determined by application requirements. When selecting a fastener for concrete, choose one that will penetrate a minimum distance of eight times the diameter of the shank into concrete. A light-duty fastener with a shank diameter of 5/32 inch must penetrate 1 1/4 inches; a heavy-duty fastener with a shank diameter of 1/4 inch must penetrate 2 inches. When selecting a fastener for steel, remember that the whole point of the fastener must appear through the reverse side of the steel plate.

3. Always use the weakest powder charge or set the fastener a fair distance into the barrel for the first fastening, when selecting a powder charge for fastening into either steel or concrete. The same rule applies when determining how far to insert the stud into the barrel.

* The material on pages 203 through 208 has been adapted largely from <u>Course in Carpentry, Part II</u> with the permission of the Instructional Materials Laboratory, State Department of Education, Sacramento, California.

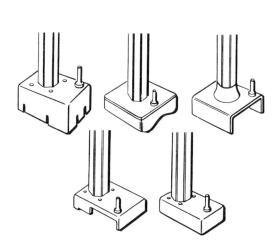

Fig. 15-3 Types of special guards

Fig. 15-4 Using a special guard to fasten 2 x 4s on edge to concrete slab

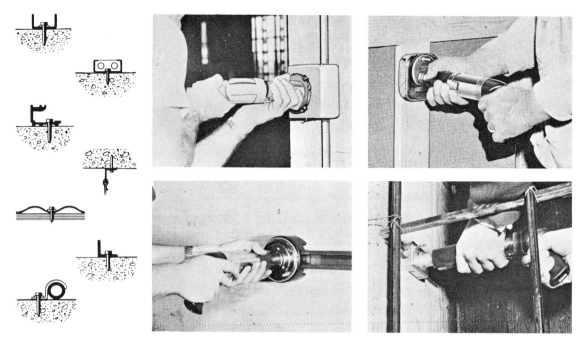

Fig. 15-5 Applications of powder-actuated drivers

4. Know the holding power of the fastener. A powder-actuated tool is designed to maintain a balance in the relationship of the power of the cartridge to the length and diameter of the fastener shank. If a fastener is selected within the proper limits, that is, eight diameters into concrete or the whole point through the reverse side of steel, the proper holding power will result.

Figure 15-6 illustrates the holding power of a properly driven fastener. This drivepin was pulled by a hydraulic jack from the concrete into which it was driven. Note how the concrete adheres to the pin. It was fused to the pin by the high velocity with which it entered the concrete and resulting compression of the concrete. Drivepins driven into steel have an even higher pullout resistance than those driven into concrete.

SAFETY PRECAUTIONS

The first safety practice to be observed is to always read and understand the instruction manual issued for a particular tool before operating a powder-actuated tool. These manuals describe the components of the kit, the operator's card, the loading and firing cycle of the tool, the parts list and parts numbers, the use of the extension, the use of the shield, the proper maintenance of the tool, and the particular precautions to be observed. Naturally, all or the safety precautions listed in the manual are important and must be observed in order to prevent personal injury to the operator or to a bystander.

Fig. 15-6 Holding power of a drivepin

1. Always have a positive guide to ensure alignment before attempting to set a fastener through a previously prepared hole in steel.

2. A tool can be fired in half-shield position, only if the work itself provides protection against ricochet.

3. Be sure the safety control rod is accurately set to prevent firing at an angle before using an extension.

4. Never fire into anything without being sure that the fastener does not have sufficient power to drive completely through it.

5. Never use a tool to set a fastener closer than 3 inches from the edge of concrete.

6. Never use a fastener closer than 1/2 inch from the edge of steel.

7. Use only factory-recommended fixtures for special fastening other than indicated in the manufacturer's instruction manual.

8. Keep a tool on the work surface for at least 30 seconds in the event it does not fire; then remove the powder charge and dispose of it safely.

9. Never leave a loaded tool lying about. If you decide not to fire it, unload it.

10. Powder-actuated tools should never be used in an explosive or inflammable atmosphere.

CERTIFICATION OF OPERATORS

Because safety is such an important factor in operating powder-actuated tools, most states require certification of operators before they are allowed to fire an explosive tool. To obtain a certificate, operators must pass a written test on the safety, operation, and care of the tool. The certificate is issued by the manufacturer of the tool, but it is the property

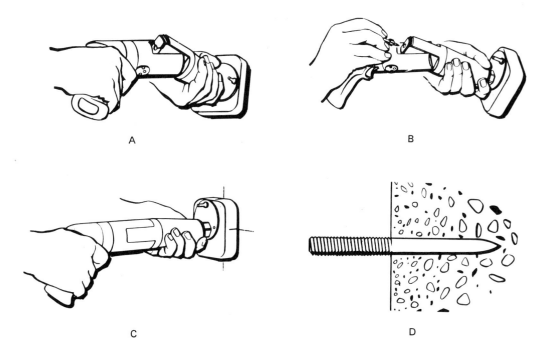

A

B

C

D

Fig. 15-7 Operating sequence for a powder-actuated driver

of the State Building and Construction Trades Council and issued upon approval of the local union representative; it is revocable for cause. It is suggested that the local regulations be studied to determine the certification requirements in your locality.

How to Operate the Powder-Actuated Driver

CAUTION: Be extremely careful to point the driver only against the material into which the stud is to be driven. Wear safety goggles and heavy gloves to protect against flying particles.

Before loading the driver, be sure the cartridge is of proper power load and the drivepin is of the correct type. If the powder load is too great, the drivepin may go through the material and cause injury to the operator or those nearby.

1. To load, open the tool and insert and position the drivepin in the barrel. Then insert the powder cartridge in the barrel and close the tool.

2. Press hard against the work surface and pull the trigger. The explosion will drive the pin into the work surface.
   NOTE: If the guard is not pressed against the work surface hard enough to prevent it from being tilted at more than a minimum safety angle, the driver will not fire. This is an automatic safety device.

3. To reload the gun, snap the breech open and the exploded cartridge is automatically ejected. The gun is now ready for reloading.

TIPS ON GOOD FASTENING

The following suggestions have been found useful as a result of actual operating conditions:

- When fastening steel to concrete, avoid over-power on fasteners less than 10 inches apart. Occasionally under these conditions shock waves cause the second fastener to loosen the first.

- When fastening into steel that reacts as though it were too hard to penetrate, always fire through a disc.

- Avoid the use of a disc when fastening plywood with 1/4-inch drivepins. As power is increased in attempting to sink the disc under the surface, the drivepin head will tear through the disc and send up a spray of steel fragments. Either use a 3/8-inch diameter head drivepin or eliminate the disc entirely.

- Never use even a light charge directly for the first fastening into cement or cinder block. Push the fastener at least 2 inches away from the cartridge, or drive through a 7/8-inch steel disc.

- A ricochet hazard exists when fasteners are driven into large-aggregate concrete. Always use the longest possible fastener and see that a substantial portion of the fastener remains in the bore at the time of firing. This engagement tends to prevent the fastener from escaping into free flight if the shank bends or deflects as it strikes aggregate.

- When fastening steel to steel, where a fastener must be flush with the surface of the steel, use a threaded stud and break it off at the threads after firing.

- When fastening into steel about which you are doubt, or which you think may have hardened, apply the following test. Remove the plastic guide from a fastener and drive it with light hammer blows on the steel much as would be done when using a center punch. If the tip of the fastener makes indentations in the steel, it will penetrate satisfactorily. If the tip tends to curl and leaves no marks on the steel, do not use a powder-acruated tool.

- When fasteners fishhook (curl up), it is an indication that the sahk is too long in proportion to its diameter. In such a case, shorten the shank and/or increase the diameter.

- Studs can be fastened into common brick, but it is more desirable to fasten into mortar joints and use a 7/8-inch disc. The disc spans the joint and permits more even joinings.

- If the fastener must be set into a hard-faced brick, it is advisable first to chip the surface of the brick with a chisel.

- Powder-actuated tools will penetrate terrazzo and hold very well.

- Rubber or asphalt tile floor coverings sometimes crack when explosive tools are used on them. Heating the tile slightly with a torch will eliminate this problem.

- A knurled shank is necessary to provide maximum holding power in steel up to 3/8 inch thickness. It is seldom necessary or even desirable in steel thicker than 3/8 inch.

- If wood is of the grain-cut type, a C clamp may be applied to the wood at the point of fastening.

- When fastening wood to cinder or cement block, use a 2 1/2- or 3-inch fastener. Position the fastener several inches away from the power charge, or use a light load if various types are available. This will leave the fastener head protruding above the wood. Use a hammer to drive the fastener the rest of the way, and the result will be a perfect fastening.

- A smooth-shank fastener set into steel 3/8 inch or thicker can be moved in the pull-out direction if sufficient force is applied; however, it will maintain approximately the same force over the entire travel of the shank through the steel.

- If a smooth-shank fastener driven into steel does not penetrate as far as necessary, it can be driven home with a series of hammer blows. The holding power will not be affected so long as the entire point pierces the steel.

- When a utility stud is set into steel, the threaded section ahead of the drivepin will stop penetration unless too great a power is applied. Thus a 7/8-inch disc in combination with a utility stud is the very best method of fastening 2 x 4s to concrete. The threads control the penetration as they pass through the disc, and variation is never greater than 1/8 inch.

- When fastening steel to uneven concrete, or to steel with a gap existing between the steel to be fastened and the base material, assemble two driver heads to a utility stud. Because the driver heads are not hardened, the first head will deform as the stud strikes the steel. This deformation causes a pushing action and forces the steel down tightly to the base material. Technically, this deformation has the effect of a gradually applied load rather than an impact load.

- All studs are very difficult to remove, but they can be broken off if necessary by repeated bending back and forth.

- Always use a 7/8-inch disc when fastening warped wood. This will pull the wood down tightly to the base material.

- Powder-actuated tools can be used to fasten aluminum or to fasten into aluminum, but they should not be used if moisture will be present, particularly intermittent exposure, since this may result in electrolytic action.

- Powder-actuated tools have been tested for resistance to vibration in both the field and The Underwriters' Laboratories. Satisfactory results have been obtained.

- A stud can be set into steel up to approximately 270 Brinnel hardness. Most construction grade steels range from 120 to 180 Brinnel hardness. In cases where such a member has been welded, it is advisable to set studs as far away from the weld as possible. However, if a fastener must be set close to a weld, firing through a steel disc will generally permit successful fastening.

- The shear and tensile strength of a 1/4-inch stud are approximately equal to those of a 3/8-inch bolt.

SPALL CONTROL

The term *spall* refers to the chipping or breaking off that sometimes results when fasteners are driven into concrete with explosive tools. Two incidental factors must be considered: the unsightly appearance; and the idea that because of spall, the fastener is not exerting full holding power.

Spall is caused by the fact that when a fastener is driven into concrete, material is not being removed; it is being compressed. This results in stress at right angles to the shank of the fastener. The stress compresses the concrete from the end of the fastener to a point where the concrete fails in shear and produces spall.

To minimize spall, the effective shear strength of the concrete must be increased or the stress must be reduced. This may be accomplished in several ways.

1. Fire through a steel disc. A disc used in this way must be a minimum of 7/8 inch in diameter but may be as large as 2 inches in diameter. It will provide resistance to compressive force and will tend to hold in place the concrete subject to shear failure.

2. Eliminate vibration and/or shock waves by column action support on the shank; for example, use double driver heads on long fasteners.

3. Keep the fastener perpendicular to the material. This directs the plane of compression straight into the material rather than off to one side.

4. Reduce the shank diameter. This will minimize the stress produced when the shank is driven into the concrete.

REVIEW QUESTIONS

A. Short Answer or Discussion

1. What do powder-actuated systems consist of?

2. Describe the three basic types of drivepins used and the specific use of each type.

3. How do drivepins for concrete and steel differ?

4. What is the purpose of the special guards?

5. Describe six applications where powder-actuated tools are used to advantage.

6. State the four basic rules for using powder-actuated tools.

7. How far should the fastener penetrate in concrete? In steel?

8. By what two means may the power of the tool be altered?

9. What is the <u>first</u> safety rule to apply in regard to powder-actuated tools?

10. Describe the certification requirements for operators which apply in your local area.

11. What safety device is incorporated in the driver itself?

12. If the charge fails to fire, what steps should be taken?

13. What is spall? How may it be minimized?

14. Why should a disc not be used when fastening plywood?

15. What is the hazard involved in driving fasteners into large-aggregate concrete? How may it be minimized?

16. What test is prescribed when fastening into steel which may be too hard for the fastener to penetrate?

17. What does fishhooking of the fastener indicate? How may it be remedied?

18. Where should fasteners be applied in brickwork?

19. What is the best method for fastening 2 x 4s to concrete?

20. Describe the safety precautions dealing with:
    a. the half-shield position
    b. use of special guards and fixtures
    c. atmospheric conditions
    d. penetration of the fastener
    e. failure of the gun to fire
    f. use of an extension
    g. position of the fastener from the edge of concrete
    h. loaded tools
    i. position of the fastener from the edge of the tool
    j. previously prepared holes in steel

B. Completion

1. The _____ of the cartridge actuates the driver.

2. If you can _____ into the base material, do not use a powder-actuated tool.

3. Some manufacturers designate the powder charge by a _____ code.

4. _____ on the shanks of drivepins hold them in the barrel and _____ them when fired.

5. If the driver guard is not pressed against the surface hard enough to prevent it from being _____, the driver _____.

6. Drivepins placed closer than _____ inches apart in fastening steel to concrete may cause _____ which loosen previously driven pins.

7. When fastening into steel, it is good practice to use _____.

8. Powder-actuated tools may be used to fasten into aluminum, but if _____ is present, _____ may result.

9. The tensile strength and shear of a powder-driven 1/4-inch stud is equal to those of a _____ bolt.

10. Probably the most important single thought to bear in mind at all times is that with a powder-actuated tool, you are handling a _____.

C. Identification and Interpretation

1. Identify the lettered parts of the powder-actuated driver shown.

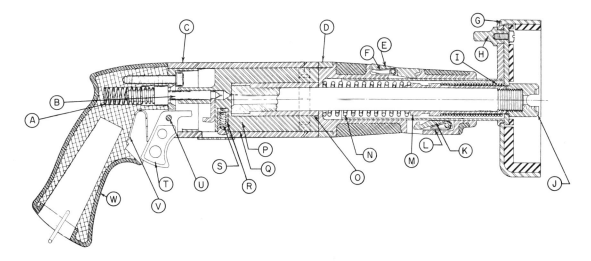

2. Sketch each of the following and include the required length and shank diameter:
   a. a 1/4-inch drivepin for fastening 1 inch thick wood to concrete.
   b. a 3/8-inch drivepin for fastening 2 x 4 sills to concrete.
   c. a 1/4-inch drivepin for fastening 2 x 4s or 2 x 6s to steel.

ACKNOWLEDGMENTS

No publication of this type would be possible without the assistance of those industrial concerns which manufacture woodworking tools and allied products. Sincere appreciation is expressed to the following manufacturing concerns for supplying descriptive material and technical data:

American Screw Company, Providence, RI
Behr Manning Company, Troy, NY
Bostitch-Northeast, Inc., Medford, MA
Carborundum Company, Niagara Falls, NY
Disston Inc., Pittsburgh, PA
Greenlee Tool Company, Rockford, IL
Independent Nail and Packing Company, Bridgewater, MA
The Irwin Auger Bit Company, Wilmington, OH
Keuffel & Esser Company, Inc., Hoboken, NJ
The Lufkin Rule Company, Saginaw, MI
Miller Falls Company, Greenfield, MA
Nicholson File Company, Providence, RI
Omark Industries, Inc., Portland, OR
Powernail Company, Chicago, IL
Simonds Saw and Steel Company, Fitchburg, MA
SKIL Corporation, Chicago, IL
Speedfast Corporation, Long Island City, NY
Stanley Tools, New Bern, NC
L.S. Starrett Company, Inc., Athol, MA
Swingline Industrial Corporation, Long Island City, NY

Special appreciation is expressed to James W. King, Rockwell International, Pittsburgh, PA, and to Carlton F. Moe, DeWalt Division of Black and Decker Manufacturing Company, Lancaster, PA, for their excellent personal cooperation in supplying technical and descriptive information.

THE DELMAR STAFF

Publications Director
Alan N. Knofla

Source Editor
Mark W. Huth

INDEX